Beneath the Stars and Trees...

there is a place

"By creating a quilt-of-the-written-word from her life in the New Hampshire woods, Janice Kolb connects the world she can reach out and touch with the faith that so often reaches out and touches her. The blend of the natural and the spiritual, like any good quilt, will warm you and comfort you, and leave you feeling a little more secure as you walk along the sometimes-confounding journey that is our earthly visit."

Michael Burnham, writer/journalist

"I have spent many happy days as a guest at Jan and Bob's place in the woods, and at the next door home of the Clancy family. I can attest to the beauty that Jan describes in her book. Jan's Woodland Retreat is a place teeming with animal and human life, and yet peaceful and serene. It is a perfect place to meditate, reflect, and renew your spirit. Beneath the stars and trees, there truly is a special place, and Jan's book will transport you there, as often as you wish."

Mark Sardella, columnist, The Wakefield Daily Item,
Wakefield, Massachusetts

Beneath the Stars & Trees . . . there is a place

A Woodland Retreat

JANICE GRAY KOLB

Blue Dolphin Publishing

Published by Blue Dolphin Publishing, Inc.
P.O. Box 8, Nevada City, CA 95959
Orders: 1-800-643-0765
Web: www.bluedolphinpublishing.com

ISBN: 1-57733-106-0

Library of Congress Cataloging-in-Publication Data

Kolb, Janice Gray
    Beneath the stars and trees there is a place : a woodland retreat / Janice
Gray Kolb.
        p.   cm.
    ISBN 1-57733-106-0
    1. Kolb, Janice Gray 2. Retreats—Miscellanea. I. Title.

BF1997 .K65 B43 2001
269'.6—dc21
                                                                    2001043041

A portion of any profits realized by sales of this book will be used to support
various animal charities.

Printed in the United States of America

10   9   8   7   6   5   4   3   2   1

Dedicated
to
my beloved
husband and soulmate

Bob

and

to my
beloved feline
soulmate

Rochester

Come with me to the enchanted forest.
Trust the magic in the air; it is real.
Take it with you wherever you go,
for the magic you feel and want
is yours if you simply believe.

Melody Beattie *from Journey to the Heart*

Sometimes a man hits upon a place to which he mysteriously feels that he belongs. Here is the home he sought, and he will settle amid scenes that he has never seen before, among men he has never known, as though they were familiar to him from his birth. Here at last he finds rest.

W. Somerset Maugham
from *The Moon and Sixpence*

Contents

Foreword

*Y*OU HAVE BEEN INVITED TO ATTEND a retreat at the author's lakeside cottage. This will be an "armchair retreat" because it doesn't require your physical presence—just the presence of your mind and imagination. You may consider yourself too busy to attend this retreat, but the rewards in a renewal of your spirit and outlook will be great. If you have ever tried to "find yourself" in the hustle of a busy office, or a home where an avalanche of activities, thoughts, responsibilities, noise, tension, and just routine living impinge on you constantly, you know that true peace and constructive personal thought is nearly impossible. You need to get apart from life's distractions—to retreat to a place, physically or in your mind where you properly order the multitude of complex factors that make up your life. You must retreat before you can advance. What the author is offering you in this book is an invitation to straighten out all that mental and emotional clutter that tears you away from the person you really are—or the person you want to be. The guidelines are here. Appropriate for your own use those thoughts that could be helpful to you, discard those that your own self-analysis tells you will not help you, and invent some of your own. The greatest resource you have is not this book, but your own ability to evaluate yourself, your needs, your talents, where you want to go with your life—and how to get there. One of the most useful skills you could ever develop is the ability to organize and refine your priorities.

Although my own methods of refreshing and refurbishing my outlook may differ somewhat from the author's, I found that her guidance and suggestions led me onto paths I had not walked before, and having walked these new paths for even a short distance, I found that my own paths led to "Higher Ground."

If we are to achieve personal goals, and develop a sense of accomplishment, we must find the time to analyze these goals. You may not call it a "retreat" but that's not important. What is important—even vital—is for you to go aside with your thoughts , block out reality temporarily, and brainstorm with your own thoughts and ideas of achieving happiness and fulfillment.

Although I didn't realize it then, the time I spent in my car travelling to my office was a retreat. When I left home in the morning, I slowly positioned my thinking to encompass the problems I would be facing that day. I reordered my thinking, and concentrated on doing the best job I could with my work. On the return home in the evening I reversed the process, purging my mind and emotions of the assaults they had suffered during my work day, and adjusted my thinking to be the father and husband I should be for my family. The car became my retreat center, separating one activity of my life from another so I would be more successful in both areas.

When I was in the Navy I became a father for the first time while I was overseas. How I longed to see my wife and my new baby girl. But while at sea I found a place of retreat under a forward gun mount where I would go every night before turning in. There I could be alone with my thoughts and emotions and find peace and tranquility even though the sea was churning and I was thousands of miles away from where my true happiness lay.

You do not have to find a spot under a gun mount, or even a spot of complete aloneness. Just sit in that armchair and join the author as she leads you to a place of infinite beauty and charm. A place where she has found her heart's home as have I. Let her share with you some thoughts and experiences which can only serve to make you more complete and fulfilled. Open your mind to a world of peace and new possibilities for your life.

Have a great retreat.

Robert A. Kolb, Jr.

Acknowledgments

*All glory to
God
And to my Christ
and
I wish to thank my
Guardian Angel
and my special Angels
who are ever present.*

I wish to express my extreme appreciation to the publisher, Paul M. Clemens, for believing in this book and to all his capable staff who helped in so many ways. I especially thank Chris Comins, Lisa Redfern, Stephanie Rumsey, Linda Maxwell, Jeff Case, Jody Black, and Barbara Houtchens for their fine work and their friendship.

I wish to thank Rochester for his constant love, presence, devotion, inspiration, and teachings throughout our life together. Because of him this book was written.

I am deeply grateful to my husband Bob for his love and support, for believing in me, and for our life together in New Hampshire. I am grateful too for the time he gave in endless hours typing this manuscript.

I wish to thank
St. Francis of Assisi
and
St. Martin dePorres
for their great love and protection of all God's creatures.

I wish to remember two beloved feline companions who entered
Heaven before this book was published and are so sadly missed.
Willy
beloved companion to Rose-Beth Woolley Pierson
and
Misty
beloved companion to
Joe and Connie Gilman

In loving memory of
Violet
entered Heaven June 5, 2001
dear bunny companion of
Dahlia June VanDorick (our granddaughter)

With much affection and loving memories
I remember
Alex
Beloved feline companion of
Nancy Dougherty and family
and our precious former neighbor
who entered heaven November 2001

May the words of this book—and the meditation of our hearts
(the readers' and mine)—give glory to God—and love and gratitude
to Blessed Mother Mary—who always intercedes.

BENEATH THE STARS AND TREES

Beneath the stars and trees
    I am alive!
        I thrive in these woods
            filled with wildlife and flowers,
and sunshine streaming through
    the tall firs and pines—
        birds fluttering from branch to branch
           and on the vines—
flying in and out feasting on seed
    at the feeders.
        And red squirrels eating perched
           with the birds—
and tiny chipmunks claiming
    the fall-out from the abundance,
        and mallards that run to greet me
           and wait by my front door.
Where else is like this,
    that one's dear friend who comes to call
        is a wild duck?
           and the rocks murmur when I pass!
I walk the soft grass to lake edge
    to behold the setting sun.
        And when shadows descend
           and twilight comes—
the peepers serenade
    from the watery cove
        and I gaze up at the heavens
           to feel the moonglow on my face.
Within the green cottage a loving man
    and a gentle cat await my return.
        Yes, there is a place—
           beneath the stars and trees.

JGK
May 15, 2000

INTRODUCTION

Welcome to the Woods

Never a day passes
but that I do myself the honor
to commune with some of nature's varied forms.
—George Washington Carver

THIS IS NOT A BOOK TO BE READ THROUGH QUICKLY. Reading it should be like a stroll in nature, slowly, so you may observe and reflect. It is to be pondered and prayed over and used to transport you, for you are being invited to become a retreatant in the woods of New Hampshire. Through means of imagination you will live beneath the stars and trees in a little green cottage by a lake, and there you will not only discover many new things about yourself, but also about all that surrounds you. Though this wooded haven is ours and we experience all I have written about in these pages, we want to allow you this privilege too through travelling in spirit to our home. You may stay as long as you wish. We welcome you! If you come with a burdened heart and need healing and uplifting, I believe you will find this on "Higher Ground." If you need to work through a problem and need time alone, this place is for you. Perhaps you have never been to the woods before and just wish to experience living alone in nature, then most definitely you will want to come here. There are many reasons someone might want to leave their present state of living and environment other than those I mentioned to be in solitude in a place far from home. Since I made such retreats myself in the past I am very aware of the need for a place where there is peace and quietude, and that is why I want to allow you to come here and invite you enthusiastically. You will not regret it. And you may stay as long as you wish until you have completed what you have come to do; heart and soul work, or merely to be refreshed in spirit in a place alone far from your everyday life. And what is exceptional is that you can return to this beautiful wooded sanctuary any time you please *without reservations* simply by opening this book and rereading, either the entire book or portions that you need more than others, or chapters that spoke directly to your heart. There may have been just one sentence or paragraph in the chapter you thought least likely to move you, and you will want to revisit it often. I know because this has happened to me in my reading which I do continuously. And so return again and again.

When we were tiny children we would be read to aloud by our parents and often over and over from the same books that caught our imagination. As we grew we too frequently read these same books repeatedly to ourselves. Our beloved books were often kept safely as we matured so that we might have them to read to our own children one day in the future. Rereading is normal in childhood and creates permanent reserves, memories, enchantments in the child's heart and mind forever. It is therefore important to do in adulthood, for no matter how well you read, it is impossible to retain everything from each book. In a book such as this—it is very important to reread and recapture things of the heart that surface while making this retreat.

It is written that a book is a magic carpet ride and I find this to be true, so come by means of magic carpet or imagination or by any means you wish, for rest and healing and peace await you.

Through this book you will also unleash your creativity which will change you and heal you. You do not have to be great in any specific field, art, music or writing, or others, just open to new insights. Your creativity can bring something new into your life and into the world, but to renew and refresh yourself is the most exciting creative act of all. When you suddenly and spontaneously have a new idea or insight, or feel led to follow a new course or direction away from your present situation, then this is exciting. You are moving away from the bindings of routine and freeing yourself, and through creativity the horizons of your life will expand.

You may even feel better and refreshed physically while spending time imaginatively in the woods, because in lifting your spirits and heart and mind through reading, and then too in participation in the closing sections of each chapter, your overall well being will become improved. When my husband Bob had a serious lung operation in 1984 in Pennsylvania, he was told by his physician to go to our woods of New Hampshire to recover for one month. The doctor believed that by spending time surrounded by nature, Bob would heal more quickly and thoroughly. And this is exactly what happened. He grew strong not only physically but in heart, soul and emotions, for a procedure like this can take its toll just as one anticipates it, plus the actual trauma of going through it. These woods, this cottage, this lake were his place of healing. It was also mine for I was drained emotionally too. Though he, myself, and several of our children were here together in actuality, one can be deeply healed by transport through imagination as well. Having experienced it often while in Pennsylvania, I know it to be true that the mind is a powerful means to transport one to another location and to bring help and healing, delight and rejuvenation. Therefore, again I invite you to Higher Ground.

Through the years I have been involved in numerous retreats. In the early 1970s as a younger woman I was asked to lead a spiritual retreat in the Pocono Mountains of Pennsylvania at a Methodist Retreat Camp. A Methodist Pastor friend who pastored the city church in Philadelphia in which Bob and I both attended as teens and that later became the church in which we were married, requested I lead this weekend retreat. I did do this and I was blessed immeasurably by the lovely people participating. We all were touched by the Holy Spirit through this gathering and it became a lasting Holy memory.

Several times in the later 1970s I attended retreats in a Catholic Retreat Home on the outskirts of Philadelphia. Though there was a speaker at these retreats, when not listening to him we were requested to keep a retreat of silence. The silence particularly moved me and the retreats were blessed experiences. The first one of these I attended several months following the sudden death of my father. I was in deep need of such spiritual help and atmosphere. I was a Protestant Methodist yet felt only mildly lonely in this Catholic place of peace. By the time I attended the next retreat there one year later in December, I had become Catholic just previous to it on December 13th, 1978. By now my Mother had also died in September of that year and a beloved uncle. Losing all three within thirteen months, and receiving *callings* to my heart and soul, led me into the Catholic Church, though still a Methodist also "within," my childhood faith and roots given to me by my parents.

All of these retreats, Protestant and Catholic, were inroads to my soul and brought me healing, solace, true help, and made me stronger within to cope with many areas of my life.

However, no retreat touched me as deeply and changed me and healed me like the retreat I made alone with only my kitten Rochester in these woods and in this cottage in September 1986. Here for one week I faced situations in my life that were overpowering and bringing me down. I prayed, read, and wrote and through all of this I felt God's healing. In the silence of nature with only bird song, creature cries and lapping lake I faced my heartaches and aggressors in the aloneness with precious Rochester. It became a landmark and turning point in my life. I do not know what would have happened to me had I not come away on that retreat.

Later in 1999 a similar retreat was rather forced upon me unexpectedly, but by now we were living here permanently no longer Pennsylvania residents. Again Rochester and I were here alone for a week while Bob went suddenly to Pennsylvania. Everything that surrounded these events was inwardly traumatic for me, but remembering always my week here alone in 1986, I turned this new time alone into a retreat again. You will read about it later in this book. Both these retreats were so transforming for me that I have basically based the concept of this book upon them so that I might try to help readers in some way, who too, have the need to be in the woods alone for reasons only they and God know and understand.

When I led the Methodist Retreat I did what I was asked to do by the Pastor, basing the leading of it on the subject that had been chosen for me to talk upon, and to help others enter into it all. The participants also, in turn, did small things that I requested of them to bring them into a fuller experience of the Holy Spirit. When I attended the other retreats following that, I did what was asked of us in order that I might have a full spiritual encounter. I share this only to point out, that if you too enter into this retreat with your whole heart and bring yourself to it fully, along with the suggested items, and especially a journal, you too will get the most from your retreat as I did from mine. If you respect what you are doing (and reading) and believe that you *are* on a retreat, you *will* be on one. Then you will receive much more from it, and enjoy too through imagination, your surroundings and experiences that are shared within the pages. Give yourself to it in spirit and it will happen!

There may be things you never before paid attention to in nature and doing so through this retreat will add meaning to your life. Some young people I know, and mature older people also, put no thought to the intricacies and beauty and mysteries of nature. They have grown up in city or suburbs and seem almost blind to the teeming life about them when they come to *Higher Ground,* because they pay no notice at all to any aspect of nature in their everyday living back where they reside permanently. I will be praying you achieve mindfulness on this retreat, something written about further along in this book. I too as a younger person having grown up in the city and then living in the suburbs, did not observe birds or bother to learn their names or give full attention to their songs, even though they caught at the outer edges of my heart and mind. It was the same with flowers and trees, I only knew the basics. I did not go out nightly to view the moon and stars or rush to be available to see a glorious sunset. I cannot believe I was so blase at times. It was not until we acquired this precious cottage in the woods that all my senses came alive and I realized the glory all about me in the natural world, the awesomeness of it all. It changed me completely and I have not been the same since. I notice everything no matter how minute, and I write in my journals about it all and create poems to capture even the mundane ant in verse. Perhaps on this retreat you can learn to become more aware of the incredible natural world about you. Your life will be enriched.

As a young girl of twenty-one and twenty-two, newly married, I left Philadelphia for the West coast to live in San Diego, and soon with a baby girl also, to travel to Bremerton, Washington to live while Bob was in the Navy. Previous to this I had never been further from home than to the New Jersey shore. The wonder and awe and amazement I felt as we travelled north through the magnificent Sierra Nevada Mountains (and the fear too at night on narrow mountain roads), and the greenness and lushness of the state of Washington from its daily rain, left me with memories that never fade. Experiencing nature as I never had before in my life, its mark was left upon my soul. Never again did I see anything similar until we discovered New Hampshire, and yes too Maine. We returned to San Diego from Washington by way of Route 101 down the glorious coast of Oregon and California, again seeing sights of over-whelming beauty unlike any others, especially the Pacific Ocean. Re-turning to Pennsylvania at the end of Bob's tour of duty, left us literally exhausted after crossing the Mojave Desert, and yet too, exhilarated in spirit because we had never experienced such a vast and seemingly unending terrain before. Entering into St. George, Utah and the utter majesty and color of the plateaus and bluffs of Utah, scenery unlike any we had ever seen in our lives, filled us with further wonder. All these experiences are forever in my memory because I paid such attention to every detail of these places I never dreamed I would ever visit. Yet back in Pennsylvania I did not have the same keenness of perception of the natural world. Perhaps because I was busy raising my six children and because I had always lived in that general area. If you pray and believe you are on this retreat, then you truly will experience what I share with you about life here in the woods. You will envision yourself here and you will be changed.

I am writing too, from a Christian perspective, but anything sug-gested in this book to do spiritually can be done according to your own personal faith or way of living. As in my previous book I will tell you that I believe in God, in Jesus, that there are Angels with me always. I believe in love, and in the love shared with my husband and all my children (and with sons-in-law and daughter-in-law for they are like my own) and the love shared with special friends. I believe that God can speak to us in any way He so chooses and I anticipate it, and too, the expectation of Angels daily making themselves known. I believe in the precious love of my little cat Rochester and that we communicate this love and all else to each other. When you believe it—it happens! I believe in the sanctity of life for all creatures as well as for humans. I believe in all of nature as other ways God speaks to us and is present to us for I have experienced Him in these ways. These are only some of the things I believe in. Oh yes, I believe in the sacred, in fun and laughter, in magic, and the more I write and pray I realize how precious life is and I experience it more fully here in nature by our lake in the woods.

I would also like you to realize that my little marmalade and white cat Rochester has been completely with me in the pages of four out of five of my last books. By his daily presence to me as I write he is also with me in this book and through his love and constancy, his help and inspiration and the joy he instills in me. Even though he may not be continually written about as in the past—*he is in this book!* This book and any other I have written only came into being because his "Angel being" came into my life. Imagine him with me as I write for he *is* with me every day as I write. You will sense his presence even if I have not spoken of him in every chapter. His love and presence are inspiring me as I write and his paw prints are on each page.

I pray that the things I share with you in this book will lift your heart and make you smile, and that the word pictures I attempt to paint will be almost as descriptive as the many photos I take.

This book, in a sense, is a journal. It is a journal recording the beauties and activities and rhythms of nature through many months, as well as other personal sharings. It is also the recording of your own personal heart thoughts as you enter into this retreat by contemplating and acting upon the *Reflect and Journal* portions following each chapter. You are creating your own book in the pages of your journal, writing things from your inner being that possibly you never dreamed would ever be put down on paper. Perhaps there are memories and dreams and hopes and silences that you did not even know were within you until they revealed themselves through your own handwriting. That is the mystery and wonder of writing. And so right now as you finish reading this Introduction, and before reading further, no later than when you complete Chapter 1, please acquire a journal for your retreat. It is necessary and will add to your journey. Choose one especially for this solitude in the woods, one that may symbolize you are living in nature, or any journal that will attract you by its size, cover and texture of pages. Keep it with you as you read as your companion. Talking to paper can be rewarding and healing, and your journal is willing to be your silent friend.

In these woods and here in this place I grow younger. My inner child spirit, my shadow, emerges more and more over time, and delight and simple living in these sacred surroundings wipe away years and tears. My life is filled with epiphanies. I am home.

Come now to your place of retreat. Envision yourself entering on a road that leads into the woods. With journal in hand and a pen in your pocket walk down the long wooded dirt road until it dead ends into an area of thick greenness. Turn right and walk ahead on the hilly terrain that goes up and down and around continuing through lovely forest. Here and there a small cottage is hidden away. Now you have reached the top of the last hill you will need to ascend. You have walked a mile! Looking down below you see an oasis of beauty, like a magic land in a story book. There is a little green cottage, a shining blue lake, tall firs and pines and trees of every sort, rocks and flower gardens and bright green grass. The birds are singing and the sun is shining. You have arrived at your place of solitude. Walk now down the dirt hill to "Higher Ground." The cottage door is open. Welcome to your retreat!

Oh yes, and may I introduce:

My Shadow

My shadow is pretty, delicate and thin
Lovely to look at and mystical within.
She wears a green dress as soft as grass—
Wildlife and elves wait for her to pass.
Oft times she dons an airy fairy white gown—
With millions of gold stars and moons upside down.
On thin tiny feet she has sandals of light—
That glimmer and glow like fireflies at night.
She has thick fragrant hair, curly and wild—
She wears to her waist as an innocent child.
A wreath of fresh flowers encircles her curls—
As she dances and sings and leaps and twirls.

JGK
July 15, 1997

My Shadow will greet you if you wish and then disappear. But you may see her at times in the woods. She is the side of me that is free and unafraid and never shy. She has come alive in these woods and has slowly allowed me to change. It is on-going. Ask that *your shadow* helps you on this retreat. If you have never met *your shadow* you can through imagination and closed eyes. Perhaps you will come to know *your shadow* on this retreat.

I came to realize the existence of mine about five years ago through the reading of a unique book that I have told you about elsewhere here in my own book, a book I have read multiple times since. Somehow and hopefully I always sensed *my shadow* with me before this but did not know her by that name. I finally acknowledged her at that time through the writing of the poem, a side of me that I wished could be more evident and alive. I could envision her through meditation and writing, and since then her free-spiritedness, joyful and energizing, has entered more and more into me. I needed this in my life. Part of me has been suppressed for a very, very, long time.

Perhaps now at this retreat, whether you are man or woman, it would be exciting to meet *your shadow* and learn more about yourself, allowing unknown essences of yourself to gradually emerge and influence your existence. When you do, changes slowly occur. *My Shadow* has already made a difference, and continues to do so day after day. Perhaps soon I will even be free enough to don one of her soft airy gowns, and then who knows what might happen!

My Shadow also has a beautiful name, one I only realized more recently. You will learn this when you visit our gardens.

These thoughts are something to consider prayerfully as your retreat begins, and to explore in your journal. Perhaps you too may want to write a poem about *your shadow* if you should desire to have this presence become known.

Again welcome. I am so happy you are here. Your cottage awaits you!

—Janice Gray Kolb
East Wakefield, New Hampshire

CHAPTER ONE

Highway to Higher Ground

Some sacred places seem filled with great power and enchantment.
Visitors feel a connection to a deeper wisdom and
may experience breakthroughs into alternate realities.
—Frederic and Mary Ann Brussat,
Spiritual Literacy: Reading the Sacred in Everyday Life,

THERE ARE PLACES OF THE HEART, places of the soul, and not having such a place even if it be only in the imagination, is enough to make the difference between living fully or dying within. When I was a child my Mother always spoke of wanting to live in a white cottage with blue shutters surrounded by a white picket fence. I do not know if she longed for her dream cottage to be in the suburbs or in the country. Often on a Sunday afternoon when I was a little girl, my parents and I would take a drive to other areas outside the city of Philadelphia, but she never found the home of her dreams. If she did find it she never spoke of it. I do not believe she could ever have made this drastic move. She was entrenched in their city row home on Third Street, and their lifestyle there. Both my parents had been raised in the inner city, and when they married and moved to this home five years before my birth, I am certain they felt as if they were living in the suburbs. And in a sense for most of their lives there they were, until the problems of the city began to touch these outskirts. My mother's cottage with blue shutters lived in her heart.

When I married as a young girl I left this home of my childhood in the purlieu of Philadelphia to live eventually in suburbia, though not far from where I grew up. It was there Bob and I reared our six children. But once I had discovered life by a lake in the woods, my heart remained in that woods until I could eventually call it my permanent "home," as my heart had previously done twenty-one years earlier. It is in this beautiful locality in New Hampshire that we have lived since January 1996 and vacationed since 1975. As did my Mother, I carried a cottage in my heart—my cottage. Only my dream became a reality, and my cottage is woodland green. In this cottage hours go by without the need to speak. My joy is so complete. My heart is so at peace.

This cottage and woods were so essential to our souls that ever since we purchased the cottage we were drawn to it again and again. We would even drive the 420 miles to spend a weekend here to become rejuvenated. Leaving Pennsylvania during the night of a Thursday we would arrive sometime Friday morning. By Sunday noon we had to drive back to Pennsylvania, but we had been touched and changed and could not wait until our next trip north. Bob would even make phone calls from his office at the end of a hard day to our empty cottage, just so he could hear the phone ring and connect, and be here in imagination. It was a form of

The cottage in the snow

healing to him. After living here permanently these past four years I can write in deepest truth that enchantment is ever present; the wonder, the awe, the joy—and this is at last, our only and forever home. We rejoice at this daily.

People say they can feel the difference when after almost a mile ride through the woods they arrive at the top of our hill, drive down, and are on our property. No matter what the season it is another world. My friend Joanne has called it "Land of Enchantment," and oh, I agree. There is not a time that I drive down that hill, alone or with Bob, that my heart does not dance, and I am in awe that this is our home. Daytime, nighttime, the magic is there! And I am grateful. Each season has its unique beauty and mysteries awaiting to be discovered, relished, and appreciated. We live in this tucked away heaven on earth with the sun and wind and snow and rain, and God's creatures, and a view of the lake outside our door that leaves me helpless at times and in tears because I am so thankful that this

is our place on earth. No matter what way I turn to look, I am lost in love, wonder and praise for this small magical kingdom beneath the tall pines and firs. It is to this sweet place of seclusion I wish to invite you, that you might share in its beauty and tranquility and healing. As you read you will sense how this home and woods have changed my life. Perhaps it too, can touch your life vicariously— through reading, writing and prayer—and just "being." I invite you now. It is written, "the best way to travel is by means of imagination." Are you willing and ready?

I try to give love from my magic cottage because it was given to us in a special way by

Photo of cross Bob made to indicate the cottage and land were given to us by God. It hangs under my writing room.

God, and I believe I am to give it to others through my writing. Through the years I was touched and invigorated in my soul and spirit repeatedly through being in these woods. I awaited each opportunity to make the trip here. The first ten to twelve years of our ownership included times spent here with our children. When our last child Janna was in college, it was then Bob and I began to come here more frequently with the intention of one day moving here. Each period spent here revitalized us.

A Turning Point

In 1986, however, I came away alone to the woods except for my tiny kitten Rochester. In despair and anguish over a family situation that had existed for years that continually hurt our immediate family, I came away for the first time without Bob or my children, in hopes that I could find peace and a way to live with this problem that seemingly had no cure. On that retreat with Rochester a new outlook and way was shown me through solitude, prayer, meditation, reading, and above all, writing. I surrendered to Christ and His means of helping me in this never ending emotional pain. It was a turning point in my life. Through the notes I kept in my journal that week here by the lake I found help, and the next year wrote a book *Higher Ground*, from my journal notes. It included a path of healing to one's own "Higher Ground," the title of the book being the name of our property here. Bob had long before named our cottage and wooded property after an old Methodist hymn by this name. He too made an essential retreat that same year at a Methodist Retreat Home in Pennsylvania, a retreat given just for men.

Your Invitation Anew

And so now, I do again invite you to our beloved place, "our secret garden"—this place of love and healing. It is my intention that these chapters may in some way touch you. Perhaps you too are in anguish as I was in 1986, or perhaps you simply need to have time alone to think and look at your life. Or perhaps you have never been to the New Hampshire woods before and you would like to come simply to be restored and moved by nature, and to rest and find solitude. Then come. It is written that a book is like a magic carpet—then may you use this book as your carpet, and spend as much time as you need in this secluded place where "God is in His heaven and all's right with the world" (Browning). I learned on my retreat that when we let God be loving Master of our own personal world then we can know the peace and security that this line indicates. I was also shown that if each human being that He created made Him Master, all these personal worlds in which He lovingly reigned would meld into one world of selfless love and harmony and joy, and then and only then, could that line from poetry fulfill its deepest meaning. This is spoken of in *Higher Ground.* I am speaking from my Christian faith, but you may make your retreat here from your own beliefs whether they be spiritual or not. You need only come here and be open to what you will be shown or given in this beautiful place of nature. Through your "arm chair retreat" you will be transported to the woods by simply closing your eyes and travelling by means of imagination. I believe it will be a turning point in your life as my retreat was in mine. Are you ready now? A retreat is a withdrawing as into seclusion or privacy, a place of aloneness, as for meditation. I believe you will fall in love with the woods, through the stories about this precious place that I will share. Too, I believe you will find the spiritual in each that will speak only to your heart in a special way.

Preparations

To prepare for your trip through imagination I would make some simple suggestions that you hopefully will adopt. In the years when we could not be here in New Hampshire often, and I longed to be, I often made these armchair retreats myself in my prayer chair. This chair was identical to the chair that sits on my platform by the lake that is my original prayer chair. Both are wooden adirondack chairs. When I sat in mine in Jenkintown, Pennsylvania with my eyes closed, I was transported to my prayer chair by the lake. It was very real to me. I felt the prevailing breezes and sun upon me, or the wind and stars of night and the moon above. It brought me joy and peace of heart to make these retreats and I believe the same will be given to you.

I would like to suggest the following ideas in order to prepare for and enhance your retreat. In all probability you will read this book and make this retreat in your own home. If you do not live alone there are things that you can do to create the aura of "being apart." My first private space was a corner of our bedroom; a long double tiered table under one of the windows, with an old rocking chair beside it. The table held my pens and books, my tape player and Bible, a framed 5x7 picture of Richard Hook's head of Christ, and some lovely artificial flowers in a vase. I became stronger spiritually and emotionally each time I retreated to this corner. Each short period there was like a mini retreat.

Though we had six children, this became my sacred space that I could go to for thought or prayer or quiet, and my family respected this. It is also where I wrote in my journal or other things significant. Because I was seeking a deeper spiritual path and was very open to the spirit, many unusual moments happened in my place of prayer. One very significant was the receiving of a group of meditations while praying in spirit and with closed eyes. These meditations by-passed my intellect and came out from me through my pen, and I transcribed them with out seeing them or creating them in my heart and mind. They were truly a miracle. Later these were published along with accompanying hymns that my husband had been given in a mysterious way also. Each hymn had come forth first. Each meditation was given for each hymn. Fifty-two in all! We called this book *Whispered Notes:* musical *notes,* poetic *notes* for the music, and the written meditational *notes.* To add to the mystery my husband plays piano by ear only, self taught, yet he transcribed the music.

Other precious things happened while in this prayer corner that I wrote about in my journal. It fed my soul to be alone there. Later, in what was my son's former bedroom, I had an entire room for prayer and writing. He had moved to the third floor in our big old home and his room became available on the second floor. Bob painted it for me, making the walls a pale blue and white, which gave the illusion through trim he put up that one was in a small chapel. I had only simple furnishings; the double tiered table moved there from our bedroom, a desk, bookcase, a short deacons bench my children would sit on if they came in to talk at length, and they did, and two wooden adirondack chairs. These were the ones identical to the two Bob and I used in New Hampshire. Now that we live here in the woods permanently these two adirondack chairs are on our screened in porch. My original prayer chair is by the lake on a platform, and Bob's chair is on the upper dock. The furnishings in my Pennsylvania prayer room were all of wood, for I wanted it all to be monk-like and ascetic, yet comforting and lovely. It truly was all of these.

Now my writing prayer room here in New Hampshire is the upper front bedroom that looks out over the lake. Here I write every day and pray, and know I have the most incredible place of retreat. I am ever thankful. My room is childlike and spiritual, filled with simple objects and many books that create inspiration. I have described it fully in my previous book, *The Enchantment of Writing*. When I step into this room each morning I am overwhelmed with joy, and feel I am in a special world, for I am.

Creating Your Sacred Space

And so, now it is time for you to think about creating your sacred space, not only for the period in which you will read this book and make a retreat in spirit, but for afterwards, so that you may always have a nook or place to retreat to in aloneness to nourish your heart, soul and spirit. It is necessary!

A sacred place can be created by placing large plants around a chair you have chosen and perhaps a table to hold things of importance to you. Or perhaps you have a folding screen that could subtly separate your area if it is in a room you share, as my first sacred space was in our bedroom. The corner of it became my retreat place. You can too, create a divider using a wall of shelves filled with books and objects of meaning to you.

A grass mat or a pretty soft rug could define your sanctuary. Placed in an out of the way corner of a room it almost seems like there is an invisible wall around your rug and chair. Even an alcove in a room can be made into *your* alcove. Some old homes have large closets. Is one waiting for you as your hermitage? Some have windows!

In warmer weather a portion of an open or screened in porch can be your personal place, or an adirondack chair or other type chair planted in your garden or beneath some trees. There are so many possibilities. Close your eyes and just visualize places of the heart you can make yours—or areas you can create, that before this you may never have dreamed could be your personal place. But if the weather is inclement there should always be a space indoors that is uniquely yours to retreat to. It is lovely to have a sanctuary both inside your home and outdoors.

Though my prayer chair on a platform by the lake is my ultimate outdoor sanctuary, immediately below it on the edge of the lake totally surrounded by thick foliage is an open space, almost a circle. I have often sat on the ground in that secret natural "room" completely hidden, to pray and think and meditate. With the birds visiting the bushes and the lapping lake immediately beyond, it is a child's dream hideaway. I am that child in spirit, but my five little granddaughters love it too. I have even retreated to it in winter when the untouched snow was piled high, yet inside that circle of shrubbery there was barely any snow at all. It was most magical to sit in a silent haven that was covered in white.

In the woods behind our cottage that rises up on a hill, there is a huge rock I often visit also and have written there in summer and fall, and meditated. One has to be a bit inventive at times. In the past summers here when our children were always with us and rain or showers would prevent me from sitting in my prayer chair in the dark, I would instead climb into our parked green Ford van that faced the lake. There I had my alone times. It was an ideal chapel or hermitage. One evening as I climbed down from the front seat I was met by one of my children who calmly announced I had a bat on the front of my shirt. Apparently I had a silent retreat companion, and it was far better that I had not known. After I peeled him from me and flung him into the air while my daughter and I were screaming, we then burst into laughter. In the morning the little bat was seen under the porch asleep. We know more about bats now and even have a handsome new wooden bat house to put outside this spring to encourage their presence, a gift from our beloved Clancys, extended family and neighbors above us on the hill. I plan to learn much more about bats for they are our friends. Back when this incident occurred that a bat grew attached to me, was in our earlier years here. I still had a lot of the city and suburbs in me and had never met a bat before. I am certain you will not meet any on your retreat.

And so, rooms, and portions of rooms, rugs, porches, large or windowed closets, chairs in gardens or woods, and even vans or cars, can be places of aloneness. You will discover others, and hopefully create your sacred space, and perhaps even have two; one inside and one outside. And you always have my special places to be in by simply closing your eyes and being here in Spirit. You are invited!

Perhaps you can sense our joy in this poem I wrote in the dark as Bob and I travelled to Higher Ground, driving at night as we preferred to do. Rochester too was with us as always. I am about to know the happiness once again of several weeks in the woods. This was one of the many, many trips we made until we eventually stayed forever. Join us in our van if you wish.

HIGHWAY TO HIGHER GROUND

In the dark we drive with ease—
No glaring sun—just glorious breeze.
There's time to put our thoughts aright—
When we can travel through the night.

Windows open—hearts are too—
Receiving now His point of view.
For mind and soul are washed so new
By wind of Spirit fresh and true.

In silence and in reverence
The breeze brings nature's soft incense.
In darkest night such evidence—
Of Spirit's sweet magnificence!

Along the miles our lives revolve
Within—and then comes new resolve.
And as the sun comes breaking forth—
We're better folk—for travelling North.

In sky—radiant hues fill all the East
We thank the Lord for night's Thought Feast.

Dedicated to   JGK
silence and night travel

Special Items for Your Retreat

Items to bring into your space will add to your retreat as you go on to read this book. The following will enhance your experience.

1. A journal that is pleasing to you. Select a new one with a cover that attracts you to write in it. You will have to decide if you want the pages lined or unlined.

2. A sketchbook. Inexpensive ones can be found on the art supply aisle in any Wal-Mart or similar store. More expensive ones can be purchased in an art supply store. I have found the inexpensive ones adequate for myself. If your journal has plain pages you may want to draw or sketch in that too. A book to draw in adds to your life. If this is new to you perhaps you will be glad to discover this delightful expression of self.

3. A favorite pen that will not run dry, or a number of pens. Perhaps you might prefer pens that write in different colors of ink to help to further express yourself. Pens are a must.

It is written that a pen is the instrument of the intuitive, and it may take you to unexplored places you never thought about deliberately or intentionally. This is true for I experience this.

4. Pencils for sketching and drawing.

5. Box of crayons.

6. Drawing pad (large).

The crayons and drawing pad can also be found on the art supply aisle and are inexpensive. These are for the "child" in you. You may even prefer the thicker crayons. I have both regular and thick.

7. A favorite small blanket or throw. If it is winter when you are reading this you might want to have this to cuddle into.

8. A cassette player. You may wish to have your favorite tape with you, or make a special one of comfort, preferably music that speaks to your soul—ethereal, relaxing, gentle, transporting.

You may wish to also consider refreshment, and perhaps you might like to have some favorite tea or coffee or cocoa on hand or anything else that appeals to you. When I made my retreat with just Rochester in 1986, I ate a small breakfast in the CooCoo's Nest, our local restaurant, following my drive home from Sanbornville where I had attended daily Mass each morning at 8 AM. My main purpose for eating out was to conquer a fear I had of going into and then eating alone in a restaurant. This was one of my fears I overcame that week by forcing myself to do it every day. The rest of the day I ate very lightly or fasted, for I had deep concerns that needed to be dealt with and I was there to find peace and healing. I also did not permit myself to leave our place in the woods once home from Mass and breakfast, for it was not the week to do anything but what I came away to do. It was my "retreat."

Only one other time have I had a similar retreat and that was this past summer when an emergency arose and I was forced to be alone without Bob for seven days. I treated this period as a seclusion, for it was sorely needed due to the circumstances that separated us temporarily. With Rochester as my sweet companion as always, and Isabel, our daughter Jessica's dog whom I was caring for, I spent the days in prayer, writing, and reading—all outdoors except for late at night. From screened in porch, to prayer chair by the lake, back and forth—and I never left our property once, not even to pick up the mail at the Post Office or to buy food. I simply needed to remain here, and I was blessed. I prayed, and I filled an entire journal along with other writing, and read several books. I did no housework except the few dishes I used, for I partially fasted each day. It was a refuge that was unexpectedly given to me and I opened myself up to all that God had to show me, and am grateful that I did this. To make it seem like my first retreat, I slept again on the living room sofa each night with Rochester as before asleep on my legs and tummy, and this time Isabel on the floor beside us. The books I read that week have remained very significant to me. I had been fearful in September of 1986 for it was my first time alone in the woods, except for the company of Rochester, and I felt safer sleeping on the sofa.

But while you are reading, praying, thinking, and writing on this retreat, you may wish to restrict yourself to just liquids or small amounts of food to create more of a retreat-type atmosphere. At least you might want to try it at first and then decide. You could eat more normally later if you desire, when you are not in your "place of aloneness."

Wearing soft comfortable clothes is also essential; sweat shirt, sweat pants or an old cotton shirt, whatever you usually like. Remember, you are in the woods! And too, you may wish to have a camera, but this is not necessary. If you do own one, however, perhaps keep it in your special space.

A Special Friend

And lastly, perhaps if you have an animal companion you might encourage him or her to be with you in your space. Perhaps he/she would normally do that without invitation as would my Rochester. I can only say I cannot imagine making my retreats without him or spending any day of my life without him. He is right here beside me as I write and for some ten minutes was lying perfectly across my hand written pages on my desk forcing me to stop writing. These are times I know he is blessing my writing for he has done this continually through the years, and I welcome him to do it. So invite your animal companion into your sacred space and to travel to New Hampshire with you.

Rochester on our screened in porch where he interacts with birds and little creatures and meditates.

Retreat in Spirit

I could not always come here physically but I did come in spirit. This gave me such peace. Perhaps in the reading of this book you can connect to this place in spirit too, our "Higher Ground," and make a retreat in reverie. I welcome you! Come and spend time in our "Land of Enchantment." I will wait while you conceive your special space, and gather your few supplies that will enrich your retreat and the reading of this book, if you will make use of them. While waiting, I will create some suggestions for you to think upon when you return, and share a poem to hopefully inspire.

SILENT VOICE

There is one who will assist—
If you can keep a faithful tryst—
'Twill help you be an optimist,
Perhaps serve as psychiatrist.

A journal may I recommend—
To keep with you as your dear friend.
A silent one who won't betray—
That calms a soul in disarray.

Have it with you like a prayer—
It will soothe you in despair,
Help you be much more aware
And keep your heart in good repair.

With blank book and pen of choice
Fill now those pages with your voice.
Live your life—but live it twice—
You'll not regret the sacrifice.

Dedicated to   JGK
Journal keeping

Reflect and Journal

☆ Perhaps say a special prayer or write one for your new journal. Inscribe it within.

☆ Create a place to keep the articles you have brought to your sacred space of retreat. Perhaps a special box or a wicker basket, or a shelf.

☆ If inclined, say or pray a blessing over your chair and the area of your retreat.

☆ Sit in your chair and just rejoice. Begin to imagine things you wish to think upon that were brought to mind as you read this chapter. Happy trip! Blessed retreat!

Come with me now whenever you are ready to the next chapter and I will share some other thoughts that may help to make your retreat memorable and everlasting, as my retreats are to me.

CHAPTER TWO

Settling In

Slow down, Be calm. Find a place where you can regularly practice silence.
There you will find the resources to revitalize your body, mind and soul.
—Frederic and Mary Ann Brussat,
Spiritual Literacy: Reading the Sacred in Everyday Life

*I*N THE PREVIOUS CHAPTER there is a list of items essential for you to have with you on this retreat. Perhaps you have already obtained some of them before going on with the reading of this book. That is good, for having these items, all of them, will enhance and enlighten your time spent apart in the woods. Hopefully too, you will continue to use these articles, for they are prayerful and fun, and will help to deepen your understanding of your inner life and existence on earth.

While there are other objects that can also be included in your retreat, there are some that should not be present. Perhaps you have never considered that certain things in your home or personal belongings have somehow brought you down emotionally, or even made you feel uncomfortable with their presence. Has this ever crossed your mind in any way? And perhaps if it did, did you let the items or item remain despite the little warning signals you were receiving? I know I did, and for years! But there comes a time when we must discard these objects or give them away, no matter how valuable. Nothing is more important in your own home than your own well being. Do not even put these items in your basement or out of sight in a closet, because their presence and energy is still there even though unseen. And you will know they are there even though they are covered or packed away.

24

It is not easy for me to release belongings because I am very sentimental. One of my daughters has stated that it would take me a year to go through a shoebox, meaning if personal items were stored in it. Sadly that is just about true. Well, maybe it *is* true. But in regard to the previous questionable objects I am referring to, I have learned to dispose of them, but only in recent years. If certain objects in your home affect you negatively, or you are only just realizing this in some way after reading here, please take time to evaluate the situation and let memories surface. Sit quietly with your journal and prayerfully ask for guidance. Then begin to write about this matter or about any objects that surfaced in your mind as you were reading my words. Write in free flow type writing without stopping for about ten minutes and see what turns up on your journal pages. And then prayerfully consider what you have been shown and act upon it. Do this numerous times, and even continue to do it periodically in the future, so that your environment is kept clear and clean of harmful things.

If there are bad memories associated with certain things in your home that you are aware of even before you do the journal writing, it would be wise to remove them. Or if there are belongings that were given to you by someone that has hurt you, or you do not feel comfortable with in actual presence or in thought, then get rid of those also. Your home should be filled with objects that cause happiness and good memories. If you think this all sounds strange, then at least put these objects outside your home in some way for a period, maybe even let a friend keep them or store them in a place not immediately near your home. See then, how you begin to feel without these negative carriers and reminders always near you and before you in your everyday life. Perhaps after a period of time without them you will understand what I am saying and be ready to move onward without them. There are ways to dispose of them that will come to you when you are ready to do it. You are worth more than any material object. Your mental, spiritual and physical health matter!

We had many things in our home of this nature when we lived in Pennsylvania until I became aware. In a large home it was easy to accumulate many such items that came in through our large family who lived there, or were gifts that had negative affects. Only through living through bad moments and continuing terrible experiences did I come to realize what was happening. It was confirmed through spiritual reading also, and I began to take steps to get rid of the things. One very large item on our dining room wall had caused me pain from the moment it was hung there, yet because I felt intimidated by the giver and helpless to do anything but let it remain, for the spot had too been chosen by the giver for the gift, I lived with it. I lived with it for years! I lived with it for years in the very room where we had sweet family gatherings, ate wonderful meals together, a room I had to walk through many times daily from my kitchen to get to other rooms in our home. I cannot explain explicitly enough the affect it had on me. No one should be told they must display something in their home they do not want and that they will have to look at day after day. Do not let that happen to you.

Finally years passed and our large dining room was divided and made into a smaller den area, and our kitchen enlarged using the rest of the dining room space. We took down all pictures to reassess and redecorate during the remodeling. In mutual consent we finally placed the very large wall item in a storage room on the third floor. This did not help me. I continually felt its presence oppressively above me in my own home for an ensuing six to seven years.

One day I came home from morning Mass, went to the third floor, brought down this "entity" and put it in a large deep metal container out in our back yard. My husband happened to be home and I invited him to join me and, though he certainly thought my means were drastic, he did stand with me as I prayed, and then set fire to the thing. It was a time of extreme cleansing, and only until it was a pile of ashes in the can did I feel released from its power. Later due to circumstances when things from another family member were stored in our barn and were never again retrieved or wanted and left with us, I found a duplicate of the item I had burned, and was devastated! Our barn was not that far removed from our home! Circumstances then did not allow me to burn it as before, and so I got rid of it in the large waste disposal system of an apartment complex whose garages faced ours across our lovely back drive. I buried it in the trash collected from all the apartments the day before trash collection.

The same is true now in New Hampshire. Since moving here four and a half years ago we are extremely careful to have exclusively items of personal meaning to us around, for our cottage is small and we want only love within the walls. Things of a negative nature that have tried to make their way indoors have failed, because I know better now and will not permit them in here. Items questionable are taken to the dump.

Our town dump, fifteen minutes away, is an intriguing place with many sections, deep holes in the ground, and huge containers for every kind of refuse that must be separated. It is an experience to be there with sea gulls calling, and circling the entire area above. It is all like another dimension. I often dump various things of a "non-material" quality while there. You too can do this in a dump you create through imagination. This poem explains a visit there of this sort. I still had not yet discovered the duplicate item in the barn of my Pennsylvania home. At times feelings like those expressed in the poem came over me.

DUMPED

Today—I am at the town dump.
Most appropriate—for there is a clump—
Of balled-up debris—within me;
With roots just like that of a tree.
It's made of junk clinging there—
It is nothing I want to declare.
But it causes such sadness and woe,
I desperately want it to go!

Right here on this spot in this dump
With the Sword of the Spirit—that lump—
I'll cut free and jump on and smash—
And leave it right here in the trash.

JGK

Actually there is nothing you cannot dump while making this retreat, in actuality with material objects, or through visualization, eliminating memories and pain.

Other Items to Enhance Your Retreat

If you are sad or depressed in any way or feel heavy in your soul, try to make your home light, especially the area in which you have created your sacred space of chair and chosen items. Perhaps if you make your area whimsical as well as employing simplicity, it will lighten your heart. Even if you are not depressed this child-like quality can enhance your feelings. I know this to be true.

Some readers may feel a sacred space is only for the deeply religious and belongs only in churches, but this is not so. We are all spiritual beings and you will find happiness and healing in your sacred place. There are other personal items you can bring to it that I did not mention in the previous chapter. I shared with you in that chapter the basics, but you can elaborate, and that would be wonderful. You may like candles, as I just mentioned, or a pretty covering or table cloth on your table near your chair. Perhaps a family picture or two of people and animal companions you love. None of these should be too big but you can be the one to decide. You may wish a religious picture also of the Divinity you love. Flowers in a small vase are nice too, but are not always available unless they are lovely artificial ones. If you use a Rosary you may wish to have it near you, or a rock of meaning. You be the one to contemplate all of this and decide. The objects you choose to add, if you do, can represent all that you love, and you will feel love when you sit there. Men will create a different sort of space than a women, obviously.

Women too, if you do not have an animal companion may like to have a stuffed animal share your space, either a beloved one from the past that has travelled through life with you, or a new one. You could make a very special ritual out of purchasing one if you do not own one, a silent companion for your retreat and forever after. Once the animal shares the retreat with you, he will also share a special place in your heart. You will see. I am an advocate of stuffed animals and many sweet ones share my writing room, some more special than others. Rochester is surrounded by them. I have written on this subject in my book, *Journal of Love,* and others have written on it also. I am not alone in my feelings for these wonderful companions. I too, have a man friend, Dan, who appreciates them and has given me several special ones, and owns several himself. I have shared about him in my previous books.

If your special chair is surrounded by objects of meaning you will be drawn to it again and again as I am to mine. You may wish to create a little ritual that is known only to you that you say, pray or perform, or all three, each time you enter your place of retreat, your sacred space. I believe as time passes you will be inventive in regard to it, especially as you grow to love being there while you read this book, and create little acts of blessing and love for your space.

Altars

In a sense, what you put in love on the table in your sacred space creates a small altar. You may want to make another one in another area of your home or apartment too, to carry your retreat beyond the boundaries of your central sacred space. I have an altar on my large writing desk that I have described in my previous book, *The Enchantment of Writing*, and also a small one on the kitchen windowsill. Bob made the sill wider for me, and this altar has mainly things of nature upon it, and is different than the one on my desk. Three abandoned birds nests, a white angel, a miniature wooden shrine of bench and crucifix beneath a tapered roof, a small woman statue bent in prayer before a drawing I made of my Christ in a little wooden frame, images of cats to represent Rochester, and a small mug with an image of a Cairn terrier that speaks of three family dogs we loved so. Also there is a lovely African violet, named "Violet" after my mother. It all is dispersed the length of the altar with a taller statue of St. Frances of Assisi and a little ceramic lamb at his feet in the middle, he who loved animals and all of nature. To me the little altar is very welcoming and inspiring as I work there in the kitchen. It promotes prayer and smiles. To the left of the window sill immediately over the

Kitchen window sill altar

oven is a continuation of the altar for me in a framed picture of my Dad, Mother and Uncle, the last picture taken together. They all died shortly after, one after the other in a period of thirteen months. I talk to them often as I prepare meals, or walk past them to go out onto the porch. I leave prayer requests with them too.

Perhaps sharing my sacred places will give you ideas for your own if you have not already created any. You may or may not be so inclined, but I believe if you at least try creating during the reading of this book you can better decide.

Solitude

Perhaps you are not used to being alone in a retreat-like setting, especially if you live with others. But new adventures can often create new patterns for life and so I hope you will find the time to at least try some of these things suggested in this chapter and the first one. I do believe they can touch you deeply. Solitude is an essential part of growing spiritually, and also being on a retreat such as you are creating now for yourself. I am speaking of a retreat alone, for I know it will change you and make a deep difference in your life. To help get in touch with your inner self, there are few things as powerful as solitude. And this is especially true if outside stimuli is removed such as television, radio, newspapers, magazines and other forms of escape. I hope you will begin to enjoy solitude if you have not started already, for it is good to be comfortable in being alone. To have time to spend on your own is delicious. I thrive in it and write in it, pray and meditate, and become healed. You can spend time thinking, communing with nature (as I hope you will do on this retreat) reading books you always wanted to read, getting in touch with your intuition, and contemplating deep questions that have been in your heart, perhaps pertaining to the universe. We all need time to nourish our spirits so that we will have new energy to live, and give to others. Perhaps this retreat will introduce you more to being in solitude, and beside the sacred place you have created for yourself, you will find other places to be alone.

In solitude you have the opportunity to confront your inner self in ways that few other endeavors offer. Out of your precious times of solitude will come unequaled occasions to connect with your soul, and find peace of mind, serenity, and a deeper relationship with your Creator.

Writer Bonnie Friedman in her heartfelt book, *Writing Past Dark*, that explores the emotional side of the writer's life, writes of how she always felt the most herself when she was alone. One of her two favorite places to be alone as a child was an orange chair. She tells how the orange chair was a perfect half-sphere, padded all around, and shares how she would push it right up flush against the sill of the living room window, climb aboard like hoisting into a dinghy, and then swirl the thick, heavy curtains so they draped around her. She states, "I was in a tiny room." She goes on to share more deeply of her feelings in that hidden place and the books she read, the things she ate. She saw a garden and tree through the window and occasionally children, and felt as if she was in a small quiet pocket separate from them, and from the discordant sounds of her family. It was in this secret place the flame inside her grew brighter. She later refers back to it as a writer.

The first time I read that passage several years ago I identified with it at once. As a child I too had an overstuffed chair in the living room at the bottom of the stairway. It was my special place when not in my room, and I would sit in it sideways with my back against one thick arm of the chair and my legs over the other arm. My cat Mitzi would settle on my lap. It was here I would read my Nancy Drew mystery books and others that I enjoyed. I could be silent in this chair for long periods reading and thinking. I had no curtain or window as Bonnie Friedman did, but it was my special place downstairs. How I wish I had had a curtain about me and a window, for my chair did not afford the same seclusion as Bonnie's.

Perhaps you will come to be drawn to the particular chair you have chosen for your retreat, and it will become more and more appealing and sacred, and soon it will call to you as mine have done through the years.

Close your eyes often as you sit there and sense an invisible curtain around you as you enter into this retreat. Use your imagination as often as you can, for imagination can take you on magic trips (hopefully to New Hampshire) where you can soar with the birds over the lake, and walk in the woods, sit in my prayer chair by the water, and enter a whole new realm. Welcome!

FLIGHT OF FANCY

In imagination
    and soul's celebration—
        I wear an acorn cap
          and flap
          and spread my wings.
                My heart sings!
I fly with an Angel and humming bird
    and I have heard
        they take pure delight
          in my flight.
Yet when I remove my cap
    and open my eyes—
        there is mishap;
          pull of earthly ties.
But I shall soar
    once more—
        o'er woods and Balch Lake's shore.

                        JGK

Will you join me?

Reflect and Journal

☆ Through prayer and journal writing consider anything you may wish to remove from your surroundings that creates a jolt to your heart, or causes feelings of negativity.

☆ As you continue on your retreat continue also to rid yourself of any negative emotional baggage through prayer, meditation and journal writing. In imagination actually take the hurt or pain to the dump, letting the poem guide you. Or you may throw it into the depths of our lake, and as Christian writer Corrie Ten Boom advised, put up a "no fishing" sign.

☆ Have fun deciding on any additional items you may wish to bring to your sacred place of retreat.

☆ Like Bonnie Friedman and myself, did you ever have a special chair or place where you could be alone to think and read? Maybe it would be nice to remember that now through writing about it in your journal.

☆ Record any other memories that surface too, as a result of thinking and writing about your childhood chair or special space of your teen years. What you remember and record may enhance your present retreat.

> *The summer I was sixteen I hid out in a hollow in the pine trees near Little Sissabagama, a lake in Northern Wisconsin. I was a certified would-be early bohemian, barefoot in cut-off jeans and a blue denim work shirt, dubbing myself "blue goldsmith." I wanted to read, write and figure out who I was.*
>
> —Susan Goldsmith Wooldridge, *Poemcrazy*

This author goes on to say she wrote rambling odes of praise to (Walt) Whitman in her journal, and with her Brownie camera photographed his book propped against tall grasses. She loved everything Whitman said to her in her private hollow by the lake. She is also the author who shared about "The Shadow" side of herself as I have shared with you in the Introduction.

☆ Try to free your inner child or teen as you make this retreat, and continue to try to remember your special chair or place (or hollow) and other memories of those early years. Think of ways you will use your camera if you bring one to your sacred place of retreat.

☆ ☆ ☆ ☆ ☆

Now as you "settle in," in your special place—perhaps I will share with you our incredible experiences with a most lovable Moose. Think of this not just as a true story, but be open to what it has to say to you personally in some way you might never dream possible at this moment.

CHAPTER THREE

Moose

One does not meet oneself until one catches the reflection
from an eye other than human.
—Loren Eiseley, *The Unexpected Universe*

MAGICAL ADDITION

When we drew open the curtain
      just after dawn—
We knew then for certain
      there was a moose on our lawn.
Exchanging glances
      with two humans that day—
She delighted in the circumstances,
      and decided to stay.
What a magical addition
      this enormous recluse!
So we began the tradition—
      to entertain moose.

JGK

DRAWING OPEN THE CURTAINS on this sunny, crisp morning in late
October is comparable to unwrapping a stupendous surprise.
Outside the sliding glass doors stands the gift of a huge moose! After

34

seconds of both exclamations of delight from Bob and me, and a deep silence in awe, grabbing a camera I slip outdoors as quietly as possible. Thus begins my relationship with this adorable creature.

Upon seeing me emerge onto our front porch, she turns and runs back into the woods to the left of our property. I begin to talk to her gently, calling to her, and Bob does also from our side living room window. Thinking two people on the front deck might keep her away, Bob remains indoors. Eventually she turns and gradually comes back in our direction, stopping to munch on branches and shrubbery along the way. She is browsing now along the water's edge, exploring our beach area, the canoe, and obviously delicious greenery as she pauses to taste. All the while I am taking pictures of her, snapping wonderful close-ups as she comes up to linger along the side of our cottage.

By now both Bob and I are on the front deck and Rochester is observing from the sofa back indoors. Having been there originally when we opened the curtains, his immediate reaction to his first moose sighting was to seek seclusion. Upon giving it all thought he returns to his primary stance for he is curious. His first reaction had been a normal one! We had been startled too! Now he goes from window to window in order to better see this amazing creature.

We watch her every move, speaking to her in low gentle tones and calling her "Matilda," a name Bob gave her almost at first meeting, the middle name of my mother. We give up all we had planned to do,

When we opened the curtain this was how we saw Matilda.

spending two hours outdoors with our new acquaintance. How often does a moose come to visit? We do not press in on her, but stay back, watching incredulously. Bob goes into his office briefly, a small building near our cottage. Matilda begins to walk from the area out front, and not thinking, I call to Bob that she is leaving. My raised voice frightens her and she runs to the left of our home and into the woods. I berate myself! Though we wait for some time she does not return, and we reluctantly go indoors. We cannot stop speaking of this glorious happening and eventually call some family members in other states to share about Matilda. She does not return, but the excitement of her former presence lingers. Later I write a poem to honor her, the one that begins this chapter.

The next day we are away doing errands and going to the library and bookstore and other necessary places in Sanford, Maine. This is a little routine of ours every two weeks, and it ends in dinner at a fine country restaurant, then returning home in early evening. Rochester indicates Matilda has not made an appearance in our absence.

She is embedded somehow within me, however, for that night she appears in a dream. Bob and I are driving through the center of Sanford just as we did in reality earlier, and suddenly a moose emerges from a side street and out onto Main Street. Bob is able to stop the car in time. The moose stands in front of our red Mitsubishi staring through our windshield at us from her towering height. It is Matilda! I recognize her as I do an old friend. The dream ends. What does it mean? I believe it is symbolic, and requires prayer and thought, and writing too. Perhaps in working through the dream in these ways, in time I can know. Already I interpret she is a "spiritual visitation."

Friday, the next day, our moose returns. Yes, by now she is "ours." She is beautiful and I am again filled with awe at her size and demeanor, as is Bob. We are so thankful she is roaming about on our property. She wanders into a deeper wooded area behind Bob's little office building and beneath the Clancy's cottage high on the hill above. I follow her and wait on the outskirts. Perhaps she is capable of going up the steep hill surrounding this area but she does not. She goes to the base of it and stands still. She can barely be seen in the trees. If I did not know she was there she would be hidden. I move in a bit closer talking gently to her. Her back is to me, and it is in this position she stands for almost one hour. Still as a statue! I too wait and stand, observing and speaking softly at times, mentally recording these unbelievable moments. Soon I write some notes on paper in my pocket.

Tip toeing away to get Bob so that he can join me for awhile, we return to find she has changed position and is now facing us. We enjoy her as she stands still at the base of the wooded hill watching us. Bob eventually returns to his office and I begin writing details about her in my mind. She is feeling more comfortable with my presence, or so I hope, for she begins to eat dead maple leaves and eventually whole branches.

A poem begins to form and I write again on paper.

CLOSE ENCOUNTER WITH A MOOSE

She is chomping branches—
  and as I move in quietly,
    she compliantly
      allows my presence—
        with occasional glances
          at this stranger.
As I gaze at the eloquence
  of this massive creature—
    and speak to her gently,
      I sense no danger.
I am a beseecher
  on behalf of the human race,
    as I intently
      speak love in this quiet place—
Revealing my respect—
  yearning to protect—
    seeking to connect
      with this wondrous teacher.

For Matilda   JGK
Moose of our woods

And so I pass the hours with this amazing moose. Normally I am in my writing room at my desk with Rochester ever with me, but I know that for several of these hours I am outdoors he is asleep on the bed next to my desk. Later I tell him all that transpired, but too, I have been sending him mental love messages from the nearby woods. We are always connected.

Sometimes I stand, sometimes I sit on the ground or on big fallen branches, but I am all the while keeping company with Matilda. When I talk to her now she turns to look at me and makes me feel acknowledged. I recall words of Thoreau that have meaning. "If you would learn the secrets of nature, you must practice more humanity than others." In these hours perhaps she has come to know more about me. She has never once since she first appeared every shown aggression to us, and she continues to peacefully eat and stroll and stay near me. She makes no attempt to leave this wooded area in all these hours we share. She is content to all outward appearances, even when I occasionally take her picture. She seems to ignore the flash. She can walk or charge past me if she so chooses for I am no obstacle. That she elects to stay makes me feel honored for, indeed, I am in the company of a great, mysterious creature.

Though we have been looking at each other for hours there comes a moment in time so incredible when she slowly turns her massive head. Her big brown eyes stare deeply into mine at closer range. I stand

Up close—when I spent the day with her

motionless held by her gaze. I cannot move until she again shifts her head. Momentarily I am in another realm. In my spirit I hear, "I come peacefully so you may know me." My imagination? I really do not think so. As her eyes meet mine I am not thinking or creating, only allowing this contact. No fear. Only peace. In a few minutes I take out my pen and paper to record the words left in my mind, while Matilda chews on a small green branch. Later I will remember a passage from a book revealing that if a deer looks at us straight into our eyes, whether it be in a dream or in actual life, it is an invitation by the deer to follow it in peace and harmony and to awaken.

The eyes of a moose have gazed into mine both in a dream and in reality, not a deer's, but the moose and deer belong to the same family. I claim the message from that passage as my own. Later I write it in my journals when I record all that is transpiring since the arrival of Matilda. I have always thought the deer to be my totem animal and there are several figures and images of them in my writing room. Now a "family member" has come in reality—a visitation!

Bob joins me again and we take pictures of each other with Matilda just a short distance behind us. We feel no apprehension when turning our backs to her. She never shows any indication whatsoever that she is aggressive. Already there is trust between us. Pictures of her are important to me. Bob leaves, encouraging me to also leave, but I stay until dark. I feel this day, these hours, this close encounter with Matilda, is all pure gift. I stay until dark in case it is the last time I ever see her, or can be with her in such an intimate and amazing way. It is hard to go away from her, and I talk to her and speak loving messages, and request that she never leave our land or these woods. I say a little prayer for her and wave good-bye. The sun is setting on the lake. Never does she go near the water in all these hours, though she is so close to it. I like to think she remembers fondly the time spent together that day, both with Bob and myself.

Inside I tell Rochester many things about Matilda, and Bob and I discuss her more deeply all evening. Is she still in the wooded area behind Bob's office? Is she right out front? I look outside beyond the curtains off and on, but she is disguised and hidden in the darkness. I thank God repeatedly for such an experience and for her.

Later I take down a favorite book from my shelf where inside there are many underlined passages. I go directly to the one I want.

Following the deer's way signifies the start of a search to find out heart's wisdom. Often the deer stands at the edge of the woods or in a clearing in a forest and calls us to enter this unknown realm to discover what we need to know.

—Linda Schierse Leonard,
Creation's Heartbeat: Following the Reindeer Spirit

To me, this speaks of Matilda—relative of the deer, and I write this passage also in my journal and claim it as my own. Matilda stayed at the edge of *our* woods calling us to discover what *we* need to know.

Moose Facts

While I tend to think upon the mysterious and more mystical aspects of this moose, Bob is more practical. He looks up "Moose" on the internet and finds interesting material. There is a special bulletin entitled "Moose News" and some of this is just for children.

Other Moose facts there tell us:

☆ Mature male moose typically weigh around 1110 pounds, but can get to 1400 or more. Females weigh in around 800 pounds (our Moose has a back height of six to seven feet—varying at different points on her back due to her hump and head).

☆ Moose eat about 40 to 50 pounds of vegetation a day.

☆ Their eyesight is not the best, but they have an excellent sense of smell.

☆ Moose can swim very well, with sustained speeds of six miles per hour or more.

☆ The Moose is found all over the Northern Hemisphere, in Europe, Asia, and North America.

☆ The Moose is the official State Animal of Maine. We live within a short walking distance to the border of New Hampshire and Maine, and half our lake is in Maine. We are New Hampshirites and there are many Moose here also. (The Deer—the Moose's relative—is New Hampshire's State animal.)

☆ Only the bull moose has antlers, and they fall off every winter.

☆ Moose are herbivores.

☆ The moose is the largest member of the deer family. In the United States the moose's scientific name is *Alces Americana.*

The Moose site on the internet invites people to e-mail them if one lives near Moose or if you are a moose researcher or Moosophile. Also if you have any information about the moose, noblest of animals, please contact this site. They would like to hear from you. They may be reached at moose@halcyon.com.

Living with Wildlife, a fine book by the California Center for Wildlife, informs me about every detail of the Moose, and I try to absorb it all by rereading. Moose feed on plants growing on the forest floor as well as material stripped from trees. (I was witness to this). They also feed on aquatic plants and will wade into the water up to their belly to feed, depending on the water temperature. Their long noses let them feed on water plants while they keep their eyes above the water line, alert for predators.

I read too, that Moose tend to be solitary because of the limited food sources in the northern winter forests. Half of all moose live alone it is

Another day she was out in front of our cottage

estimated, one quarter live in pairs, and the other quarter in groups of three or more. There are so many facts about the Moose in this one book alone, I stop reading for awhile but not before one last thing catches my eye. It is written here that Moose are very big and very wild. It also states, "Do not attempt to approach moose, as they can be aggressive when defending their territory."

This surprises me but it needs to be shared, for perhaps all moose are not like our Matilda, who lingers in our presence for hours never making a sound nor showing any signs of aggression. At one point I take a picture of her at approximately 10 feet or less while in the wooded area with her. I hope to one day touch her sweet face. Only time will tell if this can be.

Making Memories

The next day we see her at a distance in the woods, to the left of our cottage, a fleeting glimpse. We decide to wait for her to appear and not follow her. Today she remains at a distance.

Sunday follows, and we drive up our wooded hill to go to church. I feel I forgot to turn off the toaster oven so we turn back. As we pass our road at the top of this hill we are about to descend, Matilda stands silently staring at us. We stop and back up, roll down the window and speak with her. It makes us so happy to see her just a couple of feet away. We leave and in a minute are at out cottage. I run in and check the toaster oven (I had turned it off after all) and call the Clancys. Usually they are here in their cottage on weekends (and most of each summer) but this weekend they are not. They are in church in Massachusetts and I leave my message about Matilda, and we return to the car and drive out of the woods to our church. Shortly after we are home we receive a call from Dennis and Patti from their car phone. They left Massachusetts and are nearing New Hampshire. When they arrive we are all excited to see each other and Terry, Dennis' mother is here too. None have ever seen a moose, nor Sarah and Jenny, our "granddaughters," eleven years and nine years. In a moment after greeting, without further conversation, it is like we are following an unheard call, for we all file out of our cottage ·in a hurry and head into the woods to the left of our home. We are only out five or six minutes when we spot Matilda lying down on the big wooded hill eating leaves and branches. Everyone stops in silence but she hears us and rises to her enormous height. The Clancys are so respectful and still, in awe as we are. From then on we spend the rest of Sunday afternoon and until sundown in the presence of Matilda. We are observing all that we possibly can about her, and Sarah and Jenny are thrilled. Dennis takes marvelous pictures with his close-up lens that later he shares via the computer with us once he is back in Massachusetts. All week he sends Bob picture after picture. Bob and I too continue to take pictures. We talk to her gently and appreciate her beauty. It is an afternoon of memory-making in the presence of this silent, massive creature who seems only pure gentleness. With seven people near by she contentedly roams and eats, occasionally pausing to look at us. While we are cautious, for we realize we are numerous and she is only one, never is there even one moment when she indicates any aggression or threatening motions. She is sweet and lovely and we all softly keep acclaiming how beautiful she is and how these hours will be forever in our memories. We talk together later, all thankful for Matilda, before the Clancys drive back to Wakefield, Massachusetts.

Days pass and we continue to see Matilda in our woods, on our property in full view, and on the road. We are driving through our woods returning home and we glance right and left in hopes of seeing her. Suddenly Bob spots her standing in front of a man's cottage and we know he is away for some time. Bob and I talk to her and I ask her to please wait there and not go. We drive to our cottage and I dash in and grab my camera, and we drive back to the white cottage. Matilda has not moved an inch, remaining like a statue as she did for almost an hour in our woods that lovely Friday with me.

Bob asks me not to go too close to her, but she is beautiful standing there and I do not believe she will hurt me. I go very near and take her picture so that this man will have a photo of a moose in front of his home. She gently looks at me, and I remember with love our close encounter and those eyes. She moves. I take another picture and another. With a glance back at me she trots to the back of the home and into the woods. The photos await the man's return.

Another day I stand with her in the woods as she eats branches and I talk with her and listen for her mental replies. When she leaves we separate. I do not follow. Bob discovers her on our beach still yet another day, and we both stand and keep her company while she feeds near our canoe. I take more pictures. We admire her beauty and tell her so. That this massive creature is standing here before us still leaves us in wonderment. Each encounter is precious for she is precious.

Loren Eisely, a man I deeply respect, has stated:

> *Man has the capacity to love, not just his own species, but life in all its shapes and forms. This empathy with all the interknit web of life is the highest spiritual expression I know of. "Love not the world" the Biblical injunction runs, neither the things that are in the world: . . . But I DO love the world. . . . I love its small ones, the things beaten into the strangling surf; the bird, singing, which falls and is not seen again. . . . I love the lost ones, the failures of the world.*
>
> —from "The Star Thrower" quoted in
> *The Extended Circle: A Commonplace Book for Animal Rights*

Who can hurt such a dear creature deliberately? Who can believe that men take up guns and intentionally seek to kill the moose and deer? But it is so! It is hunting season now for deer as I write, and already, five days into the season, horrendous pictures are shown on the 11 PM news of dead deer tied to car tops, and lying on the road. One picture so horrible leaves Bob and me sick within and I cry, one I will not describe. That human beings do such despicable things to God's creatures is beyond comprehension. To see these hunters in their orange garbs on the road or in restaurants and knowing their intent, is heartbreaking, and we are helpless to stop the killing. Our woods in which we live is protected from hunting with signs posted on the outskirts. Matilda is safe in these woods and we are grateful, but if she strays from this blessed sanctuary she can be killed in the hunting season for moose, or mistakenly in the present deer season. Even the hunters themselves can kill or wound fellow hunters. Such an incident happens here just today, one hunter shoots another in the back! Matilda is in my prayers daily for the safety of her life.

As she continues to live and roam in our woods we have a new spirit about us. It is thrilling we share our lives with such a creature, and each day or moment we see her is a blessing. But even unseen, her presence is with us as we speak of her and anticipate our next encounter.

In my book, *Journal of Love,* I have written that a deer is a symbol of Christ, learning this some years ago. The deer is sacred to many cultures and it blesses me to read in detail about this and to continue to learn more. Extraordinary things have been written about encounters with deer, and how these encounters continue to live on in hearts, and affect lives of ones so blessed. Seeing warning signs along New Hampshire's and Maine's highways about "Moose Crossings" is a signal to both pray, and to think upon the marvelous creatures that roam these woods. Their presence is transforming to us. Animals are messengers and bring wisdom to us if we are open. Using animals as spectacles and degrading them, violates them! It is deplorable! And too, as spiritual messengers of mystery and transformation as I believe them to be, we deprive ourselves of their indispensable roll in our lives when we do not seek to learn from them and respect them. I have expressed myself deeply on behalf of the animals in my book, *Compassion for All Creatures.* The poet Walt Whitman too has written on their behalf when he reveals

I think I could turn and live with animals,
they are so placid and self-contain'd,
I stand and look at them long and long,

—from "Song of Myself"

As I continue to live in the woods and learn more about wildlife, I am grateful for this privilege. Each day is filled with miracles. I believe an enormous and precious messenger has come to us in the form of Matilda, and she is a spiritual presence reminding us of our Creator. One has only to look into her eyes to realize the holiness that is within. I will never forget those moments when her eyes looked deeply into mine and touched my soul. She has forever left her mark, should we not meet again. I am most thankful that she roams our woods, her presence gracing our home, our land, and our lives, and may she remain forevermore. Each day we call out to her in greeting when she is not present, and when she is present—oh, she most surely knows she is so very welcome. This woods is her home.

IN THE LINKING OF OUR EYES

O great brown moose—
    a delight to the eyes,
        a wondrous surprise,
            roaming loose
                in the tangled woods.
Strong, slender legs
    that stomp and crush
        the underbrush
            so lovely and tall.
Dark chocolate moose—
    soulful, inquiring, inspiring,
        is the rare, gentle, sweetness of your stare.
            O, what human and creature could share
                if we only dare.
What are you thinking?
    In the linking of our eyes lie
        mysteries untold,
            may they slowly unfold.
In these moments of silence—
    is sensed a sacred, unspoken alliance.

For Matilda   JGK

Reflect and Journal

☆ Have you ever found a significant mystery or surprise when you have opened your curtains? Write about it in your journal and try to recall the moment in detail, even if it is years ago. The more you write the more will surface in your mind.

☆ Spirituality is always happening. Deliberate questioning is not always necessary, but often it is right to stop, and just "be." This helps you to be more aware. Often when you are hassled and unobservant of the things in your life, a moose could walk by unnoticed.

☆ When is the last time you kept company with a moose or any living creature just for the pure enjoyment of his/her company, and to observe his/her sweetness? Tell your journal about it.

☆ With your crayons and using your drawing pad, create a Moose from your imagination. Hang it where you will notice it as a reminder to the delights and awesomeness of spiritual moments that come silently and often unobserved. Pray that you will see the living "moose" in your life.

☆ If something in this true story of Matilda has touched your soul, write a poem about it in your journal. Or a Haiku verse.

☆ ☆ ☆ ☆ ☆

After writing this chapter, an article appeared in a December local paper about a moose sighting in another town of New Hampshire.

A crowd of people leaving some parked cars, watched a moose on a grassy hill above a low brown one. It had happened in the same month Matilda was with us. The people stood there all day! The article spoke of the mystical quality of the moose and how there was a quietness over and inside of all watching. This woman reporting it, too felt "other-worldly" inside. She compared it to how people must have felt when they saw Moses or Mary and ends by saying, "For those of us who still believe, Mary can be seen, Moses was a real, flesh and blood prophet with God's laws in his hands, and a moose standing in a foggy field for an entire day is a visit once again from God" (Peg Lopata).

To read these words and realize that she and a large crowd of people were also so moved as to remain observing an entire day, confirmed anew all my feelings regarding Matilda. It was as if there was a suspension of time when I was with her. There was nothing else I should be doing. God wanted me there right with her.

How do you feel about rocks and stones? Like Matilda, they are from God, carriers and letters of spirit to be hopefully recognized and appreciated. For a few brief minutes close your eyes and imagine you are here, and then join me in thinking about rocks.

CHAPTER FOUR

Rocks

In their stillness and unchangeability they are comforting,
the work of nature's art, giving me lessons in how to write, make things,
and live my life."

—Thomas Moore,
The Re-Enchantment of Everyday Life

I FEEL WITH A CERTAINTY that it is not by chance that I live here in
these beautiful woods. God knows my love of rocks and stones that
remains in me since childhood, and our living in New Hampshire, the
granite state, is His chosen land for us. It is not for this reason alone we
are here but it is an added blessing for me. In an earlier book of mine, *The
Pine Cone Journal*, I write in detail of the steps leading us to "Higher
Ground" in these woods, and we can never question that our living here
is not of Him. Bob too appreciates rocks, but we are different from each
other, and so we see them differently and acknowledge them in separate
ways.

Perhaps it is because I grew up in a city, though Bob grew up in the
same city, that rocks hold a fascination—for as a child I was always
delighted to find one. One did not see loose rocks often just lying on the
ground on a city street or in a back alley. So to find a pleasing one was
exciting.

In my mind's eye and in my heart I see that little girl, and too the
teenager, walking about and deliberately spending time looking for
special rocks or stones, and upon finding them, keeping them all to-

gether. This child walks in a nearby park at times with friends, and highlighting this outing is the discovery of an unusual rock along the path. Rocks are important to this little girl, and while she has no collection of worth, she keeps them in boxes, with several rocks punctuating surfaces in her room. Only she knows the significance of each one. Through the years and throughout life as a wife and mother, I bring rocks back to Pennsylvania from New Hampshire so that I have their presence from our beloved summer home there. Now living here permanently I am surrounded by them and in my glory!

Most of my rocks signify happiness of some sort, these rocks that I keep near me in my writing room. Several larger ones are originally from the shore of our lake, but spent a period of years in my prayer room in Pennsylvania. They rejoice living once again in the woods. One rock is not a signifier of joy, however, but reminds me of an extremely sad and humiliating event and a sorrowful year to follow. This large, rounded pale gray smooth rock has a black band entirely encircling it as if the rock is in mourning. It indeed is, for it is representing betrayal that once bound me in sadness and depression so that I was not free, just as the lighter colored portion of this rock appears bound in the wide band of black around it. But the rock also gives hope for I am no longer bound and broke free of that blackness. My other rock next to it in a corner of my writing room on the floor, brilliant and sparkling with highlights of silica, makes me remember how I again came into the light. And knowing and remembering this gives me determination and new trust that God is continuing His work in me making me new and whole.

I have told you previously that in 1986 I came from our home in Pennsylvania to our cottage here, with only my kitten Rochester, to make a spiritual retreat for a week. While here I began to collect rocks from beneath and around the lake to see if they qualified in some way to bring the meaning of this week to another soul. I sat them along the water's edge to dry, side by side in a line. Each one was to be personally chosen and given to each of my friends from daily Mass at our church in Jenkintown, Pennsylvania. The rocks represented the solitude of the woods and the lake, and God's utter strength. They too signified their source, for they were granite rocks in many shapes and colors from the granite state. A strange gift perhaps, but to me it was the truest concerning my retreat.

While I was on retreat in the solitude and silence of the woods, these friends had all been praying for me. A rock was a symbol of where I had been, and what I had experienced, and it was a substantial natural object I could share with each one. Each rock had been surrounding me here in the stillness for years and during that special week. I felt each one had a message for the recipient far more than any store bought souvenir from New Hampshire. Francis Thompson has written "The Angels keep their ancient places, Turn but a stone and start a wing." Yes, I knew the angels had been with me on my retreat and the stones spoke of them also.

A number of years ago when Joe and Terry Clancy, Dennis' parents, were here from Massachusetts vacationing in Dennis' cottage, Joe suggested that we find special rocks during the week. His thought was that we exchange them in friendship at the end of their vacation when we went out to dinner together. We still have these mementos. Rocks and stones are symbolic and are treasured by many in unusual ways, not only in their natural settings. That Joe is now in Heaven makes his rock and his original idea of exchanging them, very precious, just as he is.

Bob also used rocks some time ago to add weight to the rear of our van. In driving up our big hill that leads from our property into the woods, the rear of the van would often dig it up and undo all the work Bob had done on the hill to keep it smooth. If the least bit of frost or snow was on the hill, in attempting to drive up, the rear end would impede getting the van to the top where we would keep the van until the snow was gone. Bob finally had the idea of putting one half of a fifty-five gallon metal drum inside the van near the rear doors. He piled this large drum measuring about twenty inches deep and twenty-four inches wide, with countless medium-sized rocks, filling it to the rim. It was such an attractive thing to me, though its only function was to weigh down the back end of our black and white 1979 Chevrolet van. We were never without this large drum while here in New Hampshire, for it also served its purpose when driving on slippery roads outside the woods.

One day, however, without a thought about it, we drove all the way to Pennsylvania with our huge metal drum of rocks. Bob was amazed to see it when we arrived there even though he had unconsciously packed our things all around it, and of course it caused us to use much more gas on the trip. I had gone into the house ahead of Bob, and he was met out in the garage by George and Laurel who were welcoming him back.

George looked into the back of the van in preparation for helping to carry some of our belongings down to the house, and spotted this huge metal drum of rocks. Shaking his head in shock he said quietly to Bob, "Boy, Mom really did it this time, didn't she?" Before Bob answered, Laurel ran down the walk to speak with me in the house. In disbelief at what she had seen she said carefully, "Your rocks are nice, Mom. Where do you think you'll put them?" Thinking she was speaking about two fine ones I had brought home in a bag and wondering how she had already seen them, I said casually, "Oh, on the window sills or bookcases." She just responded, "Oh." At this point Bob came into the kitchen laughing and anxious to tell me that George—and apparently Laurel also—had, on first seeing the drum of rocks, believed I had finally lost control. True at last, after years of suspicion, "rocks in the head!" Bob had already explained the drum of rocks to George, but Bob still had the fun of being able to tell the truth to Laurel. We really broke up in laughter, and Laurel confided that when she had carefully inquired minutes before about the rocks, she was really worried about me. In imagination she was seeing the contents of this huge metal drum on all the window sills and bookcases of our home. When family members can actually believe such a thing about me, I guess it is ultimate proof that rocks truly have meaning in my life.

The Magnificence of Rocks

So many people seem to have lost touch with the earth or simply have no interest in the natural world. Rocks seem to be included in this thinking. This can easily happen to those born and raised in cities and who often remain there the rest of their lives. Some also feel no accountability to the earth. This is perhaps understandable, for those who live in cities or even suburbs—are concerned with their own responsibilities and interests, and many have not explored in thinking, reading, or actuality, territory this is totally unfamiliar to them. Perhaps there has been no time in their busy lives to do this, or nothing that sparked the interest to do so. Perhaps there is even a dislike for any other way of life except for city living.

It is a combination of many things really that causes indifference or unawareness, but I pray that a spark of interest will ignite in the hearts of those reading this book, for all the wondrous natural things in God's world. What a miraculous place our earth is, and living here in the woods is "our heaven on earth" and we long to inhabit it endlessly. Living in nature truly changes one's life and thinking, and I am deeply grateful for that.

Often we say that someone is "like a rock." A person given that title speaks to my heart as being strong, reliable, stable, supportive, and someone totally dependable. Earth is formed of rock and stone and we spend our life on it. The moon too is made up of rock. Stone and rock are in the oceans with purposes we can never fully know. Men use rock and stone for building amazing homes and cathedrals, and even the incredible pyramids are made of stone. Great sculptors make elegant art objects from it and many cultures use it in sacred ceremonies. Magnificent altars in various Christian denominations are made of marble or other stone, and rosaries are frequently created with semiprecious stones such as amethyst, quartz or jade. Malas too, the prayer beads and holy rosary of the Buddhists are also made in this way as well, and too with natural seeds such as those from the Bodhi tree under which Buddha sat when he attained complete enlightenment. Yet many never give rock a thought! And to those people that do give it attention or appreciate it, the general consensus by most is that these others that do are strange folk indeed.

Edward Hays, an author of numerous spiritual books, has written that he uses small stones as prayer pebbles, dedicating each pebble to a specific intention or person in need. He suggests arranging the pebbles in a pattern on your personal altar in the morning, and as you pass them throughout the day, you will be reminded of your hopes, prayers, commitments and concerns (from *Spiritual Literacy* by Frederic and MaryAnn Brussat).

Similar to this is a little ritual I began a number of years ago when I placed a stone into the soil of one of my house plants. This stone signifies a special prayer or intention prayed each time I water the plant, and always I make certain water is poured over the stone as I pray. I will speak about this more completely in another chapter.

Right now as I write there are two enormous piles of rock outside on the hill leading up from our home. We had the hill widened and changed in areas this past summer due to the great difficulties we have in winter trying to drive it or even walk it. The great machinery that came in to do this work left the one side of the road looking raw and open, though wonderful trees line both sides of this hill. Bob had a truckload of incredible rocks delivered and dumped. It would have been impossible to find and collect such an enormous amount of rocks in the woods for this project. He is lining the one side of the road and the bared uprisings here and there with these rocks. Such beauty! As he places each rock by hand it is a work of love and it will also keep the soil from washing away where the machinery disturbed the earth. The rocks are especially glorious in the one area beneath the wooded hill, stacked carefully one upon the other on the earth ascending upward and slanting inward. I love too, to just stand and look at these piles of rocks—that still need placement. They are beautiful just as they are without being placed on the earth to support it. We will also encircle the huge Colorado Blue Spruce tree with rocks that is by our front porch door. We have watched this tree grow and it is one Bob planted years ago. The rocks will add to the tree's beauty.

Circles of Stones and a Friendship Rock

At our front door outside our screened in porch I have placed a lovely rock chosen prayerfully from beside the lake. This rock is to welcome others and carries the energy of the water and trees and sky. Our younger granddaughters that I have written about in my *Journal of Love* also love rocks and stones, so this rock has disappeared at times, taken innocently just because it had appeal. Each time I replace it. It is not as if we are lacking replacements! Another much smaller pine tree closer to the water also had a circle of stones about it like our larger tree, but they went home with the granddaughters also. I am in the process of collecting some others but it takes time, for each stone is placed there for spiritual reasons.

A circle of stones has import to me, and I have written about a sweet significance of one such circle also in my *Journal of Love*. It led me to purchase a book that I was intended to read through the innocent announcement of the words "circle of stones" by one of my granddaughters. By reading the book that I had postponed buying several times, I came to understand why I was instructed in such an unusual way to make it mine. Christ and His Angels used the stones and the innocence of

*Smaller pine tree
with a circle of stones*

Jenny to instruct me. The title of the book? *Circle of Stones.* She had made the announcement of those three simple words after completing the making of her own circle of stones. Those three words only were so profound and startling they resonated through the woods and my soul. The next time to the bookstore I purchased the book.

Circles of stones are powerful and healing whether on the earth or table top. I have one here on my large desk consisting of many different and significant rocks and stones. They encircle several animal and bird images and a collection of acorns. To me a circle of stones speaks of sacredness and stillness, and connectedness to nature. It is a reminder to listen to what is within.

In my circle of stones are several gifts from friends. Found in Acadia National Park—a beautiful two-inch smooth black and white stone from my friend Ruth, a brown and white mottled one from the hillside in Medjugorge in Yugoslavia where the Blessed Mother Mary has been appearing for many years, and a pale yellow limestone rock from friend Jeanne in Pennsylvania. A three inch long piece of heavy quartz from Dan is also displayed. I too enjoy giving rocks to others and have written about this previously in more detail. Many of my rocks are from right outside here on Higher Ground, along with several amethyst rocks and a crystal. Only recently I found half a large stone split lengthwise, revealing the amazing circles of growth within in various earthen browns and whites. So beautiful and intriguing to me! Related in the same book with the account of Jenny's circle of stones is the sharing of the day that Jenny and her sister Sarah and I went walking on rocks by our shore that had been hidden under the lake. In late September the lake had been lowered slightly in order that the dam might be repaired and these water rocks were now exposed. Amongst the many rocks collected that day was one found by Sarah. It was a natural phenomenon—a large flat rock split exactly in two lengthwise and yet the two pieces were still lying together. Sarah at once named it a "friendship rock" and was excited with the prospect of possibly giving one half away and she keeping the other. In this case, this rock had spoken and had given out its message to Sarah, and she so attuned, instantly knew what to call it (as Jenny had with her "circle of stones"), and that it would give its love and hers to another. My little granddaughter Renee also treasures rocks and stones and upon finding a dead moth, buried it beneath a sunflower. She had the perfect rock to put upon its grave as marker.

Sacredness

Obviously there is enchantment and significance in rocks and deeply so in regard to a circle of them or any boundaries made by them. In his remarkable book, *The Re-Enchantment of Everyday Life* (that I am embarrassed to reveal how many times I have read), author Thomas Moore relates of a trip to Ireland with his wife and children and specifically of a visit to a Holy Well. Their trip to Ireland was to fulfill the need to see such a well. Upon being directed to it and finding it they were "all impressed and moved to behold the gravelike oblong of water, edged with stone, at the base of a broad sheltering tree." Author Moore believes that one can renew and preserve an enchanting experience by enshrining it in some tangible form to contain the spirit of the original event and to serve memory. He believes that at one time long ago someone came upon a nymph, fairy, or holy spirit at that spring in Ireland and "had the presence of mind to enshrine it in stone and protect it from profanation." Thoughts and words like these have been a guide to me in recent years in regard to my relationship with rocks and stones, enhancing all my earlier beliefs collected in mind, heart and writing since I was a child.

Vision Quests

In the Native American tradition people often go on Vision Quests, but too, they are for those in all walks of life. These Quests are to help individuals find a sacred space within themselves and to confront troubling issues in their lives or to heal relationships or old fears. While on these Quests, the Quest seekers go into nature in solitude, and through this separation and aloneness shifts of consciousness occur. Often mysterious and unexplained things happen and a voice might be heard or a cloud looks like an angel. On occasion a song might come out of nowhere into one's consciousness to be received, or a tree becomes significant and wise. One often begins to have understanding of self and then unusual transformations may take place. Some of these entries into another form of consciousness I have experienced and have always written them down in my journal. They have come through deep prayer or meditation, not in a Vision Quest. Because I write in solitude and love the quiet life we live in the woods, this way of life I have found is conducive to "going deeper" into nature and into the realm of the Spirit. In a sense it resembles a Vision Quest. More about the spirituality and intrigue of the Vision Quest can be read in a fine book by that title by Denise Linn.

A sacred circle has significance to native people all over the world for it signifies wholeness and totality. On a Vision Quest individuals make a circle of rocks often large enough that they may lie down within it. It is sacred ground then within the circle and the individual is stepping into a place of prayer. It is also considered a place of protection and where the revealing of the true self takes place as well as a deeper connection with Spirit. The stones are to be selected carefully and prayerfully for each chosen one affects the energy of the circle. I feel certain Jenny was guided by the Holy Spirit in making her circle. Each stone and rock seemed most important to her.

Befriending Rocks

I have always felt a closeness to rocks that I have found, and that are important to me ever since I was a little girl. Each one seems to have its own personality and as I have learned more about them through the years, this does not seem so strange, at least not to me or to many others who write about them. They are like friends. In my heart I have often imagined Jesus with his disciples gathered around a big rock while He spoke to them, and in the Garden of Gethsemane an artist has painted

Christ kneeling and learning on a huge rock in deep prayer. Rocks have a sacredness about them through all time that some cultures respect and others disregard.

To give some of your rocks more credence in your life take pictures of them and keep them in your journal or a special photo album. Write down under the photos the feelings they brought forth in you or caption them with the personal messages they gave to you. Return to these pictures at times for confirmations or new thoughts.

Hal Zina Bennett, another author that I read frequently, relates that the Zuni people of New Mexico have used small stone carvings of animal figures as helpers, as conduits to another reality, and as source of personal renewal (from *Animal Fetishes*). Stones seem to teach in so many cultures.

I have always carried several stones in my pocketbook, something I began doing while living in Pennsylvania. They were stones from our property here in New Hampshire and they were most meaningful to me, and just to hold one gave me a sense of my beloved place here in the woods. I believe rocks and stones carry and hold such messages for humans. I also had a rock in my pocket frequently some years ago that I found here on "Higher Ground," one I treasured. Often I would transfer it to my small Rosary purse at night that went along to bed with me. This brown and white purse became lost once in a town in New York when our van broke down while travelling from New Hampshire to Pennsylvania. I could only imagine what thoughts might go through the finder's mind when first they opened it and discovered a rock and a rosary. A woman who worked in the motel to which we had been towed, lovingly returned the purse and contents intact by mail, learning my address through the motel registry. In writing her a letter of appreciation, it began an exchange of many letters. She apparently did not think the rock strange, and when she later made a spiritual visit to Rome she surprised me with a Rosary of black stones. God often sends "alike persons" into our lives in strange ways.

He also sent Rochester into my life some years ago and we two are truly kindred spirits. Rochester has always been attracted to my Rosary and fondles it gently at night as he drifts off to sleep upon me, usually with one little paw in my hand. I once wrote this poem in tribute to him in this regard.

SETTLING IN

Little furry face and head—
An inch from mine—I lie in bed.
He stares into my eyes and purrs—
Then walks my body—he prefers—
To settle down on legs awhile,
Then moves to tummy—he knows I'll—

Not move an inch—he's here to stay
Because he knows now that we'll pray,
I with my Rosary; now the beads—
Know too, sweet paws and purrs and kneads.
In union with the breaths I take—
He's lulled to sleep until we wake.

JGK

Afternoon nap in my writing room before "settling in" for the night

Pahtuta

Often when I am concentrated on a subject in writing, it can turn up unexpectedly in daily life. Last evening after writing yesterday about rocks on the previous pages, we watched *Nightline* with Ted Koppel as we do each evening. This segment was titled "Pahtuta's Diary" and immediately caught my attention. A young fourteen-year-old girl had kept a diary in a small book during the terrible tragedies she and her family endured in Kosovo. Like Anne Frank and others before her she had tried to make sense of the atrocities through writing. During these terrible times her daddy (she always lovingly called him "my Daddy"), a school teacher, was murdered by the Serbs. She and family members buried him in their yard with a small wooden marker before they were forced to leave their country. Upon return they found their home had been destroyed but the body of her daddy had not been found by the enemy. They exhumed his body and placed it in a fine coffin and men carried it miles to the outskirts of the city followed by an endless procession of the towns people. This man had been loved. There with proper ceremony he was buried. But back at their simple unfurnished dwelling they were now living in that her daddy had built before his death, a home they had planned one day to move into, was another symbolic marker to mark this beloved man's life. Pahtuta and her family had placed a worn kitchen chair outside the dwelling, and on the side of the road in front of this home. On the chair was a white towel or scarf draped over the back and seat, fastened somehow in the back. On the towel had been placed a large rock. To me, the towel seemed to represent an altar cloth for it was holding a sacred object that expressed this family's loss. We were told that the empty chair indicates a family member is missing. And the rock symbolizes that his presence can still be felt. To learn this moved us so much. Simple objects like a chair and a rock speaking out for this heartbroken family. His death had affected Pahtuta so deeply she cried and fainted each time she spoke of him or read from her diary, and her mother had not spoken in three months due to grief and depression.

The Language of Rocks

Rocks do speak if only we listen, and communicate in mysterious ways by the energy they give out and through our "knowing" if we are attentive. We may find a rock or stone in a most significant place and through this the rock speaks to our soul about something we may be dealing with interiorly, or just by its silent presence. Yet we hear it speak. How can we ignore them and think of them as anything but magnificent and mysterious, even most magical. They contain stories and words and are living. They can make themselves "heard" if we are aware. Rocks are venerable and mystical, and have witnessed incidents and happenings through the ages of time, and yet come to exist near us.

ROCKS

These silent witnesses
    to all that has passed before—
        hold secrets deep within.
For those that behold them now
    they are vaults of knowledge
        waiting to be tapped—
            waiting for ones who will listen
          to the whispers
                from these ancient beings.

JGK

In my *Journal of Love,* I have told how author Burghhild Nina Holzer writes about finding a large rock while on a trip to Northern California. The markings on the rock looked like ancient pictographs. She showed the rock to an old man who lived there in the mountains, a wise old man who had been "called" to live there. He touched it with both hands and seemed to read it, and then asked where she found it. She told him it had been by the side of the road. His reply was, "Well, then you better read it since it came to you." The author writes then that she drove home that night hundreds of miles to the cities, thinking she carried the journal of

*Statue of
St. Francis in
garden named
for him*

the earth with her. This passage has always stayed with me and was worthy of sharing again in this book. Her book is a marvelous book of inspiration to be read again and again as I have, and is also an excellent book that encourages journal writing. It is titled *A Walk Between Heaven and Earth—A Personal Journal on Writing and the Creative Process*. If we are sincerely attentive, things in nature do speak to us if only we listen.

As I have told about in *Journal of Love*, when our youngest daughter Janna and husband Bill chose to be married here on "Higher Ground" by our lake in August 1994, her dad made the wedding programs for the guests. On these programs we placed a lovely quotation:

> *Touch the earth and listen to the rocks*
> *for they remember.*
> *They know and remember*
> *all that has come to pass here*

—Lee Henderson

These rocks on our property truly had known and remembered Janna's life since she was a tiny girl and remembered all that had "come to pass." On that Saturday morning the rocks witnessed her marriage to Bill—and since have come to know and witness the frequent presence of her three little ones here, Dahlia, Nicholas and Rebecca. Dahlia enjoys rock collecting each time she is here on "Higher Ground" and usually takes some home with her to Riverside, Rhode Island.

A Story Remembered

As a young teenager Janna had many friends here on the lake and a special friend as well. One day she told me about a new boy, and then wanted us to meet him. Before his arrival she told me what little she knew of his background. He had been adopted with no knowledge of his past. Because of difficulties with his father he had run away, hitch-hiking to the woods of New Hampshire where his parents had a summer cottage. He was not living in their cottage but existing instead alone in the woods. He had little money and was happy and content under the stars at night and sleeping on the earth beneath the tall pines and firs. When he came to visit that night we sensed he was unusual even before conversation. The young teenager stood there with freshly wet hair, long but combed. His clothes were unkempt and mussed but did not look soiled; a loose white tunic shirt and blue jeans. His feet were bare. He reached out eagerly and shook hands with us, and then slowly we began to learn about him. Janna had told him I spent my days writing so perhaps that freed him to speak from his heart, for soon he was revealing his strong enamourment to write poetry. In writing his poems he was finding his deeper self.

As we talked I was moved to get a newly bought journal from a drawer and give him this book of blank pages with colorfully striped graphics on the covers. Telling him briefly the significance journal keeping had for me, I gave him this new one to be his own, indicating it could perhaps be especially used for his poetry. He seemed truly moved by this gift and as we three sat there together I inscribed meaningful quotations of well know writers in the front inside covers, that hopefully would inspire him to write. I also shared about Thoreau's journal-keeping and his life on Walden Pond, for this boy and his present life style seemed to bring Thoreau to mind. He was not familiar with him or the book *Walden*, so I gave him my copy. He realized he must be close to Thoreau in spirit, for he lived near Walden Pond in Massachusetts. He seemed appreciative for the time we three had shared when he left us. Perhaps in writing his deepest feelings in poetry or prose in the journal while alone in the woods, he might learn more about himself and the problems that caused him to run away. Thoreau too, would help—in some unknown way as yet—to touch this young boy that he might not live as most men who "live lives of quiet desperation."

Soon Janna confided that Josh's parents had learned his where-abouts—suspecting he might come here to these woods, but they were also keeping their distance. Through his aunt who also lived on the lake, his family had peace that he was well. He had made contact with his aunt and had shown her his journal and copy of *Walden*—and she asked him if she might read the book too. While the summer days passed Josh and his aunt entered into discussions as they took turns reading from Thoreau's journal-like account of his two years on Walden Pond. Through this new closeness and sharing, Janna told me Josh had softened about seeing his father and returning to finish his senior year in high school in September in Massachusetts. Janna too, had been encouraging him to return home since their first encounter. Though father and son still had not met or conversed, it had been established with his aunt that he would make this commitment to go back home when summer ended. He came by with Janna to tell me this news and at this time I again felt impressed to give him a small gift, an ornate pewter crucifix. He said no other words but a soft "thank you" and left quietly. Janna excitedly told me the next day that he had shown it to his aunt and she had had the perfect chain on which to put the crucifix. The next time Josh came to visit it was around his neck. In my heart there was a joy that he was wearing it for it was a symbol of the protection to a lone boy living in the woods and it was signifying God's love. Though all these phases in his life Janna quietly gave Josh her trusted friendship and advice, and he had confided in her and had taken her to meet his aunt.

Before he left that last day he asked if he and I might talk, so Janna went outdoors and he and I remained in the kitchen. Josh said he wished to show me something very special, something he had shown no one, but that he always carried it with him. Janna knew of this but had not seen it. From his pocket he drew out an object and opened his hand to let it be before my eyes. There in this young man's hand lay a black rock—just large enough to be more than a stone, but not so large he could not close his fingers around it. He waited silently for my response.

Perhaps others would have been dismayed or questioned that this dark rock was his treasure, but without one moment's hesitation I softly exclaimed over its beautiful smoothened surface and its unusual con-tours, and that "I understood." He stared at me quietly and for an instant I knew we had together touched some unknown point in communicating our feelings without speaking in that space of a moment. This passed gently, and he then pointed out the delicate white specks in his rock and that he had found it the day he left home. It had been his companion on the way, an entity he even spoke to. Again, "I knew." Because I had cherished rocks since my childhood they were extremely personal and significant to me. Often I spoke to the rocks here on "Higher Ground," quietly greeting them as I did the birds and trees and water and earth. Many times, through the years I experienced the joy of sitting silently with a lovely rock hidden in my hand, a special rock that I could not share with others because they would have doubted my mental stability. Even in the present my family often teases me about my attraction to rocks, and try not to say too much about the ones they know I carry around in the bottom of my purse. Truly the Lord had led Josh to confide in one who would deeply and instantly know how he could possibly have such attachment to a mere black rock.

This understanding seemed to strengthen him and most especially when I emphasized how he had honored me with the disclosure of his keepsake companion.

Words from an old hymn flowed within my being, "Rock of Ages— Cleft for me, Let me hide myself in thee." Jesus our Rock—perhaps speaking to this boy's soul day by day, drawing Josh to Himself silently unbeknownst to him. With each gentle palming and fingering of his beloved black rock, with each hiding and confiding of his secrets within it, with each touch of it as he would put his hand in his pocket—Jesus was there. A simple rock found on the first stepping stone of his journey alone to the woods. Christ, though still unrecognized, symbolically had been with Josh every moment through this "rock of ages" he had personally been drawn to immediately! Perhaps it is why the Crucifix seemed loved and important and was now worn about his neck. Once in his possession he could have chosen to quietly disregard it.

I watched him go out the door after our warm parting—walking barefoot down onto the beach with his long dark hair blowing in the breeze. He and Janna stood speaking their good-byes, and then sepa- rately Janna and I watched him walk into the woods and disappear. For a fleeting moment across my mind and heart walked also the well known scripture: "Be not forgetful to entertain strangers: for thereby some have entertained angels unawares" (Hebrews 13:2). I only know I was better for having met this young man in some unperceived inexpressible way.

Thomas Moore writes in *The Re-Enchantment of Everyday Life:* "We need stones around us to echo the substance of our own lives—hard, solid, heavy, timeless and subtly hued." He continues, "We use the earth and its materials to create a life full of materialistic wonders, but we have lost the appreciation for the earth as a source of our spiritual development and the life of our soul." He suggests that we are to see if our environment has enough stone in it and also to make an amulet out of material (rock, stone) that speaks to you clearly. He states, "Wear a stone around your neck." This is good, and for years a green stone heart hung around my neck with a crucifix and another treasure, a turquoise stone face of a cat trimmed in gold, a gift from a friend Charlotte. My green heart stone eventually fell from its chain and cannot be repaired and is carried with my rosary in a small purse. One day another stone will speak to me to replace the green heart. Josh's carrying his rock in his pocket was equal to my wearing mine.

Every stone is a unique spirit. Try to take an imaginary journey within your rock or stone when you are drawn to one. Each rock has a different energy. Hold your stone in front of you and observe the crevices and valleys and hills and really look at it. You will know if the stone is to be with you. Each stone has its own story to tell.

When my daughter June was younger she enjoyed the book *Stone Soup* by Marcia Brown, and incorporated it somehow in an assignment she had while in Nursing School. This story tells about how three soldiers taught a French village to make soup out of stones. Just for fun you may wish to read that story while rediscovering the uniqueness of stones.

A Place of Love

In the wooded area to the left of our cottage, and a few feet from the water's edge, is a cemetery. In this silent holy place are many large rocks that mark the graves of beloved family animal companions, animals that once romped about on this property. I have written about the first death in my book *Compassion for All Creatures*, that of lovely Katie, our daughter Jessica's beloved one. Her death and burial established this area as Holy ground. Several other dear family animals are now buried there too. Rocks mark the graves in serious and sacred placement expressing love and honor to these precious companions, both huge rocks and others of many shapes and sizes.

The cement grave markers, also a form of stone, that Bob created and I helped him simply engrave with names and dates, were placed on the graves in reverence as head stones following a Christian burial for each of great solemnity equal to that of any human's, yet precious in simplicity. If there is one thing that speaks of the Holiness of this wooded area, it is the rock and stone. It is a place I love to go to pray. Rock can wordlessly stand and be the intermediary between life and death, and speak of the presence of "the Rock," who has the lives of these innocent little ones in His Hands eternally.

One of the graves in our cemetery contains not the body of the little animal, but belongings that represent him. When the beloved little elderly dog of our daughter Janna's father and mother-in-law died, in their grief they did not retain his ashes. We felt it might offer some consolation if we suggested we bury something that belonged to Pepper, so that the family could have a spot on earth to visit as a "touchstone" with their precious animal. Our idea was deeply and enthusiastically received, and soon we in turn received a scarf, a collar, and a favorite toy. Accompanying these cherished personal items was a beautiful poem written by Mike VanDorick, one of Pepper's persons. When the ground was soft enough we buried these treasures in a water proof and air tight container, and held a Christian service just as we had before.

First we called Bill and Janna in Rhode Island, and Bill's parents so they could be present in Spirit, and then Bob and I held the service by the grave. When it was over we informed them of this too. It was a great comfort to Mike and Mary to have a symbolic presence of their sweet Pepper buried in Holy ground and marked by a rock. They were in Jenkintown, Pennsylvania throughout the ceremony but one day will visit Pepper's grave. Pepper was here in 1994 when Janna and Bill were married by the lake, and he was a perfect and gentlemanly little guest.

After the service I chose a medium sized rock that had been in the ground when we dug the grave for Pepper's belongings, and mailed it to the VanDorick's as a tangible natural object from Pepper's grave site and to be a keepsake. We were told this had significant meaning. Rocks can express the inexpressible yet seem silent. They are meant to be listened to as well as appreciated with the eyes.

A Solitary Place

Nor far from the cemetery on our back wooded hill is a large rock, possibly considered to be a small boulder. On this I have sat often when I have gone up the hill to be alone or to do a bit of writing outdoors. This rock is on the rim of a deep valley area and the little girls and I have often thought of it as a place where fairies romp. Many a time I have sat on the earth as well at the edge and let my legs dangle down. My imagination is alive and well in such a green wooded place of seeming nature magic.

Rock Gardens

My gardens express a holiness to me and I am blessed with seven of them. But first came the rocks, and then my gardens! Bob created the areas for the gardens by surrounding each with rock walls that he built. The rocks are laid down on each other loosely, but are strong and magnificent and approximately two feet high. The rocks are all sizes, shapes and hues and enhance the flowers and our property. I will later write more about my gardens.

The poem that follows tells of a lovely day by the lake with Jessica and our two granddaughters, all the while Bob was raking rocks. Yes, raking rocks!

AN HOUR IN THE LIFE OF A BEACH COMBER

He is raking rocks upon the beach.
Two little granddaughters just within reach—
Build sand castles in their play,
Wade in the lake on this Spring day.
His hair is blown and whipped about—
As he determinedly tries to rout
Each hidden rock—because he knows—
Tears will be spared from small stubbed toes.

His wife—arriving with love and affection,
Sifts through these rocks for her collection.
Smallest granddaughter's stones in her tiny hand—
Are gift to Grandmom from the sand.
Three large pieces of driftwood become debate—
He, to discard—but spouse says "wait."
They are "finds"—and she will use them—
She smiles—with warnings not to "lose" them.

To his rock wall from his new stock—
He carefully places each raked rock—
Lovely daughter stands smiling, reaping—
These family moments to her keeping!

Dedicated to the "beach comber"   JGK
and to our daughter Jessica   April 26, 1995
and Maxine and Renee
who gave such joy on this Spring Day

Stone People

When those making a Vision Quest select their stones they believe
they are like silent guardians with ancient wisdom and timeless strength.
They are your "stone people" and will help to create a circle of power
around you while on a Vision Quest. It is comforting to know that the

center of all circles of stones (or Medicine Wheels) is symbolic of the Creator (from *Vision Quest* by Denise Linn). I feel as if the circle of stones on my desk is an indoor sacred circle, for these are created often too.

Talking with Nature

Never scoff at rocks or stones for they hold mysteries. Author Michael J. Roads has written incredibly about his conversations with rock and was one of the first authors that made me realize my interest in rocks was not abnormal. His *Talking with Nature* that I discovered in 1987 will make your mind spin. You will not be able to be in nature again and think as you did before. This book was a confirmation to me of many feelings I had and encounters in nature—ever since my childhood. I could not believe I had found such a confirming book on subject matter I could not talk to others about. It was (and still is when I reread) very consoling to read

Mystery of Rocks

Poet Robert Frost has written about rock wall, so prevalent in New Hampshire and Maine, and we have seen some of his walls where he once lived in New Hampshire when we visited his home this past year. Rocks touch us in unexplainable ways, whether in the practical sense or the imaginative or the mystical. They hold secrets and have been holding them for millions of years. Though they may seem boring to some, so ordinary and plain, there really is a mystery within them and about them.

So often we think of ourselves too as ordinary and simple, so mundane, but in fact we are filled with mystery. When we find ourselves feeling boring or uninteresting we should remember the mysterious richness within ourselves given us by God. If a simple rock can symbolize this to you, then be aware of its lesson. When I view the rocks from my window here at my desk, or go outside to see them or pick one up, I feel gratitude for their teachings and for the abundance of them on our property and in our state. When we handle a rock or stone we are in touch with creation and our Creator. What can be more incredulous and comforting?

PRIMITIVE WRITING

Rocks are like primitive writing—
meant to be held and read—
examined with care and prayer.
Their mere presence is inviting.
The crannies, hues, and markings shed
wisdom and light on a midnight thoroughfare
to the inner unknown.
Befriend a stone!

JGK

Rocks can truly bring a peace. Author and Nun Macrina Wieder-kehr shares in her wonderful book, A *Tree of Angels*, about the healing rock she had as a child. She did not realize it was a healing rock back then, but as an adult when she would pray with those memories she realized what was happening at that rock. She went to the place of the rock when she was confused or afraid, and it had been a place of healing for her. She writes that it did more to soothe her soul than any confessional.

I had a soothing of soul also the day after I began writing this chapter. At the end of the first day I laid the pages I had written in the middle of my desk beneath my circle of stones that was above it and closer to the window. When I returned to write the next morning and to continue this chapter, I found four unfamiliar small white stones lying on my handwritten chapter pages, two larger above two smaller, two rows side by side. I was in total wonderment! All the stones on my desk were written about in this chapter. There are no others. No one had been in my room after I left it the night before, nor earlier that morning. Bob never goes up and Rochester goes up when I do. The door had been closed. Since Angels are a part of my life in a deep way my first thought was that an Angel had placed the stones there in confirmation of what I was writing. Each night I replace these four stones on my day's work.

Rocks go through so many things in their existence, and they become bumped and broken and worn, even moved from their original homes. Soil covers them, they get drowned in waters, but they do teach us to accept the bruises and ups and downs of life. It is often when we have been worn and broken by adversity that we eventually come into a state of peacefulness. Rocks can teach us this and so much more. And may we learn too, to be like a rock for others and ourselves, to be a gift, supporting, fortifying, strengthening and sustaining. From this moment on, -perhaps you may see rocks with a new heart and vision.

Earth without stones—
is like flesh without bones.

—Irish Saying

LAUGHING PEBBLE

I am the laughing pebble tumbling in the stream.
My squeals of delight
Turn into bubbles—
As I am bounced
Through sand,
Water grasses,
And smiling fish.
Large rocks envy my freedom.
I encircle them with my giggles,
And kiss them as I pass.

JGK
from "Enchantments"
in *Journal of Love*

Reflect and Journal

☆ Do you have a special rock or stone from childhood or from another period in your life? Perhaps add it to your treasures on your table in your sacred space. Write the rock's story and its entrance into your life in your journal.

☆ During the reading of this book try to find a rock that will be a symbol to you of this time spent in reading and while on your retreat. Write about this rock in your journal too.

☆ Have you ever been "between a rock and a hard place"? Has this situation been resolved in your life? Write freely about it in your journal.

☆ Who has been like a "rock" to you in your life? Thank God for that person right now and perhaps place a photo of him/her on your table if you have a photo. If not, draw a picture of that person with your pencil or crayons to keep in your sacred place. It can be drawn on paper or in your journal. Write about that person in your journal in deep appreciation for what he/she means to you. Not everyone has such a person in their life.

☆ Find a unique rock for this person in your yard or a park and give it to him/her as symbolic of what he/she means to you. If the person has died perhaps keep the rock on your table or somewhere else significant to you.

☆ Perhaps adopt some other things from this chapter into your life that may have spoken to your heart in relation to rocks.

☆ Find a smaller rock to carry with you. See how you feel about doing that. Try it for awhile as Josh did and as I do.

☆ Perhaps make (or buy) a soft medicine pouch with drawstring for any special rock or rocks you find, or for a feather, or any small treasures meaningful to you.

☆ Think of how much that rock placed on the chair meant to Pahtuta. Perhaps it will help you to realize how meaningful rocks can be.

☆ Never let your heart harden and become like a rock. Be a gift to others giving joy and love and peace from your heart.

Let me share with you a poem written about my dad. Perhaps you will be inspired to write a poem about "the rock" in your life too. You could write it in your journal!

LIKE A ROCK

His birthday and Father's Day fall in June—
And it is as if an entire platoon
Of marching feet trample on my heart.
For eighteen years we have been apart.
Often within I find myself careening
Into sadness, celebrating quietly the meaning
Of my father's days—
His gentle ways.
I wish him here to share in what is ours.
His absence—strong, visible, like a rock—towers
Over my life, while I recall—
He truly was the best—and still stands tall.

Dedicated to Ellis George Gray,   JGK
my father, for his birthday, June 2
and on Father's Day 1995

In all the discussions about our Moose and rocks I have neglected to tell you that it is fall, having made only one reference to it, I believe, in the chapter about Matilda. Fall in New Hampshire is the most glorious season of all. "Leaf Peepers" (tourists) come from many states by car and on bus tours to travel around the lake and mountain areas here just to view the foliage. It is perhaps unlike any area in all of the United States, roads lined with brilliant colors of orange, gold and red, and truly an awesome sight for the visitors that travel so far to see it all. Our lake reflects the brilliance of the trees along the shore lines, giving double the pleasure. I take many pictures. The poem that follows describes the glory of it all. Often there is a second burst of color from the trees and the "Leaf Peeper" season is extended.

MORNING MAGNIFICENCE!

Ah, New Hampshire in the Fall.
God has put His Touch on all.
And yet today it must be said—
Magnificent orange, yellow, red—
Appear quite different and immense—
In color—brilliant and intense!
Each shade is vivid—at its height—
Causing sighs and pure delight!
Mirrored in each lake and pond—
Glorious trees seem depths beyond.
God surely used His Holy Paints—
Commissioned Angels and the Saints—
To work all night and in a flash—
They gave each leaf a Sacred Splash!

In appreciation to God   JGK
and dedicated to   October 4, 1991
Jane and Cindy   Feast of St. Francis of Assisi

These words speak of a rainy day and how the water can intensify the colored foliage —but can do much more if we wish.

FORGIVEN

The rain is pouring down today
The fallen leaves in disarray—
Are colored splashes everywhere
On porch and ground and in the air.

The green pine needles now are brown
They too, in masses have come down.
The rainbow trees in long parades
More brilliant now in rain drenched shades!

We need a day like this because—
It seems to wash us of our flaws.
As He is washing lake and earth,
Let's claim this rain for our rebirth!

Envision cleansing of our soul!
Ah—God's made us now all new and whole!

JGK

I cannot imagine living here in the woods and not keeping a journal.
I would like to share now with you the significance of journal-keeping.
Keep your journal near you as you read, and a pen. Perhaps make a
refreshment and prepare to be inspired and motivated to write.

CHAPTER FIVE

Journal Keeping

Think of your journal as a loyal friend.
Let your journal-writing time be a sabbath time for you,
an enjoyable quiet time, even a gift you give yourself.
—Ronald Klug, *How to Keep a Spiritual Journal*

$\mathcal{I}$ F YOU ARE MAKING THIS RETREAT IN IMAGINATION and through reading this book, but have not as yet begun to keep a journal or to have even purchased one, then perhaps I can inspire you to rethink and begin to write. It is not too late to begin and once you have, I believe you will be so surprised and interested in where your writing is taking you, that you will wonder why you never before began.

Anne Morrow Lindbergh, author of many published journals and other books as well, states: "When one is a stranger to oneself then one is estranged from others, too. If one is out of touch with oneself, then one cannot touch others. . . . Only when one is connected to one's own core is one connected to others."

And this all comes about through journal writing, and I would also add prayer. I believe this combination will add a new dimension to your life. I cannot recommend it highly enough. Journal keeping is not just to record only the pleasant and lovely things, thinking that if one begins to collect a pile of woes and troubles in your journal that through rereading, these entries would bring you down emotionally. No, as a long tome journal writer I can attest to the fact that quite the opposite occurs. For a moment perhaps you will feel a sadness as you relive what you have

76

written about, but it is far from depressing and actually becomes a source of encouragement. It does! Those dark days and episodes are but a memory and to have made it through the rain and storms is a gift to yourself that you have recorded forever. It is something you can return to to reread if ever you have more pain or sorrow, for it will be a testament to a previous victory in your life, and if you attained that victory then, surely you can again. I am writing this all from experience and it is all truth! I have journals that I believed I would never want to reread, that just the writing and purging were sufficient and I got all the pain and badness out of me and that was the all in all, but I was proven wrong time and again.

Just last summer, as I previously mentioned in Chapter 1, I was unexpectedly forced to make a retreat alone here for a week. The events that surrounded the reason for my being alone caused me much sadness. I thought these feelings would all go away after that week and life would go on. But the sadness continued and I can only describe it as having a broken heart. It is not that my heart had not been broken before, it was just that this time I thought as time passed it would not ever heal. If I had not been involved in the writing of this book and in the keeping of journals, I believe I could not have gone on without some Pastoral help. The months passed (my retreat had been in June and I had just com-pleted writing a book and began to write this book in early November) and I wrote and wrote, yet still often not being able to see the paper and my handwriting for tears that would well up. Writing was my salvation (a gift from my Christ) and I filled journals while also writing this book. And I wrote many poems, as I am always inclined to do, but these poems were different and sad and bleak and depressing. Yet with every poem, every journal entry, and the continuing writing of this book, I was being pulled upward to a place of healing even though I first had to go down into the pits of pain. I still have a way to go and it is almost a year later, but without my journal keeping and my writing for this book for you I would not have been healed. I know that with a certainty! It has been an experience unlike any I have ever had. I will share one of my poems with you that will more deeply explain my sorrow and sadness again, unlike anything else I have gone through before. I have only shared it with two others, Bob, and a dear friend who also was experiencing despair and sadness. Now that I have "made it through the rain" perhaps its message will help another realize that you too, will be healed. And writing is the most wonderful way to achieve healing.

It Takes Time

One can die of a broken heart.
You slip and slide downward
      into the mire—
          a quicksand pulling
              you deeper and deeper
                    into sadness and despair.
There is nothing to cling to—
      yet you reach out to grasp
          again and again.
Your heart splits in two
      and you submerge into the depths—
          arms and hands upright
              trying to cling to Heaven
                to help you.
But you sink and sink—
      your own tears adding to
          all that surrounds you—
              all that pulls you down—
                and then you are gone
                    into the unfathomable
                      abyss.
One day you shall rise again—
      but it takes time.

JGK
February 28, 2000

When I get out the journal that I kept during that week of retreat I can re-read it, though I thought I never would want to or be able to do so. It was not the most despairing one of a collection of them, only the beginning one. I will eventually reread them all when I know I am strong enough. Without my writing in my journals, letting it all pour out from heart into my hand and pen, I would still be in despair. But I am not! The journal is like a spiritual physician or an Angel, and the act of writing like an actual act of release of the wounds and pain. Writing in a journal is a proven cathartic by many, not just myself.

R<small>X</small>—<small>FOR</small> P<small>EACE</small>—R<small>EPEAT</small> D<small>AILY</small>

Journaling into the night
    ofttimes in tears
        feeling the weight
            of all my fears—
                all that had gone wrong
                    all that took my song—
I write and write
    telling the smooth white pages
        all that hides
            all that abides
                in the secret recesses
                    of my heart.
And in time
    there is a lightness of being—
        a gradual freeing.
I pause—
    and in the sacrament of the moment
        having released the past—
            breathing freely at last—
              I sigh—
                and give thanks.

        JGK
        June 12, 2000

I have written about journal keeping in my three pervious books because it is so much a part of me. I believe you would find much support and help especially in *The Enchantment of Writing* and *Higher Ground*. My *Journal of Love* is about communicating with animals through journal writing and is different than the others, but then each book touches on journaling in a different way.

Though my journals reveal my inner state of heart, soul and mind during that difficult period, I was being healed through the writing of them, and also through the writing of this book. I wanted to write a joyful book about this woods and cottage I love so and all of nature, believing healing would come and also hopefully help readers as well. And healing did come as I realized anew this beautiful place is a gift from God and a healing grounds. Perhaps if your heart is heavy this book will help you as it is helping me through the writing of it. This chapter is being written as I near completion of this book and I realize now it belongs near the beginning of the book not at the end, so that it may encourage you to use a journal while you are reading the book and making the retreat. So though I am writing in early June it will appear before the chapter Winter," for journal keeping is for every season, and can be placed anywhere I choose. I was so involved writing about the seasons and wildlife and flowers and all I love while they were making their spring and summer appearances in proper order through the year, that I waited to write about journals for they are not seasonal. However, a journal is a book for all seasons to me.

> Open your journal
> and on pages of white
> Write all of your joys—
> and too, your "dark night."

> JGK

Yes, it is to record the joyful and the sad and anything you wish to put into it. There are no rules in keeping a journal, though I would suggest two that I abide by that are rather significant to me.

1. Date all your entries.
2. Do not share your journal with others for this will inhibit your writing.

At some point down the line you may feel you want to share a small portion with a friend, perhaps an entry or more that might help the person. I can only emphasize then, to not give the entire journal to them, but copy out the portions you wish to share for them that they may keep them. If you plan to expose your journal in entirety to other eyes you will be inhibited in your writing always. You want to be able to freely write anything that is on you heart, and for your eyes only. That is the point of journal writing. And it will free your entire being the more you write in privacy. These entries in your journal are from your heart for the edification and healing and solace of your soul, so use discretion. I have used two entries in two of my books, but never have shared any others. To write in a journal is like having your own therapist at times, and this has been very especially proven true to me this past year. I could not survive without writing in a journal if that is any indication as to its importance and strength in my life. Writing in it also makes me feel closer to God and my Angels. I keep a separate journal for my Angels for I feel it is necessary.

> *Talking to paper is talking to the divine. Paper is infinitely patient. Each time you scratch on it, you trace a part of yourself, and thus a part of the world, and thus part of the grammar of the universe.*
> —Burghild Nina Holzer

A journal is like a Holy sanctuary you can return to again and again. It is not only good for the soul but the body as well. It is well known that writing about heartaches or anything at all that is bothering you can make you feel better psychologically. Recently there has been evidence that it can also make you feel better physically, too. In the July/August 1999 issue of Remedy Magazine it was related that in a study of 112 adults with rheumatoid arthritis or chronic asthma, doctors asked two thirds to write about a very upsetting event in their lives. Following instructions, they wrote for 20 minutes a day, three day in a row. The rest of the people just wrote about their plans for the day.

It was rewarding to learn that at checkups two weeks, two months and four months later, almost half of those who had written about a traumatic experience had marked improvements in their asthma or arthritis—whereas over half the others had no change at all. Joshua M. Smyth, Ph.D., assistant professor of psychology at North Dakota State University in Fargo, says, "This is the first study to show that writing about stressful events may actually reduce the symptoms of a chronic illness." When asked "why," he states, "Trauma may produce hormone changes that affect long term health, and writing about it may help to restore balance."

James W. Pennebacker, MD in the late 1980s, examined healthy people and journaling and his research concluded that when a person wrote about the most traumatic event in their life, the participant or participants stayed healthier than those who wrote about mundane subjects.

Journaling helps those who take the time to write to get rid of those things that are troubling them. Journaling slows you down and it is a whole body experience. Pennebaker and Smyth agree, but admit they still do not know why journaling heals both the body and soul. As one who journals I can only agree that it does. Smyth and Pennebaker remind and caution that it is not just any writing that helps you to stay healthy. If you write without examining your problems then this will not bring the best results. But writing and addressing the stressful event or problem for four consecutive days and writing for 15 to 30 minutes will bring the best results. Sometimes one feels worse at first when beginning to journal about a painful event, and I can attest to this. It may take weeks or months to notice you are feeling better. (Some of these findings have been reported by Susan Luzader in an article "An Entry a Day" in the magazine *Personal Journaling,* Winter 1999.) If you decide to write in this way to explore your pain do not let others see this particular writing. Include all the emotions associated with the event and try to write at a certain time each day if you have not done this type writing or any journaling before. This helps you to establish a writing discipline. Set aside 30 minutes and also during this time explore other aspects of your life such as relationships and childhood. When you write, write in stream of consciousness writing, writing continuously without worrying about spelling or grammar. These thoughts are all to help those with both emotional pain and for those with asthma and rheumatoid arthritis, but writing such as this cannot but help other conditions in our life because we are releasing so much pent up in us when we write in this way. Stress and anxiety I know it helps from personal experience.

This way of journaling relates to those dealing with issues in their lives, but journaling is for everyone and just for pure enjoyment. To know that it has added health benefits is very reassuring.

I have several times read James W. Pennebaker's book, *Opening Up—The Healing Power of Confiding in Others*. He discusses journaling extensively in his writings and you would find this book very informative.

> Pour out your heart
>   in your journal of choice,
> In releasing your words—
>   you capture your voice.

JGK

Some people now keep journals on the computer, and if this is better for you that is fine. But I am mainly speaking of actual writing by hand in a journal, which gives a certain release and good feeling that can only be experienced by doing it. Also you can keep your journal with you to use anytime you wish and this is important for it should be your confidential friend. Enrich your journals too by describing occasionally your surroundings at the time you are writing. You will not always take time to do this but in later reading you will appreciate it.

Locked within yourself are all the things in life that have ever happened to you, the good and bad, your desires and dreams, the things that have been said and the words that have remained silent. Within your spiritual center these all exist and it is through writing that release will come as you slowly allow them to be recorded in your journals. Forever you will have them written on paper. Often as a result of having them in written form then wounds are healed or poetry is created or even the writing of books. I have experienced all three through first writing in journals.

Some like to play music while writing and if this encourages and inspires you then that is good. Certainly the more meditative music would be best since you are trying to go deeper within yourself. It is also good to pray or meditate first before beginning to write for as long a period as is right for you personally, and that will bring peace and inspiration. If you plan to spend a longer time writing you could light a candle and set a mood. You may even make a cup of your favorite tea or coffee. And yes, I repeat, keep your journal close to you and respect it. As I suggested in my previous book, if you have an altar or special table, perhaps keep it there. On this retreat you will find it best to keep it in your sacred space, perhaps transferring it to a night table by your bed when sleeping, in case you wish to write at night or record a dream.

Some take their actual journals with them every where they go in their pocket, a bag, purse, or just to keep on the car seat. Only you can decide. As I have revealed before, I never take my actual journal with me unless just outside my cottage, but always instead have a steno pad. Anything I write goes in there and I transfer necessary things later. The steno pad goes in the car with me not my journal. As years have passed these steno pads have also remained personal and not for other eyes. They contain only the briefest asides and recordings that are expanded on in depth later in my journals. But at home of course I write directly into my journals. Some writers keep folded index cards in their pockets or papers to write on. One journal keeper and poet uses small loose leaf books as journals, so she keeps a few blank pages from these in her pocket as she takes nature walks or goes out anywhere into the world. You can devise your own methods, just so they inspire you to write in your journal. You can write anything you wish in your journal. You will be guided by the Spirit and you will be surprised at times what pours forth on the page.

Creating Personal Journals

Thomas Moore, in his book *The Re-Enchantment of Everyday Life*, tells of creating his own personal journal. Having bought a manual of home bookbinding and some red leather, he stitched together and covered a large book of empty pages for writing down his dreams. He stated he never again looked at a book in the same way since that project. That he thought his dreams important enough to record also is inspiring, and you too can do this in your journal or in a separate one meant only for dreams. And too, that he actually made his own journal speaks of the significance that he places on journal keeping.

Thomas Moore is a Christian, but from the Buddhist tradition, Lama Surya Das, author of *Awakening to the Sacred—Creating a Spiritual Life From Scratch*, also tells about his writing. He writes that he needed a spiritual notebook, for he already had a black, bound poetry journal and a dream journal, and now he wanted one for matters of the spirit. At first he began to record prayers that spoke to his heart and mind on scraps of paper. Soon after he wrote them all down in a little notebook. But as this practice grew in significance he bought a special new notebook and asked a spiritual friend who was a calligrapher to copy them all down for him. He then covered the notebook with a rich red and gold fabric, and he carries this book with him wherever he goes. It had gone around the world with him several times. He prefers collecting prayers by recording them the old fashioned way, by hand. He encourages his readers to start collecting their own prayers, but states that all that you put into a prayer journal does not have to be formal. He includes words, phrases, bits of hymns and chants and even popular songs that speak to him in a spiritual and personal way. Many of them are also throughout my own personal journals aiding in my spiritual life, both through the recording and the reading, and like this author, I too, know by memory many of the personal writings of significance I collect.

Writing down soul stirring poems (our own or others), stories and other passages that similarly touch our hearts and minds, we begin to realize a power revealing itself in our own handwriting. This makes us come to the knowledge that there must be many other sacred writings than those in authority have revealed in and through the religions of the world. When we begin to collect in our own handwriting our personal selection of soul-stirring texts, and take the time to write them out meditatively, these then become like personal scriptures.

As I have always felt throughout my entire life, reading and writing go hand in hand. I could not live without either. They are good for my soul.

Francis Dorff, O. PRAEM, in his fine book *Simply Soul Stirring— Writing as a Meditative Practice*, states: "Writing and reading are actually twins, Reading leads to writing and writing leads to reading and both of them are capable of stirring our soul." He suggests too, reading something back to ourselves that we have written and this can at times cause us to discover a truth that we did not even remember or realize that we had written earlier. We then often find our souls being stirred by our own writing.

I know when I do this it often causes me to write more because new thoughts are generated or we are given a teaching through the writing, and even from our own life. When you pray with a pen you do not always write about what you *already know* or feel or think. At times you write to *discover* and come to the full knowledge of what it is. Your journal's pages begin to hold thoughts and images from your own depths that will amaze you and also heal you.

Writing truly illuminates our life and takes us places we never dreamed we could discover both through imaginatively entering into it and through the truths of our life recorded.

In my previous book, *The Enchantment of Writing*, I tell of another author and journal keeper who suggests that you wrap your journal in a lovely soft scarf or a meaningful piece of material and keep it in your quiet corner or sacred space, or perhaps on your altar table as I have mentioned. This is a beautiful thing to do, and as the author also suggests, the unwrapping of your journal can become a ritual and could include carefully folding the scarf or draping it over a cushion to add to the sweetness and spirituality of the setting. These last two thoughts are from a gentle and inspiring book entitled *Find a Quiet Corner—A Guide to Self Peace* by Nancy O'Hara. And since sharing this with others in my previous book I have begun such a ritual with my Angel Journal. Even though I have kept journals since I was a child, I am always open to thoughts of other journal keepers and their forms of creativity that enhance the act of writing in a journal and I like to share them. If at times one's interest lags, a new concept on the art of writing in a journal definitely is motivating.

Often the more we journal we are moved beyond words and it is then we may want to try to draw the images that we see interiorly. It is often surprising to learn that we can make such drawings if we were never inclined to do so before. These drawings are a form of journaling and will become precious to you. You may wish to use the different drawing materials, pens, pencils, brushes, paint etc., that you brought to your sacred space on your retreat. You will treasure what you are led to draw.

Journals and Writing Instruments

Before you go on with your retreat treat yourself to a journal if you have not already done so. That will be a significant and fun thing to do. Choose one that truly appeals to you, within and outwardly. Choose a cover that is attractive to you and draws you to it invitingly, and check to be sure the paper is a nice quality to write on. Decide too, if you wish lined or unlined pages. You can better add drawings and sketch on plain pages along with your writing, but you can draw on lined pages too. I do!

Selecting your writing instrument is important as I mentioned in the first chapter. It can be a favorite pen, or you may want to buy new ones for your new journal and this retreat, perhaps in different colors to express different moods or subjects. I used to write only in blue for years with a favorite pen. Then I began use different colored inks at times. But in 1989 Bob and I became vegetarians for the animals sake, and immediately I began to write in green only (our favorite color), for it represented nature and animals to me. After eleven years of total commitment to vegetarianism for the love of animals, I am still writing in green only; journals, letters and anything I write except this manuscript and all previous ones. For those I write in pencil on loose leaf paper. So enjoy picking our your journal and writing instruments for they are a drawing factor and entice you to faithfully write in your journal. I am forgetting to tell you that there is one other exception to my using green ink, but in my journals only, and that is on the dates of my mother's birth, death, and her wedding anniversary. Because her name is "Violet," I use violet or purple ink pens to honor her. Just a simple thing. My dad is equally honored through my writing in green on his days, for love is in all of this personal writing. And back to the use of hand writing only as I mentioned as the way I keep journals. I feel it is more personal and things can be added, and you can draw or glue things in (and I do both), and it all becomes extremely personal and "you."

You will find journals you like and it will be fun to keep your eye out for your next one, once your present one is almost filled.

When you meditate write down what comes to you in these times, or images you see on your inner eye. Everything and anything of significance can go into your journal. You are its keeper.

Privacy of Journal

Keeping your journal private if you live in a family household requires inventiveness and it is important. If you begin to use it faithfully you will find a secure place for it when you are absent from your home if you think others will read it. I do not have to suggest places. You know your own home and I do not. If you do carry it with you then you will not have that problem, but if you are acquiring a collection of completed ones then you do need to find a secure place.

If you have a family that you know will not pry into your journals then you do not have to keep them anywhere private, only where you wish them to be. One writer keeps hers on a shelf above her desk, years of completed journals. My current journals I can leave about near me for Bob would never pick up my journals and read them. My whole collection of them from years past however, is secure in this small cottage hidden away, for we often have many family members here. Eventually we are going to have to build another enclosure of some sort, a "Journal Hut" perhaps, to move all my completed journals into, unless one day my writing room here will be strictly that, and not at times become a guest room as it does. Then I could have my journals on many shelves out in the open for my own use as I do all my books that are on shelves in this room and all over the cottage. But only you can decide how best your journal can be kept from other eyes, unless you completely trust others in your home if you do not live alone.

Journal keeper and writer Christina Baldwin states in her detailed and excellent book on journal keeping, *Life's Companion—Journal Writing as a Spiritual Quest:*

> My journal is my life's companion. The format changes, the pens change, the contents vary, the cast of characters comes and goes, yet this tangible object reminds me that my life is being lived on many levels; it reminds me that I need to act, watch, reflect, write, and then act more clearly. It urges me to remember to pay attention to spirit, to be led rather that lead.

So many other writers and those who do not write as their life's work, proclaim the use of a journal. There are excellent books on the subject of journaling if you want to read further on this wonderful subject. I believe I could write an entire book on the subject for as many journal keepers as there are, so are there vast and different thoughts on this subject to share, as well as the methods and usages that many writers share in common, the very basics.

Rochester's Journal

In the past three years a phenomenon occurred when I learned to communicate with my beloved little companion Rochester. This is well documented and shared in my book, *Journal of Love: Spiritual Communication with Animals Through Journal Writing*. This book covers much more in the mysterious ways of communication, but through prayer and writing there came a break through that allowed Rochester to tell me his thoughts. I record them all in his own journal and many of the original messages are included in my book. It has been a blessing, that like our loving bond is inexpressible, beyond words. It is a means of communication that others can learn to do including you who read this now. Upon completing the book I later learned of others who communicate with animals, though not all through the written word as Rochester and I do. It is utterly amazing to experience this with a precious companion. His journals are my treasures, expressions of our love and life together.

Anne Frank

One very well known journal writer is one you may never have read though million of others have read her diary. I am speaking of Anne Frank. I can only hope if you have not read her diary that you will now be inspired to do so. She has shown the world that writing truly can sustain the human soul in all circumstances and also shown us courage and endurance, though her brief life ended all too soon. She wrote with a maturity far beyond her years and wished to become a journalist. She received her diary on her thirteenth birthday from her parents and it sustained her all during her period in the attic where she and her family were hidden away from July 1942 to August 1944 from the Nazis. When it became filled she added pages to it and she was given accounting books by her protectors so she could continue her diary. The original hardcover diary had been a red and white checkered book, her best friend whom she named "Kitty." Not only was her diary kept hidden but she was hidden as well, and writing in the diary kept her aware and alert and she wrote from her heart. Her diary has affected millions of lives, my own included, for one reading for me was not enough. I will always be reading it. She kept her journal neatly using fountain pen. Once you read her diary you will understand that there is strength and beauty in writing. More can be read about this and her diary in my *Enchantment of Writing*. But to obtain her diary too would inspire you in ways that only she can. If a young girl in these dire circumstances that ended in her death can write faithfully in a diary, why can we not all do so?

On May 2nd of this year we learned it was Remembrance Day for all the dear holocaust victims. All that week was being dedicated to them in remembrance, but Tuesday, May 2nd was the significant day, and people were taking turns reading aloud the thousands of names of people killed in the holocaust. I do not know where it took place but it was continuous. What an incredibly beautiful thing to do, to say each victim's name aloud. I wrote about it in tears in my own journal.

I said Anne Frank's name aloud many time through that first day, but continue to do it all the rest of that week to be in spirit with all the others called to do this. I also said the names of her family members aloud throughout the week. Such an extraordinary form of remembrance created to honor all those who suffered such tortuous deaths.

In Conclusion

As a record along the way, I write in a journal. My journal is bound, so that I'll take it more seriously and won't lose the pages. (I formerly jotted notes on sheets of yellow pads) It's not a diary. It is a sketchbook: furniture designs, speech drafts, silly thoughts, serious reflections, and drawings, all mixed together as life is—or should be. It is my personal equivalent of mankind's museums and libraries. It is a tangible record of the balance of my life. It makes me see better and take life with both more seriousness and more whimsey. I like it.

—Nicholas Johnson, *Test Pattern for Living*

There are so many ways to journal, but it is only in acquiring a journal and a pen that you like, that you will discover the joys of journaling and the healing that it brings. It is through journaling that we discover an inner dimension that initially may have been difficult to express. We discover parts of ourselves that we did not know existed. Other dimensions of reality can be reached by going into the mystical realms. This is especially true when we free write or use stream of consciousness writing not stopping to correct mistakes or to worry about spelling or grammar. It is good to do this often and for a substantial amount of time, perhaps thirty minutes or more. You will be glad that you did. You will discover things and be amazed at what pours forth on the paper. And in the silence and stillness of your heart and mind as you write and also meditate, you will contact the sacred. My first book, *Whispered Notes*, done with my husband, is evidence of where silence and writing freely can take you—into the mysteries of life and God.

Create a loving ritual of silence surrounded by the objects in your sacred space. At first you may think nothing is happening but if you have a sacred space and use it, something will happen. I promise you! Keep your journal with you recording all you experienced in or following an extended period of silence. Just sit silently and focus on your journal, or open it to a blank page, and you will be given a message to write down. And I again emphasize, sketch things too that you may have seen in spirit with your eyes closed. It is in silence that you will receive direction for your life. Waiting for you in silence is insight as well as direction. You are then able to continue on your quest, a quest you may not even realize as yet, that you are on. But in writing in a journal, prayer, meditation, and waiting in silence, and also valuing silence more as a part of your life, you will be led more fully on your quest. If your mind wanders do not get upset and think you failed. Just return to the silence without criticizing yourself. You did not fail.

Perhaps you will want to contemplate more deeply on the thoughts in this chapter on journal keeping and silence before continuing your retreat. If you have not obtained a journal as yet or a special pen, maybe now you will purchase them and think of them as sacred before you read further. You may even want to reread some of the thoughts and suggestions to further inspire you. Preparing your new journal once purchased will also motivate you to use it the rest of this retreat and then, forevermore. Life itself is a gift at any age and writing allows one to appreciate life in a unique way. Writing enhances awareness and the more I write the more I want to write, for I see the treasures of life all about me waiting to be forever recorded in a journal, to be reread and savored, to have forever. Like Anne Frank, giving your journal a name might be the very thing to help it seem extremely personal if you have never journaled before. Now is the time. Do not wait any longer. I pray you will become a journal writer and thereby discover yourself in ways you never knew possible. I will wait as you prepare, and I will leave a poem here on the page for when you return.

JOURNAL SPEAKING

I am your journal—
    a waiting receptacle
        for all that floats
            from out your pen—
Capturing notes
    directly from your heart—
        holding them in utmost secrecy—
           upon my pages,
Protecting them in the now
    and for all ages.
        Writings that are fragments
           of your inner being—
Spread across my whiteness,
    for your seeing—
        an extension of self
           in clear view—
Revealing a deeper dimension
    to all that is you.
        Journal and pen—
           your transport to ken.

JGK
June 15, 2000

Reflect and Journal

☆ Create a prayer to record in the beginning of your journal to bless it.

☆ Write something in your journal that you have never confided to paper before. It is like releasing it from your inner being. Seeing it on paper give thanks that you have released it. If it is something that has deeply troubled you believe now you are free of it. If comfortable in doing so, lift your journal upward symbolically offering this confidence to God, and by so doing He now will take care of it for you. You are free!

☆ Write what it feels like in your journal to know you are free!

☆ Perhaps write a poem either about your journal or anything significant in your life, or about this retreat you are making.

☆ Write each day about all the things that make you feel loved and thought about and honored, things that make you smile and laugh. This will help you to be more aware of joy.

☆ Write about a time in your life when you stayed by yourself for at least one day and one night. If you have never done this, please do it. And what did you discover about yourself in those hours alone?

☆ Write in your journal about this retreat you are making and how it is affecting you. Be attentive to any personal messages meant just for you that seem to rise up in each chapter. It could be the entire chapter, a paragraph or only a line. Do this with each chapter and go back to do it with the beginning chapters also. There will be many things for you to contemplate then recorded in your journal.

☆ At times, take some of these personal messages that rose up out of each chapter for you and journal in "stream of consciousness" writing about them at greater length. See what comes forth on the pages from your inner being time and time again. This will cause you too, to be more attentive in reading, not taking everything at surface value only. You will read more meditatively.

☆ Describe in your journal the surroundings and wildlife you see in imagination, as if you are actually here in the woods on "Higher Ground." Continue to do this as you continue to read this book.

To further inspire you in journaling, along with my book *The Enchantment of Writing* and others mentioned in this chapter, you may like to read the following, favorites of mine.

Journal to Self: Twenty-two Paths to Personal Growth by Kathleen Adams, M.A. (a Time Warner Book).

A Walk Between Heaven and Earth: A Personal Journal on Writing and the Creative Process by Burghild Nina Holzer (Bell Tower, division of Crown Publishers).

also any journals by writer May Sarton, a writer who lived in New Hampshire and then moved to Maine. Her entries are simple yet profound. She speaks of the seasons, her writing, her beloved pets, her gardens, her old home, her fears. She died in 1993, but her journals and books live on. I have them all on my shelves and reread them.

And now—bundle up "in spirit" and draw your retreat throw or blanket around you and put the kettle on for a hot drink, for you are going into the winter of New Hampshire by means of imagination. May you be extremely blessed through this experience.

CHAPTER SIX

$\mathcal{S}now$

. . . we want it to be cold, we want the snow, desire the isolation, desolation,
insulation, silence. It is why we're up here, it's why everyone's up here.
I want more snow. I want to be snowbound."
Rick Bass, "Winter" (*Notes from Montana*)

HE SNOW HAS ARRIVED AT 3:00 PM as predicted and is falling so heavily I cannot see across the lake from the vantage point here of the windows in front of my desk. It is like a thick, lacy never-ending curtain waving and blowing in the winter wind. Animal prints that had been in the snow on our deck when we woke are already covered by this fresh fall. I hear a faint hum and know it is that of snowmobiles, but they cannot be seen.

Into dark February evening, which comes early, I write with much joy and enthusiasm because of the enchantment of this wild and crazy snowstorm before my eyes. I turn on the porch lights so I can continue to watch the snow outside and the three tall white birches. Snow is thick on only one side of their trunks. These trees are my friends. I have been here all day and now go down to share the evening with Bob who has just plodded his way through the deepening snow on our property from his Birchgrove office to our cottage. Before I cook dinner I run to the basement to switch on the Christmas lights that enhance our giant spruce next to our porch and decorate our screened in porch. No one will see them but the snowmobiles or any little animals. I turn these lights on to express joy and do this year round. New Hampshirites (and Mainers) do not always put away their lights until the next Christmas, but many are kept up. It is late February as I switch on ours. They are magical.

We eat our delicious vegetarian meal as we continue to observe the continuing storm that seemingly is worsening outside our sliding glass doors. We are so warm and comfortable but with dinner over I must take pictures. It is an obsession as usual.

I venture out on the screened in porch and then out onto the open deck. Huge piles of snow fall in on me as I open the door. The overwhelming beauty drives me wild!

NIGHT BLIZZARD

There is a raging blizzard outside—
With no coat or boots—clothed only in my excitement—I have defied
All things sensible, and with two cameras in hand
Have gone out in the snow to stand—to record this grand
Display of nature. The tall blue spruce by our door—
More glorious than I have ever seen it before—
Has such whiteness packed onto its every branch—
And shining, tiny, colored lights throughout to enhance—
While millions of flakes exploding in the wind, stream
Through the tall pines and firs. It is my winter dream!

I plod about capturing the piled high benches and table
And the totally covered van, and feeders no longer able
To provide food for the birds whom I pray are secure
In some hidden hollow known only to those who endure
And instinctively survive such a whirling blast.
I await anxiously their return when this night has passed.
The frozen lake is invisible—
as are the brilliant stars and moon we made ours
In awe, as we stood last evening in the freezing woods and hours
Preceding all of this. I tramp back inside—snow-covered and cold.
But overflowing within; more than my soul can hold.

JGK

Once inside after shaking the snow from me and changing into warm clothes I pen the preceding poem that was filling me and about to explode if I did not get it written. Every line poured out of me as the snow poured forth from the night sky. Warm and secure inside—Bob, Rochester and I spend a lovely evening together.

In the morning we wake to breathtaking beauty and the snow is still falling. It is a scene that only we three are privileged to view and we are grateful.

SNOW GIFT

I am the snow.
All through the night
        I fell—
Shimmering in moonglow
        and in the radiance of starlight—
And like a wondrous magic spell
I enchanted trees and lake and lawn,
Draping them in whiteness beyond compare.
When you woke at dawn
And breathed the frosty air—
I was there in glory creating each silent drift—
And this untouched beauty is my gift.

JGK

Mounds of deepening snow, at least two feet, are on our picnic table and benches on the deck. They are just giant humps of white. The birdfeeders have peaks of at least eight inches, yet a dear Nuthatch is persistent as he feeds at the mesh container filled with suet. At intervals, huge avalanches of snow cascade down from the tall firs and pines near the lake creating unbelievable mystical beauty. All our property is totally covered with at least three feet of snow as well as the docks. No rocks, and there are many in the walls around the gardens, can be seen. I take more pictures from inside the two doors of our screened in porch, some out over the lake and the others up our wooded hill. There is no path now to Bob's Birchgrove some fifty feet away. Everywhere extreme depths,

and we are snowbound now until the plough comes, which does not
occur until sometime after it stops snowing for any snowfall here. Our
statue of St. Francis is gone from sight, totally submerged in whiteness.
Branches on all the trees are heavy laden and our property seems like it
is one from a Christmas Card. Sun falls creating lovely shadows on the
snow's surface and I am so thankful to be here.

> Little dried brown leaves
>   clinging to branches of trees,
>   refusing to sever connection—
> Do you not remember your resurrection
>   last Spring—
>   when birds would sing
>   resting in your green bough?
> Did not your Creator allow
>   rebirth?
> Set free your withered stems!
>   O little leaves—once soft emerald gems,
>   you shall grow again; now fall to earth—
> And may you ride with joy the winter winds through space.
> The snow is far too cold a resting place.

Today we can see out on the lake because the snow storm is not
blizzard-like, yet heavy. A line of five snowmobilers is out on the lake and
I am reminded of a poem I wrote about other snowmobilers in the early
nineties as I watched them then circle the island again and again from my
desk window.

SNOW MOBILERS

> Snow mobilers on the ice—
> Circling once—circling twice
> Skimming now across the lake
> Gradual quiet in their wake.
>
> Around the island out of sight
> Left in stillness from their flight—

We settle down to contemplation
Alone here in our winter station.

All is peaceful at this shore
Silence reigns as once before—
When at the island's other end—
Snow mobilers 'round the bend!

Now at dusk each headlight makes
A spot light for the dancing flakes.
Across the lake and up our hill
Ah—quietness again until—.

The Little People

Several years ago on a day such as this I let my inner child play outside in the snow and the memories of that are delightful. I recall now how I grabbed the two gnomes that are on our porch for winter but who normally stand in a rock garden under a huge pine tree I have named "the gnome tree." The name comes from the trunk's appearance of age and mysterious openings and one of my nature naturally perceives it to be a home of elementals. The gnome figures give credence to this as they stand in the garden each summer guarding the opening in the tree. One

Gnomes in the snow

has a miniature lamb around its shoulders and a walking stick, and the other carries a shovel. Today I gather them up and for small nine inch gnomes they are quite heavy because they are filled with sand so they do not topple over in wind or rain in the warmer months. I plod through deep snow with these little guys carrying them every where on our property, for I have brought my camera along also. I place the gnomes on giant hills of snow, and arrange them so they look like they are conversing. Then I let them sink down nose deep in snow, or watch them march out of holes I have dug in picturesque areas. All of these scenes I capture on film. I take them to the hidden place I often sit, beneath and in front of my prayer chair in the bushes covered in snow, and photograph them there. No matter what scene I place them in they are so realistic and colorful against the vast whiteness. I am having a ball! They even venture forth and stand in snow neck deep on top of the van. They are particularly poignant standing on the dock up to their shoulders in snow looking out over the frozen lake, with a bit of a path I clean behind them so as to appear they just tramped there. Everywhere, everywhere are these two sweet gnomes. While outside with these two little colorful men I feel like a child again. I must do this more often! The beauty of this day remains to this moment as I share it all here with you and it ever shall be with me. As I run about in the deep snow placing them and creating fairy tale like moments in unusual areas around our home and on the shore of the frozen lake I peer to my left into the woods and as a result this poem is written to always remind me of this magical day.

WINTER FANTASY

Stomping about in mounds of snow
and covered in flakes—
I am in awe watching the wind blow
masses of whiteness over the lake's
Frozen surface. It fills all of the space
between heaven and earth—and clings to my face.

I sense—as I stand there alone,
that on the edge of my vision—in the blown
Enchanted forest afar and beyond,

near the wooded shore of the pond—
A white unicorn stares from behind a tree—
and I wait for him to play in the snow with me.

JGK

from my *Journal of Love*

I eventually carry my short friends back to the porch and the photos I take turn out beautifully and bring joy each time I look at them. My intent is to one day write a story about these gnomes and use my pictures to illustrate it.

GOLDEN MUSHROOM

Golden mushroom
        floating in grass like a parachute
                above a dense green jungle—
Bring me your growth and delight
        in all darkness—
And freedom to soar
        above fear.

JGK

In summer I take more pictures of them that are most unusual. In late July to early September we have giant mushrooms that spring up all over our property and only have a life span of four to five days. That summer the child in me comes forth again. I carry out my miniature tea set and as each mushroom reaches it peak from an initial rounded dome to spreading out in full size flatness, I place my little dishes on the top of each. My gnomes are then posed on either side of the mushroom table, set with tea service, and we invite the sweet deer that also graces one of my gardens. Many pictures are taken as I utilize in turn each full size table-like mushroom. Often I leave the tea set outdoors overnight during the period of these blossoming mushrooms, while the gnomes grow drunk on tea of dew from the tiny cups. They have a continual party for the duration of the mushroom season—journeying from mushroom to mushroom for tea, as humans often do, that take part in "progressive dinners."

*Gnome
tea party*

Once we even invited my daughter Jessica's two gnomes to one of these tea affairs. Her gnomes stand outside her old New Hampshire Bed 'n Breakfast and we gave our gnomes to each other one Mother's Day. They are all from the same family of gnomes but hers carry different items than mine. She is as zany as I am, so it did not seem strange these other two gnomes from Center Ossipee should visit and get in on the picture taking and tea. But adults as well as my grandchildren love the sight of them. We all stand and just break into laughter and giggle while I continually take pictures. One day perhaps these little gnomes really will turn up in a story picture book, as well as entertain us simple folk here. Often I come out in the morning to find a mushroom's life is finished, and it has toppled over throwing the little tea set into the grass and leaving the gnomes without a table. The mushrooms are birthed as quickly as they topple in death. They forcibly sprout up out of the ground throwing the giant plug of earth all over the surrounding flowers or grass and proceed to grow and take over. One moment they are not there and several minutes later they have made this abrupt appearance! Most amazing! They even sprout out of my rock walls or create holes in the soft carpet of green grass. They are poisonous to eat.

MUSHROOM

Flowers growing in peace.
Abruptly—a new lease

on the earth—
    sudden birth
Of an intruder!
Couldn't be ruder!
Up comes the top
Almost a pop—
      tossing a dirt plug
      as if a bug!
    Like a big nose
        it grows—
Pushing, shoving an orange bloom
      making room
For the rest of its self
    a big dome—then a shelf,
    a table—flat, white—
Growing steadily through the night!

Aggressively arrives
Four days thrives
Then disintegration,
    has its ration
        of time—goes to pieces—
        deceases
           to be!
Orange marigold now free
Shaking her leaves—reclaiming spot
Sways joyfully in garden plot.

JGK

And so my gnomes of the summer learn to be winter gnomes as well, and make this arduous journey all over our property in deep snow. But they are very congenial, since I tell them I am recording all their efforts and escapades on film.

My journey of imagination with the gnomes is not the only one I have taken, by far. Here is still yet another.

IMAGINARY VISIT

Snow showers fill all air and space.
Each flake a miniature spot of lace.
It's thrilling to be outdoors where—
The sky shakes snow into your hair.

It seems I'm on my desk top now
Inside my globe of glass somehow.
And someone's shaken us about—
It's filled with flakes of snow throughout.

The Holy Family are at home
And welcome me to their snow dome.
Upside down and back once more
It snows on creche—as I adore.

It's lovely in the globe so round—
But I chose real snow earthward bound!
And as I feel the night winds pass—
I'm glad I'm here—not under glass.

JGK

Rochester at window at my desk.
Snow globe with the Holy Family in it is on sill to his left.

Blizzard of 1992

Snow has always been magical to me since I was a child, therefore living in New Hampshire seems like a childhood dream, and yet I did not know anything about New Hampshire when I was a little girl. One winter in the early nineties, in January, we learn that a gigantic blizzard is coming up the entire Eastern seaboard from the south to New England. We are in Pennsylvania at this announcement but planning to depart for New Hampshire. If we wait we will not be able to leave Pennsylvania, and we are most anxious to be up north when the snow hits. So Bob, Rochester and I hustle out of Jenkintown early and drive with the blizzard practically chasing us on the tail end of our van.

NATURE'S WELCOME

Arriving back on Balch Lake's shore
With frozen ice stretched out before—
And velvet black an arc on high,
With sparkling stars that fill the sky—
I thank Our God that I can stand—
Upon this wondrous Holy land—
Amidst the winter scene so white
With only moonglow for my light.

JGK

We arrive in the still dark of early morning after driving through the night and lie down to sleep. When we wake in early afternoon snow is piling up on our deck and outside our sliding glass doors. The beauty of this intense storm is wondrous. Hours pass, and wind and snow continue. We hear reports of all that is happening up and down the East Coast. We feel blessed to be here so safe and secure and to witness this intense snow. It continues and piles up as we sleep through the night and into the next day. It seems never ending. But the beauty and the depth increase. We could not open our door even if we chose to, which we do not. Snow covers it from bottom to top in entirety. We are truly alone in the woods and totally snowbound.

Fortunately we do not lose electricity or water and so can get news about the outside world. Our phone continues to remain in service also. This isolation continues for several days but we are warm, and going about life normally within this small cottage. Our writing and reading go on and we are so joyful. It is such an adventure!

SNOW GAZERS

My friend and I sit side by side
Gazing out of the window—we just cannot hide—
Our pleasure and joy at what we behold—
Millions of snowflakes out there in the cold.
He turns and looks at me as if to say—
"I cannot imagine a more wondrous day."
And then we continue to lovingly stare—
(He on my desk and I on the chair.)
His uplifted eyes try to follow each flake
And he guides many down to earth and to lake.

He turns once again to me—blinks in deep love—
Then his eyes seem to draw down more flakes from above.
Framed in our pane is a work of great art—
The Creator has sent it—it brightens the heart.
And while my blessed friend and I sit in the quiet—
Inside our beings is an unutterable riot.

Dedicated to Rochester   JGK

Approximately late in the fourth day when the snow has stopped, we hear the distant motor of the plough coming to our rescue, but we are not anxious at all for it to arrive. Though finally freed and plowed and now able to get off our property and out of the woods, we still remain at home. It is why we travelled from Pennsylvania—to be in this isolation and austere beauty. It is a time of stillness and aloneness we cherish, and treasure the memories and writings we have from this experience. Not many share our love and deep feelings for the woods and situations like this, but we are in continual awe that our lives are lived out in this way and that we are so blessed to experience such wonders of nature.

Many other glorious snow falls have filled our woods since then, and each has been duly recorded in photos and journals, and many in letters written to family and friends. Always we keep our eyes directed to the birds and any other sign of wildlife we can see. There is an order and a simplicity that comes to the woods and too, a joy and beauty, but I am certain there must also be suffering and death, and this breaks my heart.

HIS STILL VOICE

Snow is falling on the birds—
Silently—and without words—
For in beauty we can know—
God's voice in every flake of snow.
And as it blankets trees and ground
His still small Voice in it is found.

For the birds—   JGK
For the snow   March 7, 1996

Ice Storm '98

One recent winter was the winter of all winters, specifically the month of January 1998. Let me share with you some of my writings recorded in my journal over a period of a week.

Journal

We are warned that an ice storm is hitting upper parts of Massachusetts, and all of the eastern portion of New Hampshire and great portions of Maine and lower parts of Canada. We listen, but have never experienced an ice storm and do not become alarmed. We have celebrated quietly our wedding anniversary at home on Wednesday and wake in the middle of the night to sounds we have never before heard. We lose all power just after midnight and sit in the dark wondering what is going on outside in the pitch black of night. I hold Rochester to me.

We wake to see we are trapped on our property. Everything is covered with ice, particularly the trees. Our power remains off all day as well as the phone. The ice is so horrific there is no walking outside nor can we check on our Mitsubishi that is parked at the top of our big hill due to previous snow and not being ploughed properly. We go about our day as usual and enjoying the icy beauty of it all. I write all day up at my desk and Rochester is ever with me. Night falls and we light candles to read by and just to be able to see each other. It is terribly cold inside so we know it is far worse outside. We have no running water now, of course, but fortunately have several large bottles of water on hand for emergencies. We are thankful that in the fall we purchased a small sized new gas stove. All these years we have had an electric one and at last got a gas one I had looked forward to, believing it be a more healthful way of cooking after studying macrobiotic cooking in the 1980s. Because of our new gas stove I am able to at least make us a hot meal, and too, intermittently we turn it on for short periods only at night to let some warmth come into our cottage. We know it is not wise to do for longer periods but it takes the icy chill off each time. We go to sleep believing we will wake in the morning to find all power on but it is not so. During the night too, come enormous cracking noises and what seems to be trees and branches from our wooded hill behind our home toppling on our cottage and roof. All through the night it is as if we are in a war zone. Out front we hear a horrendous crash and can only wonder what it is. We sit in the dark surrounded by "gun shots" all night long, unknown outlandish noise that becomes out of proportion in my mind because it is frightening. I keep Rochester close to me vowing to keep his cat carrier in the bedroom for him next night if this continues.

Boughs continue to fall during the day and we have never seen anything like this. We still have no power or phones. It is freezing cold. While we are trying to go about our day as normally as possible we suddenly hear Jessica and Michael, Maxine, Renee and Clayton at the door! We cannot believe it. What normally is a twenty-five minute ride was a drive of several hours for them from their Inn in Center Ossipee to our cottage in the woods. It is incredible they drive down, but not being able to reach us by phone for some time, they come to us. They relate how all the world outside and the routes we always use are covered with trees and debris and that it is unrecognizable. Michael has a chain saw with him to cut tree trunks and branches that fill all the roads yet all the while using extreme caution due to all the downed wires. Once through our woods he ties a rope to a big tree at the top of our hill and he lowers himself down the ice holding onto this rope. He then ties it to the fender of our van at the bottom of the hill, the van that never made it to the top before the first snow storm of the winter. He helps Jessica and the girls down by this rope, and Clayton is in a plastic box with the rope attached to it that is also attached to Michael's waist. It is our carton we use to drag groceries down the hill in snow and he finds it in our car at the top of the hill.

Bob leaves with them after they stay awhile to get rested. They want us to come live at the Inn until the storm is over but we do not want to leave our cottage in case damage comes to it from falling trees. Bob talks to some linemen while out and buys a few supplies at a local store. He has never seen anything like what he is witnessing as he makes this trip. It is as if there is war, and devastation is everywhere! He returns home by way of the rope our Drakelys installed when they came to save us, and Drakelys return home to their Inn. We are so appreciative all through the day for their efforts to help us.

They return the next day and bring more kerosene lamps and candles. With his chain saw Michael cuts up the enormous branches that fell from our three birch trees out front and that fill our deck and cover our windows. After awhile they go home. We have had fun being all together making light of all the disaster. We believe there are others far more in need of help. We are fine. Jessica's and Michael's electricity returns for short periods but we have no signs of ours. They also have a wood stove they use. We continue to be thankful for our new gas stove.

Each night is a repeat of the one before, bitter cold within and without with branches cracking in the ice and falling on our roof. Rochester stays close with us as he does normally but his carrier now is in the bedroom in case we have to flee. This storm continues through the weekend and Monday, Tuesday and Wednesday are much the same. During the day I pretend it is normal and go on with my writing and accomplish much. We cannot go to church so we have our own little service together and many prayers fill the cottage daily. The fragrance of an array of scented candles and kerosene lamps is beginning to become overpowering and we begin to laugh about silly things and have fun. Everything is so surreal we cannot believe we are experiencing it. We continue our work during each day and the sun warms my writing room a bit. Rochester snuggles in a comforter on the bed next to my desk. I worry about him at night, but he sleeps on top of me as normal, but I check often and make certain now he is there. We do not think it wise to keep the oven on while we sleep yet it is freezing. We know people are dying of hypothermia in this ice storm in their own homes!

By now Bob has found a radio and batteries so we listen only for two hours each night when the entire program is about the happenings in the ice storm. It is a program called "Neighbors Helping Neighbors." It comes from Maine. We know of all the devastation and deaths, and rescues and warnings. Public service from states as far as the Midwest are being enlisted and driving their trucks to these Eastern states that need their help. Our phone has returned for short intervals and we talk to Jessica and get outside news of their lives and in our area. Often the phone dies. It has only been briefly on. We continue to melt snow for washing dishes and ourselves. It is an adventure we shall never forget. We learn again of the long lines of these public service trucks driving the highways of ice to help restore electricity and repair the thousands of downed lines.

By Tuesday night I ask Bob to sleep in the living room so we can feel warmer. The bedroom is colder and I am worried that we are sleeping in there. Many die in their sleep in this cold! He finally agrees and sleeps on the sofa, and I in his recliner with Rochester on my lap. Toward early morning we all go back to the bedroom to get warm under the covers for a bit as the sun comes up. We are blessed. Hundreds of people are in shelters afraid to stay in their own homes. Everything outdoors is an icy, mystical, wonderland by day, but at night fear sets in the bitter cold. The phone comes back on more permanently by Monday but we still lose service at times. Operators at the New Hampshire Public Service are so comforting and give hope even if the prediction that power is to come on never happens. Again and again an operator tells us the power will soon be on and then we are disappointed anew.

All our bird feeders are on the deck and most destroyed by the falling Birch branches. Also the wooden bar that Bob built to hold all the feeders. Where are the dear birds? Do they have secret places to bury themselves into in dire times like these? Again I am worrying about them.

A full week without all power is so difficult in the icy cold and yet we are grateful, for we know from the radio we are far more fortunate than many others. We thank Christ and the Angels for their protection.

Thursday arrives. By now the roads have been cleared somewhat through our woods. We hear the machines. Bob is able to go up the hill by way of the rope and actually drive to the end of our road in the woods. Out on the street

Public Service trucks are parked and men working repairing lines. Bob sits and watches believing they will soon come through the woods to repair lines for us. After a long period the men finish and begin to get into the trucks. Bob watches as some drive away. He realizes they are all going to leave and he catches one of the men to explain that work still needs to be done in the woods. The man disagrees saying all has been finished. But our lines are separate from these and had Bob not come to sit out there he would not have been able to stop three tucks from leaving. We do not know then when we would have had power! Bob leads the trucks back into the woods to our hill and all the fallen lines. He even stays out in the cold with the men for a very long time as they work to repair our lines. I stand in the dark at our kitchen window keeping vigil through it all hearing their muffled voices, watching their lamps and flash lights, and glimpses of the workers and Bob. Suddenly, without warning, right in front of me on the wall beside the sink I am leaning against under the window, a light goes on! I cry instantly, pent up tears of a week. And it is not an ordinary light! It is my Angel night light! It glows there in the darkened kitchen proclaiming the Angels have been there unseen through it all! Because we lost power during the night, that was the only light lit in the kitchen and living room. Its brightness brightens my heart and soul. It is over! I go about turning on every light to welcome Bob back into the cottage, especially the porch light. And outside a Public Service truck from Colorado, with a crew from Massachusetts and two other out of state trucks, drive in a line up our hill and proceed through the woods. I feel like they should have majestic music accompanying them as they would if it had all been a movie. But this was a real life situation, and we are most grateful to this day for having lived through it when others did not. In some parts of the other states the power was out up to eight weeks!

About three weeks after these seven days without all power in the ice and cold, many items began to be sold depicting the ice storm. I wear a white sweat shirt at times that says in blue writing dripping with ice sickles, "I survived the ice storm of '98," and a handsome Moose is in the center of the writing. We bought a number of them for family and friends, and very especially for Jessica and Michael.

This is a period we will never forget and it is well written about in much more detail in my journal. I will always remember too, when that little glowing angel lit up in the darkness before my eyes at 6:20 PM on a Thursday night, January 15th, eight days after the power went off.

The power goes off often here in the woods, but we feel certain that we have experienced the worst situation of all, and so are not alarmed at night when we are often left in darkness while in the middle of a good book or television program. *We Survived the Ice Storm of '98*—and remembering that brings assurance in other situations.

Despite these alarming things that can happen in the New Hampshire woods, they are far outweighed by the natural beauty and serenity and joys of this woodland lifestyle. I would not want to live any place but in this cottage in this woods. It is my heart's home.

Here is a poem to lighten the spirit after the Ice Storm

ON THE TRAIL

From our side window we can see—
Large hill—leads from our property.
From lake and woods and hidden spaces—
It transports us to outer places.
In winter it's a sheet of ice—
My husband's lost his footing twice—
And slid down it just like a sled!
(It's been more times than I have said.)
And I have watched him go with speed—
And realized we had a need.

So now we have a way to walk.
Rochester and I had a private talk.
Little loving soul is he—
He gave his gift so generously!
And on that hill we made a trail—
Out feet don't fall—we take the mail—
And walk right up like there's no ice!
A kitty litter path is nice!

JGK

Rochester to the rescue!

Maple Syrup Time

One of the sweetest outcomes of winter in our state, and Maine and Massachusetts, is the sweet smell of sugaring in the New England air.

It is said that all that is needed is a string of warm dry days with some nice afternoon sun and five mile-an-hour breeze from the west. Once it warms up enough to start the sap flowing, sugarers need a chance mix of warm days in the 40s and nights with below freezing temperatures. This ideal keeps the trees from budding and prolongs the syrup season that, at most, lasts a few weeks.

The maple sap begins to rise up from the roots through the trunk and to the branches where it will feed the leaves later on. The sap develops a bitter taste once the trees begin putting out leaves.

Maple producers drill a small hole in the trunk and insert a spout to catch the passing sap. The clear sap either travels through plastic tubing to a holding tank or is gathered in a bucket, where it is collected and transported to the sugar house. There it is made into maple syrup by boiling it down into an evaporator. Depending on the weather the season usually lasts from four to six weeks. It takes 440 gallons of sap to make one gallon of syrup. We receive such information as this in our local papers. In the February 27th issue of the New Hampshire Sunday News it states that in Southern New Hampshire most maple producers have tapped all their trees and many will start boiling sap this weekend. Up north (in NH) most producers have started tapping their trees but are fighting deep slushy snow. With four feet of the whiteness even with snowshoes, the men are sinking to about three feet and wallowing around in snow. Many sugar houses around the state welcome visitors. The sap does not run everyday, so maple producers recommend phoning ahead to check on boiling times. A free brochure listing maple producers who welcome visitors will be sent to those who call the New Hampshire maple phone at 1-603 225-3757.

On March 2nd on a drive to Sanford, Maine we look for the buckets hanging on the trees along our quiet route and are not disappointed. Even to us it is still a thrill. As children who grew up in Pennsylvania and only knew about the collecting of syrup through reading in school, it still excites us every March and we look forward to it. It is all part of the passage of winter up here, and a very wonderful part.

On March 15th on an errand to buy books in Bookland, in Sanford, Maine, we stop the car by a woods. This time I have brought my camera, and I walk around in the snow to take numerous pictures of the many buckets hanging on the trees. Hopefully one of these pictures will be used to illustrate this segment, and others will be shared with family and friends. While the collecting of the syrup does not take place on Higher Ground, it is a part of us, and our rural surroundings that adds to our life here in the New Hampshire woods. It is a segment of winter, and the snow, and the traditions, and the magic of it all. On a trip to Sanford March 24th the buckets are still in place on all the trees.

Snow of November and April

After we first bought this cottage in the woods we tried to visit it as often as possible, but normally months would pass between visits. We decided soon after it became ours to drive here for Thanksgiving on numerous occasions. In the late 70s we did not have the roads in the woods ploughed, for only a few people lived here year round. This meant we had to park our van on Sanborn Road at the outskirts of our woods and walk the mile through the snow to reach our cottage down by the lake. I would prepare our turkey at home in Pennsylvania (we were not vegetarians until 1989) and all the items we would use with it. We would pull our Thanksgiving dinner in on a sled in early morning after driving all night. It was quite a hike but very exciting after just having driven 430 miles. For both walking into the woods to our cottage and for returning to our van when it was time to journey home, Bob devised a system that worked. Each child had two large trash liners tied together and draped over their shoulders holding their clothes and belongings and anything else that needed carrying in. Janna, just a very little girl, (8 years old when we began doing this) carried only one item, a guitar. This was Barbara's, and Barb created music for us while in the woods on both guitar and piano. Janna had the guitar strapped on her as she plodded in—and then out. We were quite a sight I guess, this large family walking in a line through the deep snow in the woods. We would arrive to a house so freezing cold it was unbearable.. We all tried to huddle around a small heater while the rest of the cottage slowly heated. After starting dinner and some brief naps, we had a most joyous Thanksgiving dinner in our little cottage, often while the snow was falling. We would be in awe at the glorious red and orange sunsets on the frozen lake. We had so much yet to learn and experience about life in the woods.

Still to this day I have such joy over the first snowfall, or any snowfall thereafter. So many wonderful journal entries have been made, and so many poems written about the snow.

FIRST NOVEMBER SNOW

Awakening to a new day
　　I found a gift!
Winter snow had found its way
　　Into the woods. A drift
Once known as low rock wall
　　Was softly white—
Contoured most gracefully
　　From snow's descent in night.

Trees in winter now
　　As eternal spirits bared
Have heavenly covering on each bough—
　　No branch was spared.
The birds in numbers come to feed
　　They feel the need—and too, the cold—
A newer urgency—but never greed.
　　And we behold!

Tiny tracks out in the snow—
　　Belong to visitors we know.
Winter's attributes and rareness
　　Create in souls a new awareness—
Of all our treasures from our God!
　　Today? White blanket on the sod!

JGK
November 18, 1992

In direct contrast to the first snow of the winter depicted in the previous poem, is a period of heavy snow fall I recorded in three separate poems when it came abundantly and surprisingly on three days in April 1996. I was ecstatic and played outside frequently enjoying every flake. (I think I was one of them!) I knew it would be the last of the snow until late fall, and I just languished in it. Rochester watched from the window, but inside together we shared these precious days in my writing room looking out at the beauty as I wrote. They are days and moments of preciousness in my heart.

The Birchgrove (Bob's office) deep in snow in April 2001

APRIL TENTH

April tenth I shall always remember—
It resembled a day in cold mid-December—
A day I became a child once more—
And played in the snow like I did years before.
I stood and let it cover my being—
And loved each flake that I was seeing.

I carried my camera and recorded it all—
Bird feeders, lake and the lovely stone wall.

Snow covered shrubs looked like decorative laces—
Then I crawled on my knees into magical places.
And good St. Francis was up to his neck—
As he kept watch by a tree near the deck.

Though we had days of snow all week—
It seemed today to be at its peak.
Like heavy white cotton it draped on each tree
Squirrels peeked from its deepness in order to see.
Snow fell and it whirled and it swirled and it danced—
And on April the tenth I was simply entranced!

JGK
April 10, 1996

March Snow

An unusual thing has happened. As I come to the end of these sharings on snow, a major storm has hit, and since early afternoon snow has been falling for many hours. We are told it will continue into morning, and so I write in the immediacy of the present moment sharing the joy and beauty of our latest fresh fall with you. Already we have at least six inches, and yet this morning we could see patches of green grass at last asserting itself here and there from the remains of the late February storm lasting two days. The trees are dressed in lacy white, and the two huge terra cotta flower pots on the deck totally covered by snow, take on the appearance of oversized vanilla ice cream cones. Everything is exquisitely pristine with high mounds and curve of soft velvet untouched whiteness.

March 17th

And still yet another snow storm is occurring five days following this one of beauty earlier recorded. St. Patrick's Day here is not green at all, but enormously white in the already eight inches of fallen snow. It is said it will continue into evening. Again we have lost St. Francis, and our vanilla ice cream cones are larger than before. Though patches of lake water are seen near the shore the lake is far from having ice-out. The surface is as white as all the earth surrounding our little cottage. Magic outside my window panes once more!

In the early 1990s when we did not live her permanently but travelled to our cottage as often as possible, I penned this poem upon arrival back in the woods. It expresses my joy of being here once more—and for my dear little companion who is always with me as I write.

MAGIC WINDOW

Back at my magic window
To the world of snowy wood—
Gratitude wells up in me
That God could be so good.

My desk has waited patiently
That old thrill comes once more—
I place clean paper on it—
My soul begins to soar.

A pencil is selected—
From the cat mug chucked so tightly—
I know now I'm in heaven—
A privilege never taken lightly.

Pencils, paper—view from window
Shiny brass cat so small—
Picture of Jesus—and Mary too—
And Hemingway—but that's not all!
For there beside my paper
Is a priceless gift from You—
My precious, purring Rochester,
Who always shares my view.

JGK

And the poem that follows expresses my yearning for just one more snow fall before Spring comes to stay. It is a yearly wish.

MARCH SNOW

I thought that snow would fall no more.
The whiteness all had left our shore.
Brown earth again was there to see—
My walls of rocks were greeting me.

And though the earth and rocks I love—
I yearned for snow from far above.
I missed the silence of the snow—
The soft high mounds we'd come to know—

The snow flakes filling all the air—
The wonder of those days so rare—
When boughs were covered and
bent down,
And we could never get to town—

The starry sky and woods so still,
And tramping down our crunchy hill.
I missed the magic of His Gifts,
Virgin snow blown into drifts.

Untouched—its beauty touched my being.
What majesty my soul was seeing!
So I begged He not forsake—
This prayer sent forth beside the lake.

And now this night I thank Our Lord—
That once again He could afford—
To bless this one—
with pure white ground,
And grant the wish to be snowbound!

*Butterfly house wearing
a tall hat of snow—
also windchimes with
snow bonnets*

Frost Heaves

After and during any snow storm, the lovely, winding, country roads of East Wakefield outside our woods, lined with forests on either side and occasional homes, are so beautiful to see and travel. The dense woods of tall trees of many varieties is under a canopy of snow at every turn in the winding road. It is a picture far more magical than any scene from a magazine.

The roads are always kept ploughed continuously throughout any snow storm, something we have always marveled at. One sign I had never seen until coming to New Hampshire was that of "frost heaves." These signs are frequently along our country roads. One March day while we travelled in the snow to the store several years ago, I penned this poem.

FROST HEAVES

New Hampshire winter snows abound—
Sun melts—snow drains to underground.
Freezing cold again returns—
The frozen water brings concerns—
That stays beneath the travelled roads.
It raises surface—road erodes.
Cracking, splitting, brokenness—
All outward signs of inner stress.

How much like roads we humans are—
Frost heaves beneath roads leave their scar.
But frozen heart and attitude—
Defeat and stress—these too extrude
Leaving "frost heaves"—lines and traces
Of brokenness on human faces.

O gentle Spirit—Holy Informant
We need your warmth on all things dormant.

JGK

I shall close with an amusing aside that was experienced on frequent occasions in the bitter cold winters here upon arriving at St. Anthony's. It is related here through a poem that reveals all.

I Told You It Was Cold!

Today in bitter, winter air—
We hastened up the wooden stair
Into St. Anthony's Church of white—
Stepped in the vestibule—and to my right
I there extended out my finger—
Expecting it momentarily to linger—
In Font of Holy Water there—
That I might bless myself in prayer.

Instead my finger met resistance
Though I pressed with much persistence.
When in the Holy Font I peered
The Holy Water I revered—
Had frozen solid! That is precise!
You *know* it's cold—When there's Holy Ice!

Dedicated to Fr. Edmund and   JGK
our wonderful New Hampshire winters   February 6, 1993

Some years ago the font was moved from the very cold vestibule and placed just inside the inner church door. We no longer have Holy Ice.

However, we did witness a very precious Holy moment on the drive to church one cold Sunday winter morning this year, and it is a never to be forgotten moment too. We pass a home with a small farm, and outside the barn on the ramp or in the yard we often see a horse and llama. The horse used to be alone then some months later we noticed a llama was there too. Now they are always together. This particular moment captured in heart and spirit was so other-worldly that this poem arrived soon after.

ONE HEART

Driving to church down Province Lake Road—
 we unexpectedly and by chance
  viewed a precious episode
   of tenderness and romance.
Standing face to face—
 cheek to cheek—
  with but a breath of space
   between—one could only bespeak
    of it as an embrace
     in spirit—most unique.
Under the trees inside the fence,
 their eyes open and bright—
  in reverence and innocence
   the horse's and llama's one heart took flight.
    And we were given that image sublime—
     all in a moment of time.

JGK
February 3, 1999

And so, these are just a few of the many treasures I hold in my heart of winter life here in this beloved state and woods. It is the only place I want to be.

Reflect and Journal

☆ If you knew in advance you would be snowbound for many days, what items would you be certain to have with you ?

☆ Write about these in your journal and why you would choose them.

☆ Imagine that you are snowbound for a long period. What are the many and contrasting things you would do that when the period was over would cause you to feel the time had been well spent and enjoyed?

☆ Write about these things you chose to do in your journal—and why you chose them.

☆ Sketch, or using crayons, draw a picture either in your journal or on a separate paper that depicts best to you a time of snow, isolation, a cottage, woods, outdoor play. Whatever is in your heart. Draw more than one picture if you wish. It may even be a childhood memory.

☆ If you choose, write a poem in your journal about snow and winter, or one that speaks about the picture you just drew.

☆ When you were a child what did your Mother or Father make you wear to winterize you against the cold? Remember one of those times being dressed to get ready to go out in the snow. Recall it in your journal.

☆ Did someone ever give you the "cold shoulder" or "leave you in the cold"? Write about it nonstop in your journal. Then with closed eyes and through imagination, treat the situation like an entity and dump it into a brown bag and seal it. Envision giving it to the gnomes of Higher Ground. See them with their shovel digging a hole in the snow and earth and burying the bag. Believe now that healing has come and feel the warmth flood you. Say thank you to God

☆ Who were you with and where were you when you tried to catch snowflakes on your tongue? What were you wearing? Write about it and capture those memories in your journal.

WHEN LOVE CAME DOWN

It fell to earth—and in the dark.
Rested gently on its mark.
From winter sky—to woods below,
It came to say—"I love you so."
Yet without words it spoke, I knew—
And in wonderment sighed—"It's You!"
For on my cheek, it had not missed me—
With His snowflake—Our Lord kissed me.

January 1990, NH   JGK

☆ This is a poem I wrote about a snowflake. I recall the exact place I was standing in the dark under the night sky. It was ten years ago but still seems magical to me because I captured it in a poem. Perhaps you might poetically record your snowflake too.

☆ In winter, take the time to record the details of your life. If you are doing it by imagination in mid-summer, that is good too, because you will search more for details to record through memories and visualization.

☆ Can you envision the sweet horse and llama as described in the poem? Have you ever thought about such tenderness between animals? If not, it is something to consider and to realize that it happens. Explore this in any way you wish, writing, art, poetry—but consider it, for it will enrich your life.

I will leave you with still yet one more poem that was one of many I wrote about the war in Iraq. I protested it silently with my writing, very especially through a collection of poems that resulted.

When the Sun Descends

Across the frozen lake I gazed—
From upper window, and amazed—
My eyes were drawn to fiery glow—
And orange patches on the snow.
The colored rim above the trees—
Sun going down in winter freeze,
With spreading brilliance in the West —
Was God creating! I was guest!

And though the West held my gaze fast—
My heart was in the East—that vast—
Arena on the desert sands—
Where men are dying in those lands,
And missiles soar and burst and scream—

Existence seems a frightening dream,
And people long for guns to cease—
While I am here in winter peace.

O Lord, please wipe the tears this night
Of all those living now in fright—
When next they see the sun descend,
May You have caused this war to end!

Dedicated to   JGK
all those   February 1, 1991
living in fear   New Hampshire

As you come forth from the retreat, be attentive now to signs of spring, though New Hampshire's spring is almost non-existent. Listen at dusk for singing outdoors by the lake's edge.

CHAPTER SEVEN

Peepers

Let a Frog Sing to You Tonight

—Frog Watch USA

Until he extends the circle of his compassion to all living things,
man will not himself find peace.

—Albert Schweitzer

$\mathcal{I}$T IS EARLY APRIL and we have not as yet heard any peepers, but I am certain they will arrive before I finish writing about them. Most people who live in New Hampshire know peepers are the signal sound of spring, above blooming crocuses, or melting snow, or the return of many kinds of birds. It is when the tiny peepers sing their sweet symphony that spring is official. These miniature frogs have been a fascination to us for years.

Peepers are thumb sized frogs that are born in marshes, bogs and fresh water, like our lake. They spend the winter under logs and bark, but at mating time they return in spring to wetlands to seek mates. The definitive calling by the male is what has earned it the name "peeper," and it is known that this sound is irresistible to the female of the species.

A characteristic of the Spring Peeper is the dorsal marks that form an X on the back. It may not be a perfect X, but some form of it. Variation of brown, gray, or green is the general coloration and like any of the Chorus Frogs, the Spring Peeper is often heard, but not seen. I have learned there are two subspecies of the Spring Peeper, their names being;

126

the Northern Spring Peeper, Pseudocris crucifer, and the Southern Spring Peeper, Pseuda cris crucifer bartramiana. From eastern Manitoba, south to eastern Texas and east to the Atlantic Ocean are the ranges of the Northern Spring Peeper. The Southern Spring Peeper has strong markings on its belly but otherwise practically identical to the Northern species.

It is interesting that there are eleven species of toads and frogs found in New Hampshire and spring peepers are one of these. Their calls are true harbingers of spring. Their relative the wood frog, makes a duck-like quacking, and the bullfrog a deep thrumming, but the call of the peepers is truly distinctive. It is not hard either to distinguish between frog calls because they begin calling at different times and only a few species are calling at any given time. Wood frogs are calling now and they are raucous and noisy. Though we have not witnessed this, females are said to come down out of the woods to join the males. There is an urgency to the mating and everything must be accomplished in forty-five days.

It was related in a New Hampshire newspaper that declines in frog populations should be viewed with alarm. "Sixty-five million years ago, when the comet or asteroid impacted the earth and wiped out all the dinosaurs and a large number of plants and animals, frogs somehow managed to survive. If they're in decline now it does not bode well for us."

More information given on the internet about this states that over the past one hundred and fifty years, rapid growth in agriculture, industry and urban development has resulted in dramatic changes in our environment. These changes pose significant challenges for animals and plants, as seen in the decline of frogs, toads, and salamanders. Scientists have recognized that amphibian populations have declined. Once thriving populations have diminished in numbers and several species are now extinct. Some of the factors identified as influencing amphibian declines are habitat loss, ultraviolet radiation, introduced species, fungal diseases, parasites and exposure to contaminants. Understanding is the key, for the decline of amphibian populations is crucial in uncovering how people's activities are affecting many aspects of our environment. We share our environment with amphibians and their decline may indicate challenges we will have to face in the twenty-first century.

And so we await the peepers with much joy. They make you smile with their persistence and constancy hour after hour after hour.

One spring I decided to record them, not only to have their songs to listen to in months when they were not present, but to send to a young grandson in Pennsylvania. We thought he might enjoy playing the tape at night to fall asleep to, and so imagine himself here by the lake. Recording the peepers proved to be fun. After they began carrying on one night and singing their little hearts out, I went outside with my trusty tape recorder filled with a blank tape. As I softly walked down to the lake to the area from where the loudest singing was emerging, their singing began to gradually decline. By the time I reached the shore line there was not one peep! I could sense these little creatures in the lake all staring at me in the dark, or so my imagination allowed me to believe. I set up my recorder on the shore and waited. Still no sound from them. As I turned and began to slowly walk away from the lake there sounded one peep, then another, then another, and by the time I reached our porch steps they were in full swing, loud and unrelenting, and so it continued until I went down to retrieve my tape recorder after thirty minutes. Again the same routine was repeated. They became silent. I was pleased to get a sharp, clear recording of their incessant song that continued on for hours. It is lovely to wake in the night and hear them singing. With one word change of the old and lovely song sung by the Trapp Family Singers, I can report that "The woods are alive with the sound of singing," come the month of April.

You can contact your local naturalist, environmental, or governmental groups to get more detailed information about the species in your area. It was reported in the local paper that most people in New Hampshire are already familiar with the calls of several common frog species, and that the rest of the frog calls are easily learned by listening to commercially available tapes. The nature store at the Audubon Society of New Hampshire in Concord sells "Calls of Frogs and Toads" on CD and cassette. The Massabesic Audubon Center in Auburn, Maine, also plans to stock such tapes. Perhaps you are interested. There may be such centers in your own state as well. I am certain this would be true.

A good field guide can teach you life history and everything that is needed to know about local frogs and toads. However, the most practical way to learn and be able to tell the difference between the calls of different species is to listen to audio recordings of their vocalizations. I am sorry I cannot include my recording of the peepers for you in this chapter.

Here is a list of frogs and toads that can be found in New Hampshire that I obtained from this same website. There are also photographs (I have several of the peepers) and descriptions and maps available from NARCAM'S Online Amphibian Guide. Perhaps you can find what is in your area. This is the New Hampshire list.

Common Name

American toad	Fowler toad
Cope's gray tree frog	Unknown gray tree frog species
Gray tree frog	Spring Peeper
Bullfrog Green frog	Pickerel frog
Northern leopard frog	Mink frog
Wood frog	

Opposite each is the scientific name which I will not include here. If you are serious peeper and frog enthusiasts you may obtain that information on this website plus so much more.

Most frogs and toads and peepers start to call about a half-hour after sunset but if the weather is dark and rainy some frogs will call during the day. I have read still yet another interesting fact about peepers and other tree frogs, that they cling to their perches by adhesive toe disks that non-climbing frogs lack. Author Sue Hubbell makes mention of these pads when observing peepers on her floor to ceiling windows, written about in the chapter "Other Dimensions" in this book.

If you are interested in "Frog watch USA" that we have only learned about since I began writing this chapter and Bob turned to on the internet to see what he could find in addition to what we have experienced, I will give information at the end of this chapter. We surely are interested now to become more serious frog watchers, particularly of the peepers. During the day here in warmer weather we often see small frogs of various varieties hopping about in my gardens, the lawn, or on the beach. These are extremely interesting and we never let anyone harm them. Little grandchildren so often want to capture and bottle them up to be pets, but we never allow that, explaining that this is where they need to live. It is their natural environment. When we turn it around, if they do not quite want to leave the frogs alone, and ask how they would feel if a huge frog wanted to put them in a container and carry them away, the message of the frog's permanence on Higher Ground becomes clearer. They then enjoy watching without touching.

So many little creatures are harmed just by careless handling. Having seen this happen, that is whey we protect the frogs and all creatures here.

Living in the woods by a lake populated by peepers has enhanced our life here. They are delightful! We feel privileged to have them almost right outside our door. It is dusk as I finish these writings. Can you hear them singing? They are back!!! It is true!!! Such excitement! Excuse me while I run outside to welcome them home.

JEEPERS CREEPERS—
WHERE'D WE GET THOSE PEEPERS

Peepers, Peepers—Everywhere!
Their jam session's on the air.
Warm Spring evenings—twilight hours—
Peeper music then is ours.

Tonight's performance—titled no doubt—
"Singing in the Rain"—and they're all out—
With such enchanting song and sound—
Performing live on Higher Ground!

Walking close the better to hear—
Makes the tenors disappear—
Into the water—they're all air-borne!
The lake's like a pan of popping corn!

They've returned—they live to sing—
They jump and swing and have their fling!
Ah—such an evening concert here—
It's filling all the atmosphere!

Dedicated to all   JGK
the Peeper Frogs
on Higher Ground

For any reader interested in learning more about peepers and frogs or "Frogwatch USA" you may obtain information or ask questions by contacting:

E-mail: frogwatch@usgs.gov.

or

Gideon Lachman, Frogwatch USA Coordinator
USGS Patuxent Wildlife Research Center
12100 Beech Forest Road
Laurel, Maryland 20708-4038.

You may even want to become a volunteer in your area for collecting data. Children also may volunteer. This organization provides understanding and opportunities and promotes an appreciation for diversity of frogs and toads. I intend to learn more about this group and perhaps you will also.

That such a group exists nationwide is so encouraging. People often frown upon a toad or frog, but their importance is astronomical. In learning we achieve understanding, and old thought patterns and opinions often drop by the wayside. I believe this fine group is going to bring enlightenment and frogs of all sorts are going to be helped and saved, and in turn, so will our environment and world.

Man's presumption of himself as the dominant species of this world is true only in proportion to his ability to respect other species and the environment.

—Robert A. Kolb Jr.

Reflect and Journal

☆ How often do you hide in the dark away from others, and only let your song (self) emerge when alone, or with only a small group who truly know you? Journal perhaps.

☆ Is it because you feel small and helpless like peepers, or because you are shy? Or other reasons known only to you?

☆ Write about these matters posed in the questions above in your journal. Explore your feelings.

☆ When is the last time you felt like you were in *deep water?* Did the experience help you to grow and to sing *your song* again? Tell your self about it in writing.

☆ Imagine yourself by the lake on a spring evening listening to the peepers under the stars. What thoughts come to you?

☆ Again, use your journal for these thoughts.

☆ Perhaps consider investigating FrogWatch by E-mail or at the address given.

Peepers are not the only tiny creatures to welcome Spring. There are those even tinier that do a good job of it too.

SPRING'S HERALDS

Now I know that Spring's arrived
All winter they have been deprived—
Of being here within our home
Investigating—free to roam.

I do not know their winter haunts
But now they have the greatest jaunts—
All about the bathroom tub—
And right within the family hub,
Of kitchen and the counter top—
On linoleum floor they never stop!

But when they reach the carpet pile—
They just can't seem to find an aisle,
And every little nub's a hill
As if in boot camp on a drill.

They have to worry that a giant—
(and some are often quite defiant—
and certainly not at all compliant
to ones who must be self-reliant)
Will not smash them—wipe them out—

(They cannot even scream or shout!)
And then go on without a thought—
Of the killing that it wrought!

We watch them carry fallen brothers—
Struggling as I've seen no others—
Another world—a work of love,
Yet humans annihilate them from above!

I know I'm different—even strange—
Because I give them such free range.
My little cat agrees with me
He befriends them lovingly,
He studies them and pats them lightly
A seminar that he takes nightly!

To spray or crush we simply can't!
For we're respecters of the Ant!

Dedicated to   JGK
the ants

☆ ☆ ☆ ☆ ☆

Come with me now to some "Other Dimensions" that will enhance your retreat, perhaps places and areas you never explored before. A cup of tea might be nice to take with you, your journal and pen, and an open heart and inquisitive nature.

CHAPTER EIGHT

Other Dimensions

Develop a sense of the sacred. Where you're standing is Holy Ground.
—Melody Beattie, *Journey to the Heart*

F YOU ARE READING THIS BOOK and making this retreat in the spring, summer or fall when weather permits you to sit outdoors, there is a way you can take part in the flow of nature. I would term this "observing," but author Joseph Cornell in his fine nature book, *Sharing Nature with Children,* calls it "still-hunting." It was practiced by the American Indians, and a brave who wanted to still-hunt would go to a place that attracted him or that he knew well. Perhaps on a hillside or in a forest he would still his mind and in a watchful mood would sit in a quiet place. It is possible his appearance might cause a disturbance among the creatures around him, but if he patiently waited until this world of nature returned to its normal, harmonious routine he could then begin his still-hunting. Observance and learning were usually his only intent.

If you would like to do this it will add to your retreat and make you feel more a part of nature. Even if you only have a small area around your home of grass or trees or flowers, you can do this. Or you can go to a place you might know in your area that has a bit more foliage.

When you do go still-hunting, you let your sitting-place choose you. This will be an interesting experience in itself. Perhaps intuitively you will be guided to a very specific place so that you may learn a certain lesson. Depending where you are will result in different experiences. If you are in your back yard somewhere it is unlikely that you will have

134

many wildlife creatures come to see you, but things will happen that you may not have noticed before when you were not on retreat.

Once you have chosen a spot then remain completely motionless. Do not even turn your head. Pretend you are not there and imagine the world around you going on while you remain as unobtrusive as you can be. Try to imagine that you are a part of the natural surroundings. Be observant. Or feel like you are a flower or a shimmering leaf or a bird, or a darting butterfly in the air. You can be anything you choose, any animal or rock or tree. Try to experience the existence of the form of creation you choose. Attempt to feel wind, or summer breezes or snow, depending on the season. The more you take on a character through imagination, the more sympathetic feelings you will have for your subject. Depending where you are, if you remain still, curious creatures may come close to look at you, like squirrels or chipmunks, Pretend perhaps, that you are one of them. I have done this and a poem resulted.

CHIPMUNK

I am the tiny chipmunk in a huge terra cotta pot.
I pause to peer over the side—
before running to hide
in the tangled stems
of the begonias.
The enormous soft tangerine and apricot blossoms
glisten like magnificent gems
in the summer shower.
I seem to be in a miniature rain forest
and bask in the beauty
of each shimmering drenched flower.

This was written as I observed the tiny chipmunk from my screened-in porch as I sat in silence. The terra cotta pot was on the front deck just beyond the screens. It was an incredible day, one I term a "rain forest" day. Soft showers were falling, everything was green in the outdoors and flowers were wet and glistening. I did not realize what I was doing then sitting motionless as I often did, was termed "still watching." It was something lovely I read about much later. Sitting motionless often in meditation, is something I have been doing for years, indoors and out.

Now I glance toward the three birch trees in front of the deck and again I see an unusual sight and words start to form. I write them down.

BROWN MUSHROOMS

Dark brown mushrooms
  in a copious cluster
    nestled in the trunk of the birch tree—
Bring me your connectiveness
  to all of nature—
    that I may be it
     and it me.

Unusual things occur when you sit perfectly still, both around you or within. It is necessary for your inner being to observe times like this in the experience of still watching, or meditation, or prayer, or all three.

If you are in a situation that does not permit you to be outdoors to experience nature, simply sit in a chair by your window no matter where you are. I am certain you will encounter something from nature through the pane or on the pane.

Author Sue Hubbel in her fine book, *A Country Year,* tells of sitting in a chair in her living room in the Ozark mountains of Southern Missouri and suddenly become aware she was no longer alone. Her three big windows that run from floor to ceiling were covered with hundreds of inch-long frogs with delicate webbed feet whose finger-like toes ended in round pads that enabled them to cling to the smooth surface of the glass. They were spring peepers that had been attracted to the light. As I have shared with you, we are familiar with peepers in our lake in early Spring, but never have had them on our sliding glass windows, also floor to ceiling. I do not expect you to see such a sight, but you may be surprised at what will be there. Even a spider or other sort of bug can be a fascination, or a bird on a branch near the window. Wait in expectation. Perhaps even a sunrise or a sunset. Anticipate!

If you prefer, imagine that you are here in the New Hampshire woods by the lake. Close your eyes and see what comes into your mind. Let this experience continue as long as you wish. Perhaps what you are "seeing" will relate to something that is presently in your heart. Later you can record all of this in your journal. No matter where you are you can always experience nature, whether in reality or spirit. It will bless you and add to your retreat.

Shapeshifting

In my experience with the chipmunk in the terra cotta pot I was imagining that I was the chipmunk while I sat utterly still. But in shapeshifting there actually is a "shift" when you experience becoming what you have shifted into.

In my recent previous book, *Journal of Love: Spiritual Communication with Animals Through Journal Writing,* I write of this in regard to a flock of ducks I was observing as I stood on the shore of our lake. Though there were many family members all around and children playing and much activity on this August afternoon, I seemed suddenly to be totally unaware. I can only explain it as seeming to be pulled from my body and into the body of the last little duck following its Mother. Never before had I encountered such a moment. Perhaps it was triggered by my love of the ducks and being so absorbed in this scene. The experience was extremely moving and I *was* that tiny duckling! In that same book I also shared a poem I wrote immediately following that "shift."

IN HIS FEATHERS AND WEB FEET

As I stood on the shore watching a flock of sixteen—
I was somehow—somewhat mysteriously drawn into the scene.
I sensed for a fleeting moment I was a duck—
Within the small body of the last one, and with luck
I would not be left behind!
I heard the children—calling—in my mind
As they tossed bread. I felt the wind upon my face—
The water against my chest.
I was caught up in the race—
To keep pace with all the rest.

I saw the rocks beneath the lake
And saw ripples from the wake—
Of my large family.
It was me—not in reality!
All in an instant
And with the distant
Honk of my Mother
And a splash from my brother—
I was again on the shore.
A little duck—no more!

This realization was not the same as pretending I was the chipmunk or the beautiful begonias in the terra cotta pot. I became the little duck. Though I have had other similar experiences since, this was my favorite one in nature. My little cat Rochester is always with me and I believe it is very possible that he may "shapeshift" into me also. He assists me on my spiritual journey and I know his love and energy are continuously helping me as I write and in all things that I do. I talk to him as I write and often thank him for ideas that seem to come out of the nowhere into the here, ideas I know I have not thought of before and that are new. I am amazed at the end of each day of writing at all the surprises, all that rose up in my mind, that were not on my original planning or thinking when I began to write. Because Rochester and I can communicate I do not find it hard to accept the idea of his "shift" into my being.

Perhaps you can pray first, and then try to see through a beloved animal companion's eyes or try to enter their bodies in imagination to become them in order to better realize what they must see or feel. Or if you do not have an animal companion perhaps you can attempt to do this with a squirrel or other little creature you see. You will know when it happens. It is definitely not the same as imagination (or still-watching) even though you may first have to use your imagination. Since it occurs spontaneously to me I can only make the suggestion to simply pray and ask for this "shift," using if necessary, imagination to prod the shift.

Sacrament of the Moment and Mindfulness

While reading this book and making this retreat I encourage you to pray and turn to meditation. This will deepen and spiritualize your retreat and what you read in these pages. When you use prayer forms regularly I have found that the other things in one's life are deeply enriched because all things are connected. Meditation and prayer open your heart, soul, and mind, and you discover beauty and the spiritual in all things, no matter how mundane these things may be. Whatever you are doing, live within that moment and do not try to constantly slip back into the past or even into the future. Appreciate and live in the present moment! It is all that we have! Through my readings in my own religion of Christianity I learned years ago about living in "The Sacrament of the Moment." This type living blesses me when I earnestly put it into practice. Naturally there are times that I slip and that is my loss. In writings most inspirational, and conforming to directives in the Christian way of life, Buddhist Thich Nhat Hanh speaks about "the miracle of mindfulness" and how we must not only be conscious of the positions of the body but "we must be conscious of each breath, each movement, every thought and feeling, everything that has relation to ourselves." Whatever we do we must be conscious of it, and of "the blue sky, white clouds, green leaves and the black, curious eyes of a child—our own two eyes. All is miracle."

Thich Nhat Hanh writes that everyday we are engaged in a miracle which we do not even recognize, and mindfulness is the miracle by which we can master and restore ourselves. He continues to explain that the miracle is that we "can call back in a flash our dispersed mind and restore it to wholeness so that we can live each minute of life." As in *The Sacrament of the Moment* by DeCaussade, we are to live in awareness. Mindfulness makes it possible to live fully each moment of life and frees us of forgetfulness. Perhaps you will want to try to better live in "the sacrament of the moment" and practice "mindfulness" while reading this book and being on your retreat.

Of course, sometimes it is difficult to remain in the present and it is essential to visit the past. We may need to rid ourselves of an old feeling or hurt hindering us in the present, or heal an old belief that is binding us.

But do not linger in the past. Make the visit brief. And yes, we often have to make plans and envision our paths, and so we sometimes need to think of the future. But to wander there too long can spoil our present moment. The past and the future will be in their proper places in our lives if we live in "the sacrament of the present moment." Author Melody Beattie writes, "Stay in the present moment and the magic will return." It is true!

Hypnogogic Imagery

In this form of prayer one sits as in meditation and gradually becomes aware of the images that appear on the inner eye. Perhaps you have been doing this for years or maybe you have never experienced it. I have been shown things in this way before I knew its name and learned the term through reading *A Guide to Christian Meditation* by Marilyn Morgan Helleberg some years ago. It is a most unique form of prayer and meditation. Images arise that are absolutely remarkable and usually extremely clear, as if you were viewing them on a screen. They come and go and often stay and always mystify, that such a phenomenon can occur. I have notebooks filled with prayer times recorded of the details of these images. It is also referred to as "twilight imagery." I have seen things that utterly amazed me, scenes out of nowhere containing people I have never met and perhaps never will. Often they are like dreams, seemingly making no sense at the moment, but if recorded it is possible that in the future sometime I may realize the message of one or many of them. And I have. Mainly I have experienced images of angels, animals, stars, and unicorns. They come and go in different scenes bringing peace to my heart and soul. I have seen dolphins flying out of the water into the air, one at a time, and changing appearance by turning into Angels. Often the images appear in scenes I recognize, as one recorded after a period of meditation when I asked my Angel to speak to me. I saw too a large unknown angel on my inner eye in a dark red gown with arms lifted high. She was out over the shore line of our lake, for I too saw our trellis in the foreground, the one under which our daughter Janna and son-in-law Bill were married, the very trellis Bill built. Then the Angel's chest seemed to become transparent and a white globe of light could be seen through this transparent area and it floated out over the lake and into the heavens and disappeared. To show the contrast, later that same day in hypnogogic imagery, I saw a sweet little yellow table with turned wood legs, and sitting in the middle of it was a plate of Rochester's cat food. A strange thing, yet it was a pretty picture.

Yesterday before I began this writing I meditated, and saw not only Rochester and Bob in our living room (I was here upstairs in my writing room) in hypnogogic imagery, but three very large pileated woodpeckers in a circle around one of the birch trees outside my front window. The scene was as defined and real as if I was looking out my own window at that tree. The chance of seeing three rare pileated woodpeckers at once encircling the same tree, however, would not be a reality I am sure. But last week, after a period of about eight years, Bob and I did see one pileated woodpecker in our pine tree by my prayer chair. We were thrilled to have spotted it. Was this perhaps surfacing in a multiple way in my hypnogogic imagery in prayer?

From lovely angels, stars, doves and unicorns, the images can change to more practical scenes of people. One I recorded reminded me of a Norman Rockwell painting for I saw so clearly a young man in brown pants and suspenders with white shirt and sleeves rolled up, and a hat on the back of his head. It was a hat with a brim all the way around it, not a cap. The boy was running to jump onto the back of an old truck that had steps going up the back, flat against the rear of the truck. He ran and made it, and jumped on clinging to the rungs of the ladder or steps, and rode off on the back. It ended. It was so clear it was like viewing a movie.

I share these to show you the extreme differences of the various images. Some are spiritual and some from every day living. Some, like the cat food on the little table are more like unusual images one sees in dreams.

What can it all mean? I do not know, but in isolated cases I feel I have discovered why certain ones appeared on my inner eye. I believe it is all from God.

Like dreams, I felt them significant to record in order to reread and refer back to out of desire to learn more, and also to see if there are any connections to things in the present. My notebooks contain treasures to me. Perhaps you will begin to record your images.

Dreams

Dreams too are important to record, at least while you are making this retreat. Because of what you are reading, and hopefully writing and exploring in your journal as a result of the reading, you may actually have dreams that relate to this retreat you are making now. Perhaps God will speak to you in these dreams. Perhaps through the reading, other things have been stirred up in your subconscious, and these will appear in dreams and through your writing. So if at all possible treat your dreams with importance at least on this retreat. In doing so, perhaps it will lead you to continue to record them in the future if you have never done so before.

Keep your journal by your bed at night with a pen, and even a small flashlight in case you want to record a dream briefly in the middle of the night. The more you listen to your dreams and write them down, the more this is a message to your unconscious that you give them importance.

Dreams you want to or need to remember have a way of staying with you often, but that is not an absolute. You must respect this whole process. Writing them down shows respect.

Like hypnogogic imagery, it may take a long time before one or any of your dreams is understood. Always save your dream journals and some day or month or year later reread your dreams. You will be shown then how you were guided at times, or warned, or other deeper desires may be revealed. Never treat your dreams with disrespect as strange as they may be at times. My dream journals are very meaningful to me even though I have not always faithfully recorded my dreams. When I have failed for a period and then go back and reread my dream journals, this process always inspires me to get back to recording my dreams. May you be inspired to do this too.

Learn also to find within yourself that secret place of stillness. Stillness has power. May you find this. Seek out stillness each day, very especially in your sacred spot or in places of nature. Just be at ease in your mind and soul and then in your place of stillness you will experience joy, healing, peace, miracles, and yes even magic. It is when we are still that these appear.

And so—may these subjects written about in this chapter touch you in some way, enough to change you and cause you to write more. When you put things down in writing you will definitely be changed, and you will validate your life's experiences in a wondrous form that men and women have done for centuries. You will enter a whole new realm, for writing is a force unto itself. Just be present with pen, pencil and journal. Soon you will understand if you have not already been shown. Writing will take you places you can not even imagine. I promise!

Reflect and Journal

☆ Today and throughout your retreat and reading of this book, practice still-hunting in some way. Write your experiences in your journal.

☆ Has any particular moment or experience during your periods of still-watching inspired you to write a poem? If so make sure it is securely written in your journal.

☆ If you have experienced shapeshifting write about that too. Even if you have not yet experienced it, explore in writing what you would like to shapeshift into and why. If you do not want to shapeshift, write in stream of consciousness writing for at least five to ten minutes and perhaps your desire not to shapeshift will be shown in deeper ways to you.

☆ Make time for peaceful meditation daily. Practice living in the sacrament of the moment as much as possible.

☆ In meditation pray and ask to be shown hypnogogic imagery. Write in your journal anything that appears. Pray about it, and write down what you are given by God and how it affected you. Continue to do this daily.

☆ Have you had any significant dreams since beginning this retreat? Did they pertain to the retreat? Record any dreams in your journal so that you may always be able to refer to them.

☆ Just relax in the present moment and meditate.

☆ Beside writing in your journal, try to draw any images you may see in meditation or hypnogogic imagery. Capture them with colored pencils or crayons so you can think about them and view them. If you wish, ask for an interpretation in prayer if unclear to you.

Writing "Other Dimensions" has brought Rochester to mind for he truly is from that realm. It is important I share with you more about him so you can realize his importance in my life. Again, this could affect you and your thinking and your retreat. As you read about him imagine him on my lap—

PRETZELED

He lightly springs onto my lap
Preparing now to take his nap.
He bumps his little head on mine—
To give anew the precious sign—
That I am his, not visa versa
Then circles down into inertia.

Pretzel shaped—all round and warm
His tail secured around his form—
His back leg then juts out above
And little chin turns up in love.
White front paw drapes 'cross his eyes
And then begin the purrs and sighs
A leg adjustment—one last twist
And then with sleep he makes his tryst.

Dedicated to   JGK
Rochester

I introduce you now to Rochester.

CHAPTER NINE

Rochester – Feline Angel

I can't imagine in all the world a better friend than you.
—D. Morgan

ROCHESTER

R   eflective and rare
O   verwhelmingly patient and precious—
C   ompassionate, constant, contemplative and cherished.
H   onorable, humble, beloved friend—
E   nlightened and empowering encourager—
S   acred, sagacious supporter—
T   ender and thoughtful confidant
E   minent and everlasting Angel
R   ochester, renowned, radiant, remarkable companion

Written to honor him and in thanksgiving   JGK
for the day he came into my life

THIS POEM WAS WRITTEN JUST THIS YEAR, one of so many poems I have written for and about Rochester, my dear little companion. His love and presence are inspiring me as I write this book, as are his thoughts and words, for we communicate deeply.

145

The words in the quotation that open this chapter speak of Rochester. They appear on a pillow given to me by my friend Connie who loves and protects animals and is a rescuer of homeless cats. On the pillow two cats sit side by side and are viewed from the back as they gaze out the window at a beautiful scene. The words make my heart melt each time I look at the pillow. Rochester and I truly are eternal friends and soul mates.

Herman Hesse, author of the well known and inspiring book, *Siddartha*, and many other books too, has written:

> *Where we find something that resembles music, there we must stay; there is nothing else worth striving for in life than the feeling of music, the feeling of resonance and rhythmic life, or a harmony that justifies our existence.*

This expresses my life with Rochester and the music he has put into my soul, and of Bob also and the existence we three share in a harmony and rhythmic life here in the woods. We have found something indeed, that resembles music and we must stay. Happiness is love and that is our blessed experience. Rochester has intervened in ways that changed me, and if you read my other books those changes are woven through them. Angels do that, they change us and fill us with love and help us to heal. And love alone gives life meaning.

It is not necessary that Rochester is written about in every chapter of this particular book. He is here while they are being written, every word, and his essence and spiritual presence too are here. I cannot ever imagine life without Rochester. God sent him to me and he is all love, a precious soul, and I pay tribute to him now and always, and to all the spiritual joy, love, companionship and writing he continually gives to me. He is my Angel! He is an Angel that came to inter-

vene in my life that was filled with sadness and to show me the path of endurance and spiritual growth. He imbues me with spiritual wisdom, compassion, and a healing of heart, soul and spirit. It has been a daily ongoing ministering to me.

Today in the *New Hampshire Sunday News* well known author and resident of Peterborough, New Hampshire, Elizabeth Marshall Thomas is interviewed at length about her new book, *The Social Lives of Dogs*, with accompanying pictures. Though I completed the writing of Rochester's chapter yesterday, I believe you would be interested in this article and so I am inserting facts from it. She states "Animals come into our lives in a deep way. . . . Society doesn't recognize these relationships, but they're among the most powerful in our lives. We communicate on a nonverbal level in very deep way."

She remarks that it is not on the same level as with family or kids, but she confides that she prefers the company of her animals (five dogs, five cats and three exotic birds) to more than half the people she knows.

Elizabeth Marshall Thomas goes on to share in the interview that humans typically concoct social structures and put humans at the top ignoring the many nuances and subtleties that define life in the animal world.

When criticized that she is practicing anthropomorphism she maintains "that our cultural elitism prevents us from observing and experiencing the reality happening at knee level or below, in our own homes." She claims the behaviors, traits and reactions are all there for us to see, but if you identify these qualities using "the vocabulary that we use for people," then you are accused of anthropomorphism. This interview I have quoted from and shared here is well written by Union Leader correspondent Gil Bliss. Elizabeth Marshall Thomas has written two other books I have read and learned from titled *The Hidden Life of Dogs* and *The Tribe of Tiger*. You may be interested too.

On the same page with the article about Elizabeth Marshall Thomas is a moving account of another author and his new book telling how he was truly sustained by his two dogs following the death of his wife of thirty-four years to cancer in 1989. He claims they were beams of light and kept him going, so much so this book, *Second Thought On: How to Be as Terrific as Your Dog Thinks You Are,* is dedicated to his two beloved dogs Bogey and Golum. The book is written by Mort Crim former senior editor at WDIV-TV in Detroit and who also anchored night newscasts there. Since remarried he now travels with his cat Zoey (becoming a cat person as well because he learned from his new wife about cats), logging eighty speaking engagements annually. Animals truly affect our lives and minister to us and communicate in ways so incredibly deep if we are only open to listening and spending quality alone time with them, giving them the honor and respect you would give a human.

Rochester continually inspires me to write, and poems also, and many poems I pen just for him to attempt to express the various ways he ministers to me and fills my life with love and joy. The following recent poem tells of a past period in my life that his presence and abiding love brought healing.

ANGEL OF LIGHT

Angel of light
bright sacrosanct one
that shone in my darkness
and plight—
You radiated
that dark night
in the starkness
of pain and tears—
And in embracing you
in my arms
and feeling your soft fur—
your Angelic purr,
You banished my alarms
and fears—
instilling healing
comfort and peace.
Tears cease—and
stealing
my heart anew
you fill it with joy.

JGK

I believe with a certainty beyond comprehension that Rochester, this beautiful creature, is an Angel in the form of an animal. It is written "Angels appear to make us want to live" (unknown) and Rochester came to intervene in my life at such a time as this. He also has been my inspiration to do what I had always dreamed of doing, to write books. Too, he led me to meet head on the issue of Animal Rights and to speak out, which I have done in my *Compassion for All Creatures* and two other books that follow. He is a constant in my life. Rochester was the one who taught me the meaning of *Ahimsa*—non-violence, non-killing—and as a result I became a vegetarian for the sake of the animals in 1989 as I have written before, as did Bob.

And, although Chester has never "meowed" and remains silent as the contemplative that he is, he has communicated his knowledge to me, teaching me to mentally and telepathically communicate with him. Because I have always recognized the Divinity in him and listen in the daily solitude and stillness we share, he has brought forth this gift within me that I could never have known without him. I write down all I am learning, and through this telepathic communication we have become even more deeply bonded and I have grown spiritually and entered a new dimension of interspecies love and relationship. Together we wrote a book, *Journal of Love: Spiritual Communication with Animals Through Journal Writing* (Blue Dolphin, 2000).

Chester has been the only one present when I have had other Angel encounters written about previously. Would these encounters have occurred without my Angel's presence also?

Rochester's story also appears in a marvelous book titled *Animal Miracles* by Brad Steiger and Sherry Hansen Steiger published in 1999. In this book you will read incredible and loving true stories of animals believed to be angels and the impact they have made on humans' lives. Telepathic communication between animals and humans is also discussed. Rochester and I are honored that his life story is included.

Chester is not always serious and ministering as it may appear, although he ministers through his humor too. Angels are lighthearted and he is very playful and precious and he enjoys gentle rough-housing together on the floor, or a good mouse chase as I have written about in another chapter, though he never harms the mice. He warmly greets people with respect who come in our cottage and is in turn treated with respect and love by everyone. He is an indoor cat, of course, for he could come to harm outdoors in the woods, just as he could have in the suburbs of Jenkintown, Pennsylvania, his former home with us. It is wise to keep our feline friends indoors for many reasons, but Chester has a wonderful screened-in-porch he spends time in, with up close encounters of birds and chipmunks and red squirrels that run about in branches of a large Colorado Blue Spruce whose branches on one side touch the screening. It is like a giant television set for him featuring only natural wildlife encounters. He often sits and stares into the tree for endless periods, his head moving as he follows all the wildlife within. A little shelf at each end of the porch built for him by Bob are his alone and afford better views into this tree and of other places wildlife scurry about. He really is a sweet presence and very amusing at times. He knows I am a giggler so he is excellent at making me laugh.

The last verse of one of dozens of poems written for him, this one titled "Angel Being," tells of the way we end each of our precious days together.

> Beneath my heart he sleeps each night—
> And keeps it whole—warm with his light.
> There is no need to see his wings—
> Just seeing him—and my soul sings!

> JGK

And before sleep each night this prayer written by Bob and included in my previous two books, I pray aloud for the three of us. It is worthy to again be included for it blesses us so, and hopefully will bless readers.

> As we lay down to sleep each night
> Please keep us safe 'til morning light
> Grant us sleep and needed rest
> And fill our dreams with happiness.
> For Lord we know that with you near,
> There's nothing that we have to fear.
> Please guide us where You want to lead,
> And be with those we love and need.

> Amen

Though Bob wrote it in the singular I have converted it to the plural since it is for the three of us.

Rochester and I truly were given to each other and I am new and changed forever by a little Angel of God. I can never doubt an Angel was sent to me and each day of my life I tell God of my love and gratitude for His ineffable gift.

I will close with a secret I forgot to tell you. Rochester also is known by the name of Harry as well as Chester. This is a love name given to him by Bob when he was a tiny kitten and is explained in my *Compassion*. It was something Bob needed to do, in order to help himself know a little kitten for the first time in his life. I had thought of the name of "Rochester" on our drive home the name of the town in which we adopted him, and Bob decided "Chester" as the dignified nickname for it, yet once in our cottage he began to call him "Harry." He calls him "Harry" to this day! It is said when someone is deeply loved they are called by many names. (I will not even tell you some of the love names I call him.)

HARRY

H   arry, handsome, honest helper—
A   lso known as
R   ochester.
R   eassuring soulmate—
Y   ielding, loving advocate.

JGK
June 2000

Oh yes, and I will tell you another secret too. In my previous book I have written that Rochester sits on my lap and we hold hands. He has done this with me since he was a kitten and he initiates it. It is spoken of in my poem titled "An Angel's Touch," and how his paw is "like the brush of an Angel's Wing." He places his paw on my hand, then I place my other hand on his paw and he then puts his other paw on me. I think of it as "our little stack of love an affection" and it brings tears. It is repeated again and again. The poem that closes now this chapter speaks of this tender paw not only on my hands but on my cheek.

SOUL'S TOKEN

"My kitten's tender paw, thou soft, small treasure"*
Upon my cheek or hand—brings joy unspeakable, and pleasure
That cannot be written—nor spoken.
It is his giving of love, his token
From his soul—expressed in merest touch.
And I receive—and love him, oh so very much.

Written for Rochester   JGK
With love for his birthday   *Quote by
May 30, 1995—In gratitude   Heinrich Heine (German poet)

Reflect and Journal

☆ Have you ever loved an animal? Does my deep love for Rochester
   seem strange to you?

☆ Answer these questions in your journal and write for at least five or
   ten minutes on this.

☆ If you personally cannot comprehend such a love for one of God's
   creatures explore that through writing also, and in prayer.

☆ If you do deeply love an animal have you ever sensed he/she was an
   angel? Accounts of people sharing their beliefs in this are in many
   books and inspirational magazines. Maybe you never considered it
   before though there were many signs given. A dramatic rescue (or
   similar action by an animal) is not the only way an animal Angel is
   recognized. I have shared my beliefs concerning Rochester as Angel. Explore this concept as it relates to your personal experience or
   thinking in your journal.

☆ If you love an animal deeply draw a picture of this animal using any
   of your art supplies. Do you take photos of him as I do? Perhaps do
   that regularly also recording his life in art and photos.

☆ Above all, write in your journal about your beloved companion too.
   You may even want to keep a separate journal just for him. Both

ways are lovely, to combine his life with yours in your journal, or to use a separate one. It is up to you. But writing about him will be a gift to you. Perhaps write a prayer for him.

☆ Have you ever considered being a vegetarian, of never again eating anything with a face, for the sake of the animals—and not for your health, though that will benefit?

☆ Write a poem in your journal about your personal animal companion or about an animal you encountered at some time in your life, even as a child, that touched you deeply. Often rethink your connection to animals as you read this book and long after. Ask God to open your heart to them if you are not personally caring for animals now. You will be blessed.

You have read about my personal Angel, and now let us look at some little "Angel-like" creatures that enhance life in the woods. You will be amazed at their multitude! They have been an education to us and are a part of all our days. Rochester too is in awe of them, but is passive as he watches from window or porch. We are really blessed to have the vast variety that we do here in the woods. Come closer to the window, or perhaps even read this chapter outdoors. Settle in and enjoy.

CHAPTER TEN

Birds

"the winter is past,
the rain is over and gone;
the flowers appear on the earth;
the time of the singing of birds is come. . . ."

—Song of Solomon 2:11-12

WE'RE HOME

A frozen lake—a large expanse—
But then with just a casual glance
I saw an opening in the ice—
Just big enough it could entice—
With fluttering wings and in a flash,
Two brown ducks to swim and splash!
Out of the nowhere into here—
The first sweet ducks we've seen this year!
For months they waited for that break
So they could swim upon their lake.
How they played—and with each quack—
They called to us that they were back.

JGK

*A*ND THUS BEGAN THE RETURN OF THE BIRDS, to join the others that had stayed the winter in these woods, the Chickadees, the Nuthatches, the Woodpeckers and more. These year round residents remain here and witness the arrivals of the spring and summer residents as they come and seek a haven with us on Higher Ground and in surrounding woods. We welcome all and await them. One could give up everything else in life just to be a beholder of the birds.

Wordsworth has written, "The birds pour forth their souls in notes of rapture from a thousand throats," and that is sweetly descriptive of all we are experiencing now as the birds gather here and continually fly in and out to the feeders and to the trees, each singing and calling in their own bird song and language. It is why I never listen to music as I write, no matter what the season. I am in awe of all I hear, yet cannot always identify each song with its owner. But I am learning. Too, I read, that "bird song" usually refers only to songbirds, but many non-songbirds, such as herons, owls, shorebirds, and woodpeckers make song—like sounds that have similar territorial and mate attracting functions. One can learn this and much more from a very beautiful book of writing and photography titled *Music of the Birds: A Celebration of Bird Song* by Lang Elliott. This book contains an audio compact disc featuring songbird concerts and solos. I have only obtained the book so have not yet read it and have only heard fleeting songs from the disc. It is a joy I look forward to in quiet times when not writing.

I have learned from other reading through the years that song has numerous functions. It helps in mating and attracts mates to unmated males and also helps them feel secure. Once mated the song tells the other bird her mate is nearby. Also song expresses territory, possession or ownership, and through singing a male resident then alerts other males of the same species that he will defend his territory and that it is occupied.

Songbirds produce not only songs during spring and early summer when it is breeding season, but they also produce "calls." Calls are usually brief and simple and both sexes produce calls, and both mature and immature birds do this. There are so many functions for calls and they have different qualities and reasons for occurring. There are feeding calls, flocking calls, alarm and begging calls, and aggressive calls to name a few. Songs and calls are easy to differentiate but I have read that some songbirds have call-like songs and we have heard these. It is amazing that birds can communicate all sorts of messages that are useful to them just with their sounds, which are small in number. We feel a reverence for all we experience here through the songs and calls of the birds.

In the book I have previously mentioned I noted a quote while browsing that moved me by Gilbert White, an eighteenth century English naturalist and poet. Through his own personal observation he stated "the language of birds is very ancient, and like other ancient modes of speech, very elliptical; little is said, but much is meant and understood." It is lovely to wonder what a bird feels and thinks as he sings, but that is all a mystery. Poems and writings can explore this and provide human interpretation, but still, it remains a mystery. Even though it is believed that birds sing to one another, we as humans like to feel they too, are singing to us. Their songs lift our hearts and fill us with joy. As I write I often am overwhelmed by the beauty of the songs, and Bob and I often pause together to listen. I would like to believe that we are all connected spiritually—the birds and we humans. So many unusual things have occurred between birds and ourselves that I cannot think otherwise. We have had interchanges that are other-worldly. Author Lang Elliott also states that "Whatever the truth, is it not our birthright to listen, to enjoy, and to be moved by their songs?" I cannot imagine living now without the presence and songs and calls of the birds filling my days. It has all caused me not to want to hear any music but that of nature's own, dismissing for the most part the classical and ethereal type music I once listened to often. There are of course exceptions at certain times for some, but one composition however remains to be heard nightly before sleep that I have written about elsewhere. That is "The Fairy Ring" by Mike Rowland. Along with the bird song, this has been my healing music for the past eleven years. That I never grow weary of it, just as I never grow tired of listening to the birds, tells my soul it is of God as are the dear creatures at the feeders outside my window, and all creatures of the earth. And so I borrow the words of poet Percy Bysshe Shelley and write: "Teach us, sprite or bird, what sweet thoughts are thine."

And I believe if we give rapt attention to our bird visitors and speak to them in spirit or verbally, there will come an unusual closeness that we can only recognize as coming from God to enable bird and human to become one in spirit in Him. I have experienced such moments and intend to seek them through awareness and availability to the birds, and in the singing woods that really knows no utter silence. It is alive with the heavenly presence of songs of the birds, God's music for us wrapped in the feathered bodies of his ambassadors on earth to cheer and lift spirits of all who listen.

Robert Louis Stevenson has said, "My bedroom, when I awoke this morning, was full of bird-songs, which is the greatest pleasure in life." That is how we are awakened daily and for this I am ever thankful. We fall asleep to both the spring peepers and feathered friends and awaken to the birds calling us into the new day. How blessed we are!

The birds sing at dawn. What sounds to be awakened by!
—Henry David Thoreau

Bird Houses

TREE HOUSE

On the edge of the woods tall birches stand
By a small dirt road—in a little band
Drawing aesthetic response. Trunks beneath soft dense green
Are stark white—knotted—shaggy and serene—
Holding the fullness of the leaves that conceal boughs.
And from one limb hanging string allows
A brown wooden bird house to be nestled there—
Swaying in breeze, under leaves—free of sun's glare.

Little house so safe and blest
Waiting for a bird's sweet nest.
In this scene I love immensely—
I sense God's Presence most intensely.

Written for Janna—
who built the bird house

JGK
September 6, 1993

*Bird house
(made by Janna)*

This little poem was written to thank our daughter Janna for a sweet wooden bird house she made for us. Despite its being outdoors for a number of years now it still is attractive and has held a number of bird families. Three other bird houses are about our property; a blue one with an Angel at the door from extended family Patti and Dennis, a pottery one of blue design from friends, the Richards, and a natural wood one from Fran, Jessica's mother-in-law. Birds surely know they are welcome here. Extending like a divider or fence from Bob's Birchgrove office is a wall of bird houses he created. Since he wanted to shield and keep from view the large propane tank that heats his trailer office, he built the fence solidly about eight inches deep and three and a half feet high, making rows of holes in graduated sizes for birds of all kinds who might like to rest or be protected. It is like a bird motel or condominium. We try in every way possible to communicate to the birds that they are welcome here.

Bird Feeders

UNION STATION

Little birds fly in the air
To our feeders we've put there—
Outside our windows for their use
And now we have not one excuse—

To better know these friends so small
That feed on seed and come to call
Not to learn each trait and name—
God given—that each bird can claim.

But our feeders are unique
For as each tiny little beak
Pecks at its meal in such a hurry
Seed falls below where chipmunks scurry.

And they in turn eat up their share
That comes to them from out the air—
It's Higher Ground's new Food Chain Diner
In all the woods there's not one finer.

And often eating right together
Side by side—the birds of feather
And the chipmunks take their lunch
On the railing in a bunch—

Where the furry chippies' bowl
Takes very little to cajole
Nocturnal caller with the mask
Who eats in dark and does not ask.

And so again in early morning
Suddenly and without warning
The Food Chain Diner opens up
And birds and chipmunks come to sup.

JGK

This is a poem written some years ago also but that still accurately
depicts the activity that takes place daily on our porch. In fact it has
increased immensely because we are permanent residents now and word
has gotten around. The only creatures not mentioned in this poem are
the squirrels. Mainly we have red squirrels, so sweet and intelligent, that

feed on the feeders at the same time as the birds, side by side! They also hang in every position imaginable to reach food. And they have even taken to eating suet this year which is not a part of a squirrel's diet. There is complete camaraderie between the squirrels and birds as they feed together, and with the tiny ground feeding chipmunks as well. Occasionally a larger gray squirrel joins the gang and he too goes through many gymnastics to reach the feeders and to stay secure while feasting. I have shared more about this with you in the chapter "Diane and Friends." The raccoons come only at night and their visits have diminished somewhat this year.

Our deck each day looks like Dr. Doolittle's living room, if you have ever seen the wonderful old movie starring Rex Harrison as Dr. Doolittle. We do not have the larger animal he had but all the same small ones and birds, of course.

Woodchuck

Just this week another creature has made its appearance around our cottage but is not feeding on the deck with the rest of the crowd. A little groundhog, also known as a woodchuck or marmot, has been spending time around our cottage and in the fringes of the back woods. He seems to be enjoying himself and is certainly fascinating to Rochester who is observing him from the screened in porch. But birds fly in and land near him and there is never any conflict. I was surprised to learn from my nature book, *Living With Wildlife*, that this little fellow (or girl) is a member of the squirrel family. Unlike other marmots, woodchucks live in a complex tunnel system and they live alone, and usually near the edge of a forest. This explains the appearance of our latest visitor. They are tunnel diggers and dig a series of them then move on to another after several months of inhabiting one. In winter they burrow in protected woods and in summer choose more open grasslands. Their tunnel systems are very complex and the main entrance is most conspicuous, with a large mound of dirt. This is used as a lookout an a spot where they also sun and groom. Like ourselves I have learned woodchucks are vegetarians eating grasses and flowers, soybeans, alfalfa and clover. They are good climbers and easily reach fruit on trees. Woodchucks do not venture far from their burrow so our new little friend's burrow must be somewhere on the edge of our woods near our cottage. They hibernate in winter and awaken gradually in spring to rise for breeding season. I have learned too from reading that they make a whistling or chattering sound when cornered. They cannot run fast and are fierce fighters if cornered yet are also timid and easily frightened. This little woodchuck is typical of the description I have found and has a heavy body, short strong legs, and curved (and I would imagine strong) claws on his front paws for burrowing, and a short furry tail. Males are larger than females, about seven to thirteen pounds and eighteen to twenty-two inches long, excluding his tail. Females are only five to ten pounds and sixteen to twenty inches long. This little wood chuck with us has a course coat, grayish brown with a red cast. The legs are dark brown with black feet. I learn today that litters are two to seven in number born in May or June, so perhaps we will have a little family of "grandchucks" soon. (We already have granddoggers and grandcats, and for many years had a grandpiggy and grandbunny.) Why not some grandchucks? If they are born before I complete this book and before your retreat ends, I will announce their births. I can only summarize him by saying he is very pleasing to see and sits on his back legs upright on our dirt driveway holding a little treat in his front paws, and looking like a little creature from a story book. But I am warned through reading not to approach a woodchuck for he will retreat to his burrow, and if cornered will attack and fight. That is not the image he gives when I watch him. He is shy and peaceful, sort of checking us out and seemingly content. I hope he has come to stay. No one here would ever give him cause to worry or attack. I think he senses that.

Bird Visitors

I am going to share with you the names of the birds that have been visiting us these past weeks in spring, and that will continue to visit in summer also. Other new ones will also arrive and join them. They are all amazing beings.

Baltimore Oriole   Mourning dove
Red-Winged Blackbird   Chipping Sparrow

House Wren
Goldfinch
White-Breasted Nuthatch
Black-Capped Chickadee
Grackle
Ruby-Throated Hummingbird
Great Blue Heron
Blue Jay
Robin
Mallard
Crow

Yellow Warbler
Rose-Breasted Grosbeak
Purple Finch
(New Hampshire's State Bird)
Downy Woodpecker
Pileated Woodpecker
Canada Goose
Osprey
Common Loon
Song Sparrow

There are others, but these are the ones we can identify.

Robin, Osprey and Red-Tailed Hawk

Not all the birds listed feed at our feeders or on our deck, but the majority of them do, at least twenty of them in the list. The Robin is a ground feeder so he hops about on the grass feeding, all the while checking out the activity on the deck. The Osprey stays high in the trees when he visits waiting to attack and clench a fish from out of the lake and fly off with it in his claws. The head of the fish is always facing forward in the line of flight. That we have observed. This is so distressing to me because I value the fish's life, even though I realize the Osprey was created according to God's plan. Nevertheless I have cheered when an Osprey has lost hold of a fish he was flying off with and it was returned to the lake. I can only imagine the underwater joy when the fish are dropped through accident. Since the Osprey can be anywhere from twenty-one to twenty-four inches, his appearance is rather commanding. Often it completely disappears under the water to get its prey and then after shaking off the water takes off with the fish, with a wing spread of about five feet or more. As beautiful as they are, seeing the live fish in its claws is disturbing to me. It is also known as a "Fish Hawk."

I have had a vision or hypnogogic image occur during a meditation (these are mentioned in another chapter) of an Osprey in a tree up near Dennis' cottage. He looked exactly like the Osprey I have seen in reality and he was facing away from Dennis' looking into the woods. Dennis and

Patti's cottage and the trees and sky were all in full color as in reality also. It was like seeing a photo in meditation.

We have also had the Red-Tailed Hawk in the trees on occasion but never observed him carry off prey that includes mice and other small mammals. They will even take chicks from a farm yard.

Pileated Woodpecker

The Pileated Woodpecker is present with us now this past week and we hear his knocking on the tree trunks. He is a great black and white bird about eighteen inches with a flaming red crest. This Woodpecker is as large as a Crow and the only Woodpecker of that size, and the only Woodpecker in North America that has a crest. The noise this creature makes while it goes to work on a tree, often sounds as though a person is chopping wood. I have read that often a woodchopper at work will find that the blows of his axe have actually "called" a Pileated Woodpecker right to his very vicinity. The Pileated digs out bugs or beetles with its long tongue and all the while makes the chips fly with his bill. We have rectangular hollows of good size that have been hewed out on some of our trees from past visits of the Pileated. Some woodpeckers' tongues are so long, they have to be rolled up in the back of the mouth when not in use. They also find their food of insects in stumps, and he is capable of ripping off heavy strips of bark that no other of the family could begin to remove.

Canada Goose

The Canada Goose migrates through our area and is seen on the lake or in the sky with many companions who migrate in a V-formation. These birds come in great flocks out front on the water and have powerful voices. Often too, great flocks of these birds are heard before they are seen in the sky. We observe them en route South and when they return in Spring. It is thrilling to hear them for they are great "honkers" and never fly in or over silently. Though we have many here at times, they do not stay. They vary greatly in size but are anywhere from thirty-four to forty-three inches. It is surreal to hear them especially at night.

Canada geese (male and female with three baby chicks)

Much to our surprise while I am writing this chapter, and the day after I wrote this passage about the Canada Goose, we had an amazing gift and surprise. As we were about to go out our door, two Canada Geese, male and female strolled across our lawn with three tiny fluffy chicks walking with them so small one could fit in my hand. The Canada Geese however, were very large, the male the larger. It was an astonishing sight. Previous to this we had only seen them in flight or in water. We ran softly behind them taking pictures as they walked down onto our beach and into the water. I think they wanted to have a bigger write up about them in this book. It was a thrill and we are thankful.

Great Blue Heron

SILENT VISITOR

Sitting at my desk I wrote.
Looking out to see the boat—
Whose motor's hum told of approaching—
(on nature's sounds was now encroaching)—
I saw a handsome creature standing
On the beach, silently demanding

My attention; majestically still,
Great Blue Heron—long neck and bill.
Thin stilt-like legs gave him such height—
Pleasurable intrusion in soft sunlight.

All in a moment it occurred.
And then as if to call he heard—
With enormous wings soared over lake.
A legacy of wonder in his wake.

JGK

This majestic bird walks out of the water and up on our beach strolling behind my central rock walled garden named "The Beach Garden." He looks around and then circles down around the trees and onto the next beach and into the lake in the cove. There he wades, or perches on an old stump by the grassy and tree filled peninsula in order to fish. His wing spread is impressive too when we watch him take off in flight, said to be forty-two to fifty-two inches. They are noted to be lone hunters. I have read they belong to a group called "waders" because they search for food in this way. He stands about four feet tall and cannot be ignored. Herons fly with their long legs stretched out trailing behind and their necks folded back in a flat "S" loop. I have read more than once it is the tallest native bird that you will see standing on two legs. So when he walks up our beach we are grateful if we have been fortunate enough to see him. And we do see him often silently standing in the cove.

SILENT FLIGHT

Over the waters the large bird soared—
And landing in our cove—could not be ignored.
His very majestic presence—and stance
(By mere chance we had observed)—seemed to enhance
The scene. Could this great blue heron in his pause
Sense our appreciation and souls' applause?
In the silences of two humans and a bird—
Only the gentle uniting wind of the Spirit could be heard.

J.G.K.

Common Loon

This is a bird that we truly admire and feel so privileged to have on our lake. Even as I write this very minute there is a Loon calling out his eerie, haunting call over and over again, which is a delightful syncronicity. He is right out front on the lake, and though the Loons returned to the lake in late April and we have seen them and heard their cries in both night and day, I have not heard one in over a week. That it should appear and call (I will assume he is calling to me and knows what I am writing) as I begin this portion on Loons, is "other dimensional" just like his cry. You are never quite the same again once you have hard a Loon. It becomes a part of you somehow to hear them deep in the night, awakened by them from some dark part of the lake, is unforgettable. Then an answer will come seemingly from another direction and then a repeat call from the first Loon, and back and forth they cry out. A mated pair perhaps is communicating. It seems there is wisdom and the unexplainable essences we are absorbing when listening and waiting. So many nights through the years once in bed we have experienced this, and yet each time it is like the first because it is mystical and unlike anything else heard.

WAIL OF THE LOON

I am the wail of the loon echoing over the waters—
    bringing a touch of mystic
        to each listener's ear.
I skim along the smooth surface of the lake
    that holds the shining image of the moon.
I am an ancient mystery
    that cries out of the unknown
        into the here.
My secrets—carried through the trees
    on a gentle mist ,
        keep a tryst
            with all who seek
                and are moved
    by the wail of the loon.

JGK, 1997

Loons belong to their own order, Gaviiformes, and they are not related to geese or ducks. They fly in loose flocks during migration and do not take on the V formation of Canada Geese. They fly individually, north or south, in small flocks, sometimes as many as fifteen. They call to each other as they travel if a distance occurs between the birds. They arrive here after ice-out and we understand these loons winter on the coast of Maine.

END OF APRIL??

The Loons are back on Higher Ground.
They float on by without a sound—
Out on the lake; we now count five!
What joy to see they did survive!

'Twas just two weeks ago or so—
That "ice-out" came—released the flow—
And word went through the Loon grapevine,
And they returned 'neath fir and pine—
Greeting Heron and cruising slow.
Did God not tell them the forecast's snow?

JGK
April 25, 1992

There is such excitement when we hear our first loon, and then we are continually waiting to hear another. Then we begin to spot them on the lake and it is so thrilling. They establish their own territory and often it is the males who arrive first to establish where they will settle. Loons are in constant danger of raccoons and gulls and other predators and have far less chicks survive than other birds. In our area we had had boat patrols organized by teenagers to patrol the lakes near shore lines to keep the other noisy and larger boats away from the shores, to allow the nesting of the loons to continue safely. Unfortunately they give birth sometime in the immediate area of July 4th when there are so many vacationers and so much water activity, and so these patrols have tried to provide protection. The loons are valued and deeply desired to be on the lake. I have read where it is known that loons can go year after year with no young raised. The loons too, must be able to fish and the water must be clear enough so that they may see the fish. Islands are wonderful places for loons to build a nest, for then hopefully if it is far enough from shore, a raccoon cannot swim to it. However, even an island can have some raccoon residents, so the loon is constantly in danger. Even humans can drive them away if they build homes on the islands.

But if a male loon has found a suitable site after ice-out, then often the male loon of a pair already mated will return again and again to the same place that he and his mate have nested in before. The male may arrive two weeks or more before his mate. He makes known to other loon that this territory is his through a wild yodel. He will rear up on his tail and too, point his bill at the intruding loon and flap his wings wildly in the water. He announces his territory again and again with his yodel.

A loon will run over the water and then suddenly dive and come up far beyond from where he went down. To see these performances right out front on our lake is exciting and moving. We feel honored they are here. Loons spend most of their lives in water since they are awkward on land. A loon truly is a loved bird.

A Common Loon in summer has a shining greenish-black head and neck, a white breast, and a general body color that from a distance looks all dark. If one inspects more closely, however, there is a delightful checkered pattern of little white squares and dots on a black background. There is a horizontal white patch on the side of the dark neck with vertical black lines running through it, but to see these markings you would have to be very close. A loon is anywhere from twenty-eight to thirty-six inches. They migrate in Autumn in great numbers to the coast. It is said they have been caught in nets 90 feet below the water (how sad) when diving for fish. They use their half closed wings in swimming through water as well as their feet. People who have witnessed this say the birds seem to be flying through the water. We too have witnessed so many pleasurable sightings we feel very fortunate and blessed to have them visible here in front of our home.

They are altogether comfortable in water but waddle awkwardly on land because their feet are not formed to walk on earth properly. How sad the term "Crazy as a Loon" is used, for Loons are wise birds. This reference came about due to their eerie calls, but they are marvelous and other-worldly, and calls that we yearn to hear. I cannot imagine anyone degrading these beautiful birds.

NIGHT SHADE

At dusk I sat in chair and prayed—
Surroundings were the woods of jade
Hauntingly birds sang serenade
As if to usher in night's shade.

Immersed now in this mystical tune—
That called all nature to commune
I saw straight out from our lagoon—
On lake before me—gentle Loon.

So majestic did he appear!
His wail added voice to atmosphere—
And added affirmation to endear
This lovely creature so austere.

Survey of waters and a glance
Saw wail brought forth the slow advance—
Of two more Loons that did enhance
Twilight—and gave it soft romance.

How incredibly privileged to be part of it all—
When three Loons on a June night came to call.

Dedicated to the Loons—   JGK
of Lake Balch

There is so much to learn about the loon and this is worthy of anyone's time to learn more. There is much written about them, but one book we have turned to often since owning it is *The Loon-Voice of the Wilderness* by Joan Dunning. You may be interested also. The art work too is excellent.

I can only say we are thankful to be in the presence of the loons.

Mallards

MIGRATORY VISITORS

From out the sky a whirlwind came.
A flock of birds without a name!
But with binoculars aimed at that crowd—
And vision clear—we cried aloud—
"They're Mallard Ducks—oh, what a sight!"
(Migrating on their southern flight!)

With head so green—neck ring of white—
Blue patch on wing—and appetite
Each tipped their head in rain-drenched lake—
With bottom straight up—'twas no mistake!
It's how they feed—in vertical bobbing -
A social time—with much hobnobbing.
We counted twenty-six—and then
Saw four brown females with the "men."

In mid-day meal—for it was noon,
Not one lake fish did they harpoon!
(They feed on pondweeds, rice and grass—
Only health foods in their repast!)

Of all the places they could roam—
They chose to eat outside our home!
I think they sensed—vegetarians are we—
And with their menu we'd agree!

JGK

This poem written almost ten years ago was to celebrate the Mallards. As we came to spend more and more time here in our cottage we gradually began to take a much deeper interest in wildlife and we were learning. It was a very exciting time.

The Mallards have truly endeared themselves to us and my journals are filled with sweet and unusual encounters, particularly with one exceptional female Mallard. I feel like her Mother and the "grandmom" of her babies. But mallards in general that we encounter daily are a joy to us and we love them around. The females are shades of brown in definite designs on the outer feathers with white trim, and a white tail, and though considered plain in comparison to the male, we think they are very beautiful. They have a patch of iridescent color on the secondary feathers, that of blue, known as the speculum. The males have beautiful green heads, a white neck ring and a brown throat and chest. Their outer feathers on their back are also handsome in a brown and white vividly striped V pattern pointed to the tail, and not in the same more complicated design as the female's pattern.

The mallards arrive here right at the time of ice-out, just as the loons do. It is as if they all wear little waterproof wrist watches (well, ankle watches). Because there were several April snow falls here this year extending into the latter part of the month I was concerned about the Mallards that had already arrived. They are continually on our porch and grounds and on the lake and beach. They had to weather the snow as only they knew how but they survived. Though there are a good amount of Mallards that appear, there is one special one who has endeared herself to us and I simply named her "Mrs. Mallard" several years ago. Though to all outward appearances she resembles other females, there is a definite familiarity from and with this Mallard. I know her from the others and she makes herself known by her ways and her sweet conduct with us. I realize some may doubt, but I have an inner knowing this is the same Mallard who loves to be here in our company. When she is approaching from the lake or out on the grass and I come out the screen door, she runs to me! It is the sweetest scene to see this dear Mallard running to greet me! It is not because of the bread because I do not always give that to her and her mate. Too, they rap on our front windows with their beaks to tell us they are on the porch then move to the door to wait for us. The other Mallards do not do this. "Mrs." is truly my little friend. I have had other experiences with her to definitely believe she and I know each other on a soul level. "Mrs." taught her mate to rap on the window too. She was the only one who had ever done that.

This year has been unusual because a pattern has been broken. In years past the Mallard couples are about, but always using our "Mrs." as the source of knowledge, once the mallards mate the female is on her own. Day after day in the last several years, in April after mating, "Mrs." would always come to us alone. When her babies were born she continued to bring them to us many times a day throughout the summer. It was wonderful and she was part of our life.

Last year one of her eight had a twisted foot that turned backwards. The baby had been normal at birth but some time after, she brought her babies as usual to us and on this occasion he was crippled, perhaps having been attacked by another creature. It was heart breaking. He could not keep up with the others and fell often. I would toss bread just to him and yet still his siblings tried to get it. It broke my heart to see him, yet in the water he could swim and stay close to his family. Seeing the baby day after day like this as I fed them all made me so sad. I prayed for him each day to be healed or to be able to adjust in life. Then one day several weeks later, he was healed! He came with "Mrs." and his family walking and running like the rest, his little foot straight forward. Prayers had been answered and in some mysterious way God had touched him. The babies were so dear and we watched them grow until they eventually matched her in size. "Mr." was never with her after April or the mating.

Two years ago we had the extraordinary experience of witnessing the actual mating of "Mrs." with her mate on April 22nd. I will repeat the account of this I shared in my *Journal of Love*. This event occurred at sunset, and a great disturbance had preceded the event which caused us to be on the scene. Other males were fighting over "Mrs." under our dock, and we rushed down not knowing what the noise was about. Once the male meant for "Mrs. Mallard" claimed her, he ushered her to the base of my prayer chair and platform, and there in the waters it took place. It seemed to be something we would only have seen on the Discovery Channel, the two of them silhouetted against the brilliant setting sun for fifteen long minutes. Again like the angel deer's appearance, it was beneath the holy place of My Prayer Chair.

After this mating the male swam off but our dear little "Mrs." exhaustedly swam back under our dock and then almost crawled up onto shore. She nestled into the earth against an incline of the land and laid there with her sweet little head on a rock. We stayed there a long time immobile, but I continued to softly comfort her and tell her our love. I wanted to go to her and hold her and comfort her, but I knew that I had to let her be and believe this was all nature intended. Since during the mating it seemed as if she would drown, for he held her under for many minutes before bringing her head up for air, then submerging her again and again, I was concerned about her and if she would recover. We were deeply relieved to find her rapping at out glass once more the next day. But "Mr." was no longer in her company thereafter, nor had we particularly noticed his undivided attention in the weeks previous.

Now this year we are bewildered and waiting to see what will occur next. The male with "Mrs." is continually with her and it is the third week of May as I write. All these weeks they have been together and he has been courting and fending off other males with a furor. If one approaches "Mrs." out on our deck or lawn, her "Mr." with head lowered to the ground in a war-like position, charges the intruding male. One male in particular has lost most all his brown chest feathers from "Mr." charging and attacking him to keep him from "Mrs." Often he will fly after any male and he attacks him in the air to protect her. These defensives are repeated many times a day. The noise on our porch is so loud at times when other mallards come near our "Mrs." If another couple comes close, "Mr." goes after the female as well as the male in war-like defensive actions. He is devoted to "Mrs." The wonder of it all is, why are they still together at the end of May and he still courting, as are other mallards? It is long past when they usually mate and it is unusual to see the males here continuously. Has some great heavenly plan taken place to change the mating rituals of mallards? Are they later in mating and longer in wooing and courting due to the snow continuing to the end of April? Did they forget to wear their little wrist watches? Have they already mated, and did God decide the males should stay with the females preceding and during childbirth like responsible fathers should? Only time will tell. I will report what eventually occurs before the ending of this book and your retreat. It is a mystery. But we love the mallards and they are here even as I write and Bob is feeding them. When another male or female or both come near our "Mrs." and "Mr.," their little beaks open and shut and they make low noises. I record everything in my journal. These noises are of alarm and agitation that others are in their territory. Our grounds belong to "Mr." and "Mrs.," you see.

In past years I had had precious experiences with "Mrs." and this is why I love her in a special way. This is the fifth year she has come to us. Perhaps longer, and I was not aware because I did not live here permanently before then. The interchanges we have had were other-worldly, particularly when she came to me while I was on my hands and knees in a garden. Inches from my face she stood and stared into my eyes. I talked to her aloud the entire time she remained, calling her "Dear" or "Mrs. Mallard." I feel I was permitted to experience something divine. Bob discreetly observed it all. This poem tells of the experiences she and I shared as we came to know each other. We continue in the present to commune.

MRS. MALLARD

I remember the day I came to call
        and knocked on your sliding glass door
            with my beak.
I had visited often before
        to feed on your seed
            but this day we did not speak.
Through the glass I could see the delight and surprise
        in your eyes.

And I remember the day you were working in the earth
        on your hands and knees—
            inside the circle of a raised rock wall—
And as softly as you please
        I again came to call,
            suddenly appearing
                and endearing
                    myself to you.

I flew up into your garden
        and inches from your face—
            staring into each others eyes—
                we knew this was a sacred moment and place.

As you spoke to me
    I padded among your flowers
        never bending a one.
Then with my eyes
    I said good-byes,
Flew down—
    and waddled across the grass in the sun.

It is a wonder to live here in the woods and be privileged to learn first hand from God's creatures.

There are other ducks about in summer also known as black ducks, but they are really brown. We have had interesting encounters with them also and everything has been recorded. Actually they resemble the female Mallard, but are darker and lack white over wings and tail. The males have red legs, rather bright, and yellowish bills. Like the Mallards they prefer fresh water. Perhaps if I share a group of poems I wrote about each encounter their

Mr. and Mrs. Mallard

stories will be told as well as if done in prose. I enjoyed writing the poems because the happenings and the black ducks were and are so dear to me. But Mrs. Mallard is queen of all ducks!

The first poem tells of a specific sweet incident of a duck coming to call. The second poem describes a funny true occurrence also that I observed from my prayer chair one morning. And the third poem speaks of a convergence of ducks on Dennis's dock that once stood in the cove but is no longer there. Each afternoon as I sat writing, these ducks would gather on the dock for about an hour, all facing out over the lake and lined up in several rows. It was most unusual.

And lastly, the fourth poem describes the efforts of a tiny duck to keep up with his mother and brothers and sisters. It was heartbreaking.

Bob and I and our friend Dan Deane who was visiting, sat on our dock at sunset and silently witnessed this tragic little scene and prayed the little duck into the safety and warmth of his disappearing family. Upon arrival at our cottage Dan presented me with a beautiful creation, that of a soft life-sized replica of a Loon. It is a treasure to me and has always remained on the guest bed here in my writing room and watches over Rochester when he is settled there too, in the thick folded quilt to act as advisor as I write or to take his "cat naps."

PLEASE HONK FOR SERVICE

A little black duck today came to call.
He walked up the beach and o'er the rock wall.
He waddled around—made a honk now and then—
Announcing arrival and also his yen—
For pieces of bread that he knows are in store,
(For his family has visited this cottage before.)

The nice man obliged and threw him the treat—
(The duck has no preference—either white or whole wheat.)
We watched him devour each piece on the ground
That fell to surround him—then turning around—
He gazed at us steadfastly with dark little eyes—
Walked back down the beach with honks of good-byes

JGK

THE UGLY DUCKLING

A group of ducks were swimming there
A sea gull came—and in despair—
They scattered and they wondered why,
That he should swoop down from on high
And interrupt their morning tryst!
My goodness—didn't he get the gist?

Why they were ducks—he some strange bird!
Look at the trouble he has stirred!
But as he stood in their convention—
They saw friendship was his intention.
And soon that white gull splashed in fun—
Amongst the brown ducks in the sun!

I think with him this crowd is stuck!
That big white guy thinks he's a duck!

Dedicated to   JGK
the ducks and gulls
of Lake Balch

DUCK DOCK

Little ducks all in a cluster—
Feathers shining with sun-touched luster—
Are gathered silently in meditation
Obviously deep in contemplation.
Deserted red dock tucked in the cove—
Has become their treasure-trove—
Where dreams are spun—at least begun—
They sun-bathe there in summer sun.

Gazing out upon the lake—
They now partake in quiet break.
For just as humans go apart
In silence and for peace of heart—
So too, dear creatures sun and pray—
Commune with God in their own way.
Ducks are fortified for life's long swims—
In these sweet daily interims.

JGK

MAMA! WHERE ARE YOU?

Across the shadowed waters came—
    at twilight time, a tiny form.
Quacking, quacking Mother's name—
    while in his precious heart a storm
Churned up anxieties and fear—
    because his Mama was not near.

He swam towards us on the dock—
    hoping we had seen his flock.
Quacking, quacking, all the while—
    to tell us of his frightening trial.
I called to him consoling words—
    but he just longed for other birds.

And so he passed us on the lake—
    distraught—with quacks left in his wake.
We watched the little duck swim west—
    into the sunset on his quest—
Outlined against the orange ray—
    that ended now this August day.

As stars broke forth in heavenly dome—
    this tiny duck cried out for home.
Each measured call that floated back
    just broke my heart with every quack.
He disappeared into the black—
    diminished quack—and quack—and quack.

Dedicated to   JGK
Dan Deane August 21, 1992
on his first night on "Higher Ground"

Visitors at Feeders and on Deck

The daily visitors who come to visit and feed and socialize on the deck are really a joy. Incidents happen every day that are both humorous and interesting and we observe and I take notes.

During the night or in early morning before we were awake a confrontation between the male mallards took place. They were the last birds I had written about, and the brown ducks, before ending my writing here last night. Even as I write two male mallards are crying out and just took flight off our deck, one in attack after the other.

We know there was a fight on the deck earlier because feathers were everywhere. I gathered up nineteen, both large and small. We had only to wait to see who was missing them. Our "Mr." and "Mrs." arrived soon after and it was not him. He still had the same few marks on his chest as yesterday. Soon the other mallard couple arrived and it was obvious this male lost the fight and had intruded on "Mr." and "Mrs." territory. Hopefully they will learn from it and not come here when "Mr." and "Mrs." are feeding or visiting with us. This other male has a very bedraggled looking chest now. I will tell him I am saving his feathers and perhaps it will cheer him up. They are safely in a little box on my desk.

Grackles

Yesterday late there was a confrontation between two grackles. As I was writing, a male and female flew in, and the female went to a feeder below the long wooden bar that holds all the feeders. The male sat above on this bar. Another male flew in and immediately the first male grackle began to inch closer down the bar to where his mate was feeding. The other male followed him. Suddenly the first male opened up all his feathers until be became rounded and twice his size. I was shocked! I had never seen this display. The other male did the same, and just when I thought they would attack each other, the female flew off. Instantly her mate followed, soaring after her with the other male behind him. I have never seen aggression like this between birds other than the male mallards. The Grackles are about twelve and a half inches, and in a sense are large Blackbirds with extra long tails, I have read. The common (purple or bronze necked) Grackle has a long diamond-shaped tail, much broader in the middle than at either end. At times their tails may be V-shaped with a "crease" at the center and this apparently is part of the courting process and display. The males actually crease their tails. Their voice is a prolonged loud crackle and they travel in flocks.

Baltimore Oriole

This is a friendly and beautiful bird. The color combination of brilliant orange and black is so striking and their song is melodious. They are daily visitors we are happy to see, and they often sit and sing on the bar and look in on me at my upper window as I write. I have read that they like the company of humans, men, women and children, and even of horses and cows. It has one white bar on each black wing. The female is not as brilliantly attired but is also lovely. She is more olive-yellow with white barred dark wings. I have learned the female prefers white yarn that she will combine with plant fibers and grass to weave into her nest. Some birds do not mind what color the yarn is. They add beauty to our lives, these lovely Baltimore Orioles.

Red-Winged Blackbird

These wonderful birds about nine inches long are beautiful also. Only a small patch of the wing is red but it is what makes the bird identifiable. This red shoulder patch always shows when the bird is flying or half spreads its wings. The female is not as colorful. I have learned it makes its nest near the water in low bushes.

In a fine coloring learning book entitled *Birds of New England*, given to me by my daughter Janna, it tells that after breeding Red Winged Blackbirds fly into the sky and form flocks of hundreds of thousand and sometimes millions!

House Wren

I do not know much as yet about this small bird who is only about five inches. There are so many different wrens in North America, perhaps a dozen or more. But this little one is sweet and small, brownish with underparts that are lighter. His bill curves downwards slightly and is small. I have just read in John Kieran's wonderful book, *An Introduction to Birds*, that a House Wren will build a nest most anywhere; far away in an orchard, in a nearby hole around a barn or house, in the pocket of an old coat or in a mailbox. It has a bubbling song all day and night and is a bustler. He is a welcome visitor here. Perhaps his nest is nearby though undetected.

Goldfinch

These are always a thrill to see, small like the House Wren but so bright. The male has a brilliant, shining yellow body and black wings that have white bars. It seems to be wearing a little black cap tilted down over its forehead. As is usually the case, the female is much duller in color and does not have a cap. Often they are confused with wild canaries and their song is like that of canaries.

We have noticed how they are always chattering even when feeding or just resting, but they call so sweetly to each other (and hopefully to us) all the while they are here. I have recently read that the male loses its black cap in winter and its plumage turn to the same olive color as the female. They are a loved bird here and everywhere and we always await them. They are like darts of sunshine in the air when flying. I open John Kieran's book right now and he states that the male feeds the female while she is brooding and is a good provider for the young until they leave the nest. The female makes a thistle down cradle in an outer branch or fork of a branch and actually builds the nest late (July) because she waits until the thistledown ripens and lays four to six eggs. Such amazing things birds do, so wise in what is needed in their lives and for their young. We just gaze and enjoy their presence, yet they are responsible for matters we know nothing about.

White-Breasted Nuthatch

This little bird of about five and a half inches has always fascinated us. He moves down trees head first and that seems to be what he is most noted for. He does not have bright colors or an outstanding voice but we always enjoy seeing him. The Nuthatch always seems to be with the Chickadees here and the Downy Woodpeckers. We have observed that for years, but I only recently see it remarked upon in a book as well. He often eats suet with both these birds at our suet holder, and of course feeds at our feeders. A Nuthatch is blue-gray in color and white underneath with blackish tips on the wings and his tail feathers. He has a little black cap. He eats mainly seeds or insects and we enjoy his presence on the deck year round.

Black-Capped Chickadee

This is a precious little bird about five inches that also graces our deck and feeders year round and has a cheerful call that actually sounds like it is saying its own name. We feed these dear birds well all winter and all their friends. It has a little black bib and black crown and is a black and white pattern all over. The Chickadee is known for this little black bib and cap. It seems so kind and sweet. This spring I have come closer to them than before and several have allowed me to place my hand immediately next to their bodies as they sat on a perch at the feeder. I have also touched a tail and the Chickadee remained. I am hoping for more, perhaps one will sit on my hand. They do not seem at all afraid and allow me to take close-up photos inches from them. The Chickadee is the State bird of two of our neighboring states, Maine and Massachusetts. All official state birds are named by state legislatures and in some states, school children have suggested state birds.

I wrote a poem some years ago describing the activity on our feeders, and it was the Chickadee I especially had in mind for its politeness. I hope you know some Chickadees too that grace your yard and porch.

THE WAITING BRANCH

So many tiny birds exist
And there in early morning mist—
They come to feeders filled with seed
Yet one can never witness greed—
For each bird flies right in to eat
And takes his turn to help deplete—
The food that's there—and without shoving!
There's no impatience—only loving!
All through the day they come and go
I believe they truly know—
To bide their time on waiting branch
To be polite—give each a chance
To eat, complete and then retreat—
This procedure they repeat!

We humans can this lesson learn
To always show love and concern—
Not be impatient, push, advance—
Perhaps we need a waiting branch!

Cowbird

These are familiar visitors here and are about eight inches long. They have a round head and a short bill and I have learned they are the smallest of all native Blackbirds. They are always polite here but I do know they put their eggs in the nests of other birds when the female owner is not present. Sometimes it is noticed, other times not, but usually once hatched it is overpowering and the resident birds that are hatched with it do not often survive. I certainly did not like learning about that some years ago. I went to John Kieran's book just now to see if it is mentioned there, and yes, he states that often more than a hundred different kinds of birds have been swindled in this manner by the Cowbird. One would never guess for they are well mannered here.

Ruby-Throated Hummingbird

In another chapter I have discussed this tiny bird. We had our first sighting of one on our deck this past weekend (third week of May) before we have had time to put up a feeder just for him. Soon it will be waiting for him. I know they like water and even birdbaths and sprinklers. We have witnessed this. Their wings become a blur when flying and they can fly backward as well as forward and can also be seen swinging from side to side. They dart about like magic and the sound they make is a squeak or a very tiny buzz. We are thrilled when they choose to spend time here. They are like little fairies in the air, splashes of color so amazing!

Blue Jay

What a handsome bird! He is about twelve inches long and visits with us often. He has a lovely song as well as some harsh notes. He is a joy to witness and is so beautiful still or in flight. He often seems to be watching me as I write while he is on the bar outside my window. There are a negative things said about Blue Jays often but I can never confirm them for my encounters with these birds have all been positive. There is a very unique account about them titled "The Bashful Blue Jay" by Hal Borland in a book we have owned for ten years called *The Joy of Songbirds*. That essay won me over immediately and I share interest in them and approval as does this author. We always welcome them and admire them. They are glorious to see, sky-blue with stripes and patches of black and clear white and with a sharp crest.

Another poem tells of the Blue Jays and others recently mentioned here feeding together, and just joyfully proclaims the birds.

WINGED RESIDENTS

The blue jay comes each day to check
To see if feeders on the deck
Are filled to brim
For likes o' him
And lingers there to leisurely peck.

Chickadee too, is on display
Through winter snow we know she'll stay
She breaks her fast
And takes repast
We see her mingle there with Jay

Her Nuthatch friend comes here to dine
From early morn until compline
Oft upside down
On trunk of brown
She patiently waits her turn in line.

Black and white warbler is our guest
Flying in to gain his quest
Of delicious seed
On which to feed
Each tiny presence makes us blest.

At times we see an entire flock
On ground or rail or on the rock
Word's reached each ear
That food is here
They eat their fill not ruled by clock.

Each species at this woods and lake
Is beauty just for its own sake
The Egret white
Soars into sight
And Loons in distance their wails make.

We thank Our Lord for such as these
Such precious lives who dearly please.
Behold each bird
And heart is stirred
As birdsong wafts through tall pine trees.

Dedicated to   JGK
all the Winged Residents

Crows

Ah—the crows. They seem to travel in armies and descend here and fly about communicating with each other like no other bird. Males and females are alike but it is said that each one is really a character and most unique. You can hear them cawing all through the woods and about our home. They caw in a series of caws, sometimes four or five or six or more, then an answer will come back through the trees. Their early morning communications are often like alarm clocks, but these caws can be heard day or night. It is said there are so many variations on their caws that an entire "crow language" we can surmise might be built around this simple caw. They also have odd sputtering outbursts at times too, and soft piping notes, but these can be heard mainly by those close by. Even though they do not sing, pairs at times have a rambling series of intimate softer calls they exchange.

They strut about our lawn and come upon the deck to ground feed, but mostly just visit and observe without eating. They are so big, nineteen inches, that when a group are together they are rather commanding.

Mourning Dove

The Mourning Dove is the most widespread pigeon in the New England region. When preparing their nesting area, the female builds the nest and the male brings the building materials, like twigs and leaves. It lays its two eggs, and if a nest has not been made, will lay them on the ground or in an abandoned nest of another bird.

When in flight it has an unusual "winnowing sound" and is unlike any other sound of a bird flying. Other than that it only makes its moaning coo that we hear come Spring. It is a rather mournful sound and is how this bird received its **name**. It is said to be one of the quietest birds in contrast to the Blue Jay and **Crow**.

We enjoy its company **and** it always seems docile and sweet. It ground feeds on our deck eating the fallen seed from the feeders above. Often it just sits and meditates while other birds or chipmunks bustle around it. The Mourning Dove is about twelve inches and is a fine tan to brown all over with shades of blue, pink and deeper brown here and there and some black spots on its back. When the Morning dove takes off you can see white in his tail feathers. He has a long pointed tail. We are always happy to have this bird arrive. There is a gentleness about him.

Chipping Sparrow

This little bird is about five and a half inches long and one of the smallest sparrows. It has a little cap of reddish chestnut below which is a white line fringing along the lower edge by a thin black line running through the eye to the base of the little dark bill. The bill is conical. It is so clearly marked, this sparrow is easily distinguished from some other small sparrows. It does not have a musical song but a succession of "chips" strung together sung rapidly. It is almost like a trill and for a tiny bird it is loud. It is said not to be fond of woods yet it is a daily visitor here to us. But it also likes a well-kept lawn, which we have, and the company of humans, so how lovely these little friends come to be with us.

Yellow Warbler

The Yellow Warbler, about five inches, is bright yellow all over and is called a "Wild Canary," as is the Goldfinch. The male however, has some reddish stripes on its underparts. They like many kinds of trees and so they are at home here around our cottage. The female does most of the nest building and creates a nice little cup shaped nest of grasses and fibers from plants for her three to five eggs.

Rose-Breasted Grosbeak

This little bird, about eight inches, seems to be the model bird and is a delightful singer. He is black and white with a thick, short white bill and a startling triangle of rose on its white breast. The male Grosbeak is said to be affectionate to his mate and children and brings food to the female and even takes turns sitting on the eggs in a crude nest. He is also a good provider to the fledglings. The female and babies are streaked brownish colored and broad white wing bars and have the appearance of having white chin straps.

Grosbeak

The Grosbeak has a beautiful song, like a warble. I have read that once you recognize the song you realize you have more Grosbeaks with you than you realized. This is true. It is only recently that they have come to our woods and home and we are glad of it.

Purple Finch

State bird of New Hampshire about six inches and described as delightful, we only see one on occasion yet it is said they are everywhere. Actually they are more rose colored or raspberry and only the male has much purple. The female and young are gray to brown with dark streaks. It has a delightful rolling warble of a song and has a distinctive call note. It is a lovely little bird to represent our state.

Downy Woodpecker and Hairy Woodpecker

It is said the Downy is the friendliest of the Woodpecker family. It is described as the midget member of this great family by John Kieran. It is black and white and the male has a red patch on back of its head. It is about six and a half inches long and is friend to Chickadees and Nuthatches as I have recorded earlier. Downy Woodpeckers are constant visitors to our suet holder, and feed with their friends there winter and summer, and we enjoy their company. With my new zoom lens camera I have been trying to photograph them as they feed.

The Hairy Woodpecker, another member of the family, looks almost exactly like the Downy but is almost twice the size of the Downy. The hairy too is a daily visitor to our suet and often the Hairy and Downy are there at the same time. I have read the Hairy is not quite as abundant as the Downy and that too, is not quite as friendly. Several times the Hairy has made us laugh with his show of authority, for on these occasions he found the suet all gone after much feasting. He actually stood on top of the feeder at these times and really scolded us through the sliding glass window door for allowing this. I mean he really carried on! Naturally we filled it again for him, and I believe his thank yous are his constant visits. The call of the Hairy is much louder and his cry has a certain pitch, but the Downy has a cry that rather descends at the end. We feel honored they are here daily with us and they seem like they are gentle and caring towards the other birds—and to us. And most certainly, they are beautiful to see.

Song Sparrow

This little bird is about six inches long and found all over North America and most certainly on our deck. They are sweet and are rather plain and brownish and some have streaked breasts. The Song Sparrow has a dark spot on each side of its throat and a heavier spot in the middle of its breast where the streaks on the breast seem to meet. It also has three spots in a triangle on its streaked breast and throat. It is just a friendly little bird, so small and lovely. We welcome them as they feed with all the other visitors. John Kieran describes their cheerful song as "Tea, tea, tea! Polly-put-the-kettle-on." Their songs are also described as clear whistles and buzzy sounds by author Lang Elliott. Three amazing full page close-up pictures of the song Sparrow in color appear in his book.

Henry David Thoreau has written: "A thousand birds . . . gently twittering and ushering in the light" and this is what it too seems to us, even though there has been song throughout the night as well.

NIGHTSONG

This night God called a sweet convention
Upon my ear this intervention
Lifts my soul to new dimension
Far beyond my comprehension.

To my hidden observatory
Come strains from a conservatory
That fill the night and so resound
Throughout deep woods that here surround.

Celestial choir of migratories
Bring to earth their heavenly glories—
Chords so utterly spiritualistic
Incomprehensible—haunting—mystic.

Birdsong—O such lilting sound—
And little creatures so profound
Join the choirs of God's creation
Giving my heart jubilation.

Insects, beasties—birds of feather
Blend sweet harmony together
All tiny voices sing in fervor—
Nightsong Gift to this observer.

JGK

Puccini was Latin, and Wagner Teutonic,
And birds are incurably philharmonic.
Suburban yards and rural vistas
Are filled with avian Andrew Sisters.

—Odgen Nash

We are honored to have a bird in our woods and around our cottage that teaches us persistence, and also gives fun and pleasure. As far as we know we have never seen this bird who seems always to be in the branches singing his little heart out from the time we wake until we go to sleep. He has only two notes (one more than the famous Johnny One Note sung about), but he sings them out continuously. When he eats or sleeps is a mystery, unless there is a couple, and one takes over at times. The song is like the sound of one drawing in and out on one note on the harmonica. Over and over! It just makes me giggle. We often just break out laughing. It is the background song to everything we do and to the songs of all the other birds.

One humorous incident occurred regarding this little bird. Janna and Bill asked us to come to Rhode Island a couple of years ago to babysit our granddaughter Dahlia while they had settlement on their home. As we drove out of our woods in the early morning the little bird was singing as always. When we arrived in Rhode Island three hours later and stepped out of the car, the first thing we heard was the song of this bird. We were just hysterical with laughter! And he sang the entire time we were in Rhode Island! We were convinced he hitched a ride down on the roof of our car. One day we hope to meet this little singing star. Bob has an affectionate little risque name for him but perhaps it is better I do not include it here.

LISTEN

Listen!
    Tiny birds compose their songs
        even on a morning of gray—
           and hearts are brightened
             and heightened
In the dawn of a new day.

JGK

It has been years now we have been listening to this little songster but we are patient and hope one day we will suddenly spot him in full view singing his harmonic two notes. It is a lovely mystery really and mysteries are needed. When we finally do identify this elusive singer, this bird will be even more special. Wordsworth wrote a poem about a cuckoo whom he always heard but never saw and calls him "a voice, a mystery, an invisible thing," yet he is to him "darling of the spring."

Whenever it is possible to do so it is important to find the little singer and watch it make its music. Songs we hear in the woods penetrate the soul but those heard along a street of a city are not as moving. It is a shame for the sweet birds to perhaps not be as deeply appreciated there and often thought of as annoyances. This is so sad. Each little song echoes from a living creature formed by God and we should appreciate the songs and calls whether they be in the cities or forests. When we learn to identify the songs it brings great pleasure, just as it does when we can observe the birds. Listening to the birds is a joy and their songs bring on a healing effect. Their songs have been subjects of poems through time by famous poets, who turn to this form of expression to explore the deep mystery of the birds and their soul stirring songs. Thoreau writes about the healing effect of bird song also in 1852 and ends by saying, "Nature is always encouraging." There are many words of love and wisdom on the subject of birds by Thoreau. Poems written by the famous poets stir our emotions in regard to birds and for me, they inspire and encourage me to continue to carefully observe and learn. Birds have day time songs and night songs and learning about them is a wonderful pursuit. To be surrounded by these amazing creatures and not appreciate them or learn from them or about them, is ignoring gifts from God.

Just recently in Sanford, Maine as we walked along a residential street we heard the most glorious birdsong, and what seemed to be an enormous choir. As we approached a medium sized tree we were not familiar with, we knew instantly it was filled with birds. We stood by it listening to the most melodious and precious singing, and could see the many birds, for the tree was not tall. None flew out because of our presence, and the heavenly choir continued. People passed by us but none stopped. We, however, were in awe for this music could be heard at a distance and over the flow of the traffic. We pass this tree often, but never again heard what God sent to us as a gift that early evening. How I wish I had had my small tape recorder with me, but it is still in our minds and hearts. God's gifts are everywhere for us, waiting to be discovered and appreciated, even on a city street.

"THEY WILL INSTRUCT YOU"*

Bright beings from the Hand of God
To grace life's path on which we trod—
In glorious plumage—flaming, rare;
O—divulge one secret if you dare!

Birds of brilliance on the bough—
Grant us your wisdom—please, somehow!
In your shining eyes so bright—
Your souls' revealed; No, don't take flight
Until you teach us unknown things—
And then with blessing—spread your wings.

*Job 12: 7-8   JGK

Years ago in the first year of our marriage when we lived in San Diego and Bob was in the Navy, we visited San Juan Capistrano at the mission on the coast of California. We learned about the Swallows who returned there every year in the month of March (if we remember correctly) and lay their eggs in dozens of holes in the adobe walls of the mission. We have never forgotten our visit there. And this is comparable to what occurs on our deck and in our woods when the birds I have written about here return to New Hampshire, and specifically to our "Higher Ground." It is a wonder and a mystery. We watch them daily and feel blessed.

Loren Eiseley

I am only a novice observer and a deep appreciator of the birds, but there is an author who has so much to teach us about them. In his book, *The Immense Journey*, the naturalist Loren Eiseley tells of a time he was present when a group of birds passed judgement upon life. It is the true story of an enormous raven who was on a branch in a woods of pine with a red and squirming nestling in his beak and what followed. The response from the song sparrows and the way this author relates it is never to be forgotten. It was *their* judgment of life against death in notes tragically prolonged. One has to read this account in the author's own words and then a bird can never again be thought of in a casual or uncaring way.

And too, this man who is writer, poet, and anthropologist, Loren Eiseley, shares also a passage that stays in one's mind and heart once it is read in his book *The Night Country*. I included this in my book *Compassion for All Creatures*, but it is worthy to repeat. He writes:

A little later in a quieter bend of the shore, I see ahead of me a bleeding, bedraggled blot on the edge of the white surf. As I approach, it starts warily to its feet. We look at each other. It is a wild duck, with a shattered wing. It does not run ahead of me like the longer-limbed gull. Before I can cut off its retreat, it waddles painfully from its brief refuge into the water.

Eisely goes on to relate how the sea falls heavily and the duck dives awkwardly, but with long knowledge and instinctive skill, under the first two inshore waves. He watches the duck's head working seaward. A huge wave rises and crashes and the black head of the duck disappears. Eisely states, "This is the way wild things die, without question, without knowledge of mercy in the universe, knowing only themselves and their own pathway to the end." Loren Eisely ponders this duck and scene as he continues up the beach and says "I wonder if the man who shot that bird will die as well."

In Conclusion

We feel so blessed to daily have the birds surrounding us and with their joyful songs. How could anyone harm them? They are little unique personalities that bring joy and knowledge and sweet comforting presence. We can learn so much from them. As a child I barely knew a bird. Growing up in the city of Philadelphia I was only aware of the robins and sparrows but nothing more. As a young Mother in the suburbs my attention was on my family with little knowledge of the birds in our yard, yet always appreciating them. But in New Hampshire these past many years birds are indeed noticed, loved, appreciated and at the center of our lives. We learn from them and see them as distinct little personalities and treasure their existence and the privilege of their presence. I hope you have enjoyed too learning about the birds of "Higher Ground" and related reminiscences, and that if you have never before noticed or shown interest in birds, that hopefully something stirred within you as you read, and that from this time forward you will never be able to view a bird again without interest and desire for more knowledge of these extraordinary beings.

A final poem expresses the dear little ways of the birds and their responses when we presented them with a new feeder and an unusual addition to their menu.

WHERE THE ELITE MEET

A new bird feeder we installed
At first the birds were all appalled!
No one touched it for five days
Continued in their usual ways.
They loved two feeders that were there
They certainly did not want a spare.

They ignored it very well
'Til a Nuthatch broke the spell—
And now they fly in—wait in line—
To try this cute new place to dine.
Birds we've never seen before
Stare at us through our glass door!

Cooked brown rice we also gave
To the daring and the brave.
We laid it on a wooden bench
Soon there was a dug out trench
Where they nibbled and made haste
So it would not go to waste.
Macrobiotic birds have we—
And now rice balls are in our tree!

Dedicated to all our birds   JGK

There is serene and settled majesty to woodland scenery that enters into the soul and delights and elevates it, and fills it with mobile "inclinations."

—Washington Irving

Reflect and Journal

☆ Try to listen to the songs and calls of the birds, especially if you have never paid attention to them before. If possible sit in a garden or your yard, or if you have neither, then go to a park or wooded place. Just enjoy these beautiful sounds as you sit in perfect stillness. Perhaps record their songs with a tape recorder.

☆ As soon as possible after this experience write about it in your journal in some detail, describing the experience and what it meant to you. If you can, write about some of the birds you saw, naming them if possible.

☆ From now on be more aware of the birds for they will enrich your life. Take notes about them and continue to record incidents that occur when you have been observing.

☆ Write a poem about what you have been experiencing in watching them. Perhaps you may want to single out one particular bird. Whatever you choose. Continue to write poems the more you observe the birds.

☆ With your colored pencils or crayons or watercolors, create a picture of the bird or birds you have written about, or about any bird that is meaningful to you. Display this somewhere in your home, especially if your home is not in an area where you can bird watch in reality. Create many pictures and too, present one to a friend.

☆ Try to recall your encounters with birds in childhood and write about any that you remember in your journal. Sketch in your journal too to illustrate your writings if you wish.

☆ In your journal write about a heartache you have that you are praying to be set free from, using a bird as metaphor in some way in your writing. Perhaps in some miraculous way the heartache will take flight on the wings of your bird to be carried off and released forever.

☆ If you are in a position to do so, perhaps put out a feeder for the birds, but realizing once you do it you must be constant in keeping it full for the birds grow to depend upon it. If not a feeder, perhaps a bird house in some obscure place away from any busyness and disturbances.

☆ Appreciate the birds Talk to them and be aware, and come to understand how incredible they are.

☆ Perhaps try to find a book on birds. Birds are like little angelic messengers to me. The bird books I have mentioned in this chapter are exceptional. Also the Golden Press puts out a nature guide on birds, a small sized book. I have had mine for years. Another book that will truly amaze you that I found at a library sale is *Birds as Individuals* by Owen Howard, who calls her home Bird Cottage. She lives in Sussex, England. This may be out of print (published in 1953) but perhaps a copy could be found in a bookshop carrying old books or on the internet. It is published by Double-day and Company and endorsed by well known naturalists as John Kieran (mentioned earlier) and Roger Tory Peterson. It is unlike anything I have read, but all the books mentioned in this chapter are truly worth owning.

> *Two birds fly past.*
> *They are needed somewhere.*
>
> —Robert Bly

Think about this little poem when you see the birds flying by. Each of us is needed also. Perhaps write the poem in your journal and anything else that comes to mind in regard to its message.

☆ Imagine that you are a bird. What kind of bird would you be and what colors? Relate this to your life. Following is a poem written as I travelled by car from Rhode Island back to New Hampshire. I imagined I was making the trip as a bird and I tried to visit and use all the unusual names of places we encountered, beginning with the name of the street my son lived on (Rochambeau), and from there on towns, bodies of water and another road. Become a bird and make a trip to somewhere you would like to visit. Write a poem about it. Really try to enter into its body in imagination.

A BIRD'S-EYE VIEW

I fly North from Rochambeau
     and glide slowly over Pawtucket.
With a little luck it
     will be noon—
          and soon
I will rocket
     over Woonsocket.
I soar over the Neponset River
     beneath a fluffy white cloud—
Miles later see Totten Pond
     wear fog as a shroud.
Mishawan Road now directly below
     is but a fine line—
And I swoosh ever North—
     until New Hampshire is mine.

Written using unusual names   JGK
collected in Mass and RI on the trip
from Providence, RI to New Hampshire
September 21, 1997

☆ ☆ ☆ ☆ ☆

Come now from the lofty heights of the birds to our wooden deck once more and meet many acquaintances of the birds who congregate there. Rochester and I are going to take a little "ice cream break" indoors first. Will you join us? Rochester is only permitted to have a little vanilla ice cream occasionally, and of course, never, never anything that is chocolate! This is dangerous and deadly to dear cats! A word of caution!

SHARED FARE

I do not know if it's nutritious—
But O my gosh—is it delicious!
I'm not the only one that knows—
He's on my lap in silent pose—
Watching with big golden eyes,
As he awaits his little prize.

He sits just inches from my face—
And lets me eat at my own pace—
Until the chocolate coating's finished,
And ice cream too, is quite diminished.
And then he knows it's now his turn—
For this his feline taste buds yearn!

With little tongue he licks his share—
Vanilla ice cream—ah, such fare!
Now it's gone—there's just the stick.
What joy to eat our choc-o-pic!

Dedicated to   JGK
Rochester

CHAPTER ELEVEN

Diane and Friends

Every creature is full of God and is a book about God.
—Meister Eckhart

PART OF THE MAGIC OF LIVING IN THE WOODS on Higher Ground as I have written, is that we share life here with the wildlife creatures; loons, ducks, heron, egrets and other water birds are in our lake or about it on our shore and elsewhere. The view from my upstairs front window at which I sit writing at my desk each day is a vantage point for wondrous sights that nature lovers like myself feel blessed to observe. Raccoons, beaver, chipmunks, opossum, foxes and squirrels are in the woods and many choose to come out to make the acquaintance of their human neighbors who live in this small green cottage. As you have read, birds fly in and out to our feeders that hang in front of our sliding glass doors and the pleasure this affords can not get fully expressed. All make the scene before our eyes a joy to behold. We feel favored when a large family of Black ducks, sometimes as many as twelve, walk up our beach from the lake with the Mama duck in the lead. You will remember them quacking their greeting as they come to say hello and hope that we will remember from the last time they came to call, that they love bread and are most appreciative of the pieces we fed them. Sometimes they just stay and socialize with us on the dock. And our hearts are touched as we watch them swim away in a line with the young ones all following their Mama dear.

Raccoons love to make an appearance on our deck at twilight or shortly after dark in summer. One seems to wear a watch, he is so punctual in his arrival each evening. At times little raccoon families come, three or four, and the babies are so cute and childlike. In silence they peer silently through our windows and screens, quietly observing us, often before we realize they are there. They wait patiently for our reaction to them and continue to stare in at us, and I often talk to them through the screens in summer, or if cooler and the sliding doors are shut, I tap on the window and greet them in a friendly way as I would children. There is one who repeatedly climbs a tall wooden pole at the end of our decks to reach the goal of a little red barn bird feeder at the top. There he lies over the red barn, big chunky body in this odd position while he eats from the bird feeder and looks down at us, his eyes shining red in the dark. Raccoons are our mysterious little masked friends, but who yet somehow seem to want to know us more. To see a little family walk off together after their visit with us and disappear—is a touching sight—like a picture from a child's story book.

Raccoon on feeding bar

THE CLEANING CREW

Little figures small and brown
Are here to clean up what falls down—
From the feeders overhead
The seeds for birds and crumbs of bread.

Their little mouths are open wide.
Their tummies fat and full inside.
Dear little chipmunks—such a stir!
Vacuum cleaners made of fur!

JGK

Chipmunks are precious and scurry around on the deck outside our front sliding door eating all the seed that has fallen from the feeders. They too observe us, and Rochester loves to sit and watch them at this vantage point through the screens or glass. Often he is nose to nose with them and the squirrels.

SANCTUARY MUCH

My little cat is not a roamer
He's a steady stay-at-homer.
So in our lakeside cottage green
He oft times checks the woodland scene—
From all the windows in this place
And lies on sills with ease and grace.

But full length windows—top to floor
Are in the front—each sliding door—
Allows more beauty in the view
And gentle breezes to come through.
It's here Rochester loves it most
As daily he is peaceful host—
To birds and chipmunks who eat there
Right before his quiet stare.

Chipmunks greet him nose to nose
Between them creature friendship flows.
He watches as the chipmunks dash
Back to their bowl to eat their stash—
Of birdseed that falls from on high
From feeders closer to the sky.
The birds all flutter out and in
As if Rochester is their kin.
He watches as this all takes place
Right before his very face
A pastime that's his greatest fun—
And passes hours in the sun.

A sanctuary with tiny creatures!
And Rochester in the front row bleachers!

Dedicated to   JGK
Rochester

    The chipmunks can disappear in a flash through tiny holes in the slats of the deck floor and their actions are so sweet to see. There are also many holes dug in the earth at the base of the front steps under the bird feeders where the chipmunks run into to hide. One day recently Bob went down to the basement to create at his work bench and there sat a little chipmunk on his florescent light hanging over his work area. The furry little creature did not even seem afraid of this big carpenter friend, but paused to check him out before scurrying away into the wall somewhere. Obviously he had found a little hidden hole and had a secret entrance into our basement. I have had a chipmunk run across my lap as I sat with closed eyes in my prayer chair by the lake.

    As I have shared before, Rochester enjoys too sitting on a little shelf inside our screened in porch that Bob made for him during all the lovely months from May through early Fall. Immediately on the other side of the screen is the huge Colorado Blue Spruce mentioned earlier that we planted when it was a baby. Now it towers above our cottage and is a haven both for chipmunks and small birds, a living, breathing wildlife sanctuary seemingly meant for Rochester's solitude and enjoyment. He sits in meditation gazing into that tree for extremely long periods with only an occasional turn of his head or a pat on the screen with his tender paw if a chipmunk comes on a branch under his gaze. Occasionally he looks at me to make certain that I am aware of his joy. I am.

LITTLE GRAY FUR BIRD

Little squirrel upon the rail
Eyeing feeder for the birds—
Shot of gray with spacious tail
You are just too fine for words.

You'll maneuver 'til you win
The prize of seed high overhead—
And as you climb and leap, I grin.
Such acrobatics—to be fed!

There you sit upon the spout
Where all the seed comes tumbling out.
And when you spot me watching you—
You pause and sit and watch me too!
You say your Grace—paw touching paw.
Rarest bird I ever saw !!

LGK

Now squirrels—ah—they are a story unto themselves and daily we look at them in wonderment. Here in the woods we have gray squirrels and the smaller red squirrels. They are out there doing what they are doing side by side and chattering at each other all the while. We see regularly squirrels and birds eating at out feeders simultaneously and having no problems. Yet squirrels continually scold each other or humans. We watch as they run up and down our screens outside out sliding doors with their cute little white furry tummies vulnerable to Rochester who pats them through the screen and attempts to follow them up from the inside.

From the screens they leap onto the wire that holds our feeders—or onto the feeders themselves. Their abilities are amazing! Completely skilled at this, yet sometimes they do fall but try again. We have come to learn more about the squirrels by choice because we daily live so close to them. Gray squirrels mate in spring and in five weeks the babies will be born. The female makes a nest by finding a nice safe place in a hollow tree and this she lines with bits of her own fur and grass. The babies have no fur or teeth when born and cannot see or hear, but in a week or so fur begins to appear but their eyes still are not open. At four weeks they can see but still drink milk from their mother. By summer the babies are seven weeks and have a few teeth. The baby holds onto the mother and curls its long tail around her and in this way the mother protectively takes her young from the nest for food for them and for herself. In late summer the young squirrels can leave the nests on their own but must ever watch for danger. They make new nests and prepare for winter and some of these young will have families on their own in the spring. And so the cycle goes. Gray squirrels love peanuts but they also enjoy acorns. One little guy several years ago dropped an acorn in an open water pump pipe after he got into Dennis's cottage up on the hill. It was such a safe place for winter storage but jammed Dennis's water pump when he tried to start it. Only through deep investigation did he find the acorn and now Dennis makes sure his pipe has a cover on it.

My friend Marie shared a story so moving with me about a squirrel that I included it in my book, *Compassion for All Creatures*, and it is worthy of again sharing now. Marie was a woman of great compassion who fed homeless cats for years and ministered to them when wounded. She wrote me about a little gray tabby cat that she and her husband gave their five year old son for Christmas. The cat was truly a member of the family. At age twelve, the cat was injured, and the veterinarian said he would never walk again. It was summer, and the saddened boy and his parents made a comfortable little box for the cat and would take him outdoors with them., He was a mild little cat and never tried to hurt the birds and squirrels that Marie regularly fed. Among those was a sassy little squirrel the family had nicknamed "Ralph," who always ate the birdseed. Marie would gently scold him but eventually bought him his own peanuts. The squirrel became very tame and would come running if they called his name. He often hopped on the picnic table and patted the family members who were there, to remind them to give him his peanuts. He would gently eat them from the hand that held them out to him.

When the family brought out the little injured cat in the box, Ralph came over to investigate and realized the cat was sick. He returned to his own peanuts, took a peanut, and went over to the cat, and laid the peanut in the box beside him. Marie wrote that it was as if Ralph was saying, "I'll feed you. I know you are sick." From then on, he always looked in on the cat. Contrary to the veterinarian's opinion, the little cat did walk again though not in the same way as before he was injured.

This true story struck me so, and it brought to mind a quotation spoken by Meister Eckhart.

> *All creatures desire to speak God in their works: they all speak Him as well as they can, but they cannot really pronounce Him.*

Most certainly this little squirrel Ralph was "speaking God" in his works, as well as he could. His ministering to the little cat with his own peanuts was truly a form of prayer in the creature world, and in the human world also. Our work and our deeds are forms of prayer, and little Ralph was "praying his friend well" with each peanut and visit. His prayer joined with the loving prayers of the cat's family—and the cat walked again.

Last year my sweet friend Marie passed away and went to Heaven. I believe she is pleased I have again shared this story. Perhaps it is she who prompted me to do it.

Red Squirrels

Red squirrels too like nuts but they also like pine-cones. They often make piles of them and when they eat one they bite it from the tree and bite all of the scales off the cone and consume the seeds within. They enjoy these and chew such hard things into small pieces to keep their teeth from growing too long. Their front teeth grow all the time—thus this choice of hard food. They hide acorns like the gray squirrels, sometimes in hollow of trees, sometimes in the ground. To find where they are, perhaps in water pipes buried in winter, they must sniff for them. They eat berries also. They are in constant danger of hawks and other animals because they are small and can be preyed upon. When this happens and danger is sensed by their ears that hear tiny sounds so well, and their noses that seem able to smell danger, they hide in their nests in hollow trees. They prefer the tall pines and firs which the gray squirrels do not favor. The gray ones are partial to oak and other tall trees and open spaces. One fact we know for certain is that squirrels are intelligent, and frankly, there is no outwitting them. Bob is a fine inventor and creator of numerous things, and in his creations are a collection of bird feeders. With the exception of the red farm feeder on the tall pole, and one other, all others are of his design and making. They are never static, he ever continues to create new ones and revise former models. He has even made tiny hummingbird feeders from small clear plastic film boxes that attract a wonderful hummingbird population to our deck. The bright red liquid shines within and the minute spout protrudes for these whispers of birds to sup through. Such beauty! They are a thrill to watch.

In the course of creating the bird feeders we learned most emphatically the intelligence of the squirrels. No matter what model feeder Bob would proudly hang outdoors, within a day or so they had taken it over and begun to eat through parts of it. If it contained plastic parts, they chomped on those. If it was a glass feeder they chewed the ropes that held it. They did let the birds eat, of course, but tried to make the seed more accessible for those with larger appetites like themselves.

Red squirrel

Diane

One incident we shall always remember for it truly brought Bob down a peg or two and caused him to give up a title he valued highly. In the course of designing feeders there was a period when he was making them out of green soda bottles, turning them upside down with PVC plumbing sections as spouts on the necks of the bottles. They were really excellent and even matched the green cottage and held much seed. He would cut the reinforced bottom off a second soda bottle and put it over the reinforced bottom (now the top) of the bottle that was now a feeder, thereby making it stronger to defeat the squirrels teeth. We watched daily as a little red squirrel continually tried to get more seed from one of these feeders proudly hanging from the wire. She wanted more than was flowing through the PVC for birds, who loved to perch there on the white spout and eat their fill. It was the same little red squirrel, for she had a diamond shaped mark on her back that was not the same color as the rest of her red fur. Bob called her "little Di" because of the diamond, but I called "Diane." She never gave up trying to get into that green bottle! She would sit on the top of it and look directly at us, and scold us heartily in frustration.

One day it happened. She began to somehow have the strength in those little teeth to begin to gnaw through the heavy plastic. She began at the top, not on the thinner sides of only one thickness, but on the doubly reinforced top! And on she chewed. We could not just stand around and watch for we were each involved in our own work, but we left her to be, believing she would never succeed. This feeder was different! It had the touch of genius upon it! Stronger—fortified—unlike the others! In fact we both forgot about Diane in the hour or more that followed. Suddenly I heard a yell from Bob and I ran down to the living room. There he stood in disbelief, his hands clasping his head, "Look!" he exclaimed. I followed his pointed finger to the "green soda bottle double reinforced top bird feeder." There was a sight so amazing and funny I just broke up on the spot. Like a ship in a bottle, there sat "little Di" in her newly won prize! She had gnawed through double thicknesses of plastic on top until she could squeeze into the bottle herself. There she sat on the huge mound of bird seed facing into our living room looking at us through the bottle and through the screens. Holding the seed in her little paws I had to admit she looked cute as the dickens and she chattered and scolded us as she ate. She had already eaten a considerable amount, for the feeder had been full. In order for her to be sitting on the huge pile that she was, she had had to eat her way down to that level. Bob and I were in awe, and he was enjoying it as much as I was, though utterly amazed that he had been defeated anew. We watched as time passed and I took pictures of her for posterity. Diane sat within the green bottle defiantly eating and watching us, and the pile of bird seed gradually depleted until there were only the dregs. Diane had stayed until she ate it all! We waited for her to burst! How could that tiny body hold a one liter bottle of bird seed? She made her way out through the top of the gnawed bottle, did acrobatics on the wire that held the feeders, and dropped to the deck and scurried away. We just stood there incredulous at this performance that had taken place these past several hours! Out of the prolonged silence Bob finally muttered, "I give up. I'm now the second greatest mind of the century!" We absolutely roared—for Bob is constantly telling us in great confidence (and jest) how wondrous are his deeds in any field he attempts. Of course this lack of humility is in fun, but acclaimed so confidently and magnificently in such concert that we often wonder. That Diane should now hold the title he had to forfeit was surely a blow! We did not see her for days—probably sleeping off her gigantic food binge—but when we did, her presence was a continual reminder to Bob of her fame and intelligence. He continues to design bird feeders, always working in competition with the greater intelligence of the squirrel world, but a slap to the ego that it was, he still gives credit where credit is due—to "little Di—Greatest mind of the century!"

Reflect and Journal

☆ Have you ever personally encountered a raccoon, squirrel or chipmunk, not merely just seen them, but perhaps had an interchange of some kind?

☆ Write about this in your journal. If it happened long ago perhaps it will cause other memories to surface not related to the little creature.

☆ Write about these other memories too, at least jotting them down. You can write more about them in depth at a later time if you do not wish to today—but at least record them before they are forgotten.

☆ If you do not live in an area where you daily see wildlife creatures, did these reflections shared in this chapter open your mind and heart and cause you to want to know creatures in new ways?

☆ If so, perhaps seek to do this by walking in a park or visiting a wooded area. Perhaps take a camera.

☆ Use your journal to ruminate about your thoughts that surfaced while reading this chapter or on your walk. Later paste in any photos you took on the walk.

☆ Have you ever felt like a squirrel in a bottle? Tell your journal about it.

☆ Have you ever been "squirreled" in your life? Write about it. How does it apply to the squirrel in wildlife? Can you see any connections? Explore it.

☆ Close in a peaceful meditation in your place of prayer.

Earlier I told you about the ants of "Higher Ground" poetically, and now as we are about to visit my gardens, this poem will reveal the temporary plight of one of the little bugs here that reside outdoors, but occasionally come indoors to visit.

Down, But Not Out

A black and rapid little bug—
Abruptly gave my heart a tug—
When I spied him running there—
Within the tub on legs of hair.

I knew he searched for freedom now—
The slippery tub did not allow.

His silent message promptly heeded—
I realized then that I was needed.

Between two tiny cups I caught—
The little bug, but now distraught—
I saw a leg was tightly clasped—
By the cups rims—and I gasped!

Oh no, I tried to give him life—
And now I've caused this awful strife!
I took him outside on the deck—
Released him there, that tiny speck—

That leg—that line—
Was on the cup—the fault was mine!
Without that leg he lay so still—
On no, oh no, now did I kill?

I talked to him and prayed my heart—
And moments later—with a start—
He moved—and scampered cross the board—
And I just sighed while my soul soared!

JGK

And making mention of the ants reminded me of an ant who, like the
bug in the previous poem, was wounded but—well, you read. I cannot.

TO AN ANT

Tonight as I made dinner—
On the counter top I found—
(O dear God was I the sinner?)
An ant so bound and round.

He was wound into a ball
And he could not get undone

And his hair-like legs so small
Tangled so he could not run!

Had this giant that is me
With a pot or glass or dish—
Hurt him so unknowingly?
O dear God 'twas not my wish!

I tried fervently to free him—
With thin paper—gentle touch—
He was crippled—hope was dim,
He could not know how very much—

I prayed—and then with tears—
Made a place for him until—
He'd be found by all his peers,
On my quiet window sill.

O Dear Lord—it is a life!
Forgive me if I caused it strife!
But if I did not harm him—please—
Won't you put my heart at ease?

Is he screaming there in fright?
O help that tiny ant tonight!

JGK

I invite you now to come to my gardens in spirit. They are so beautiful to me that I think you will love them too. If it is spring or summer as you read, perhaps you can sit in a garden with this book. If not the scent and simple charm of my gardens will draw you outdoors to them in imagination. Feel the presence of the Angels.

CHAPTER TWELVE

Gardens

The kiss of the sun for pardon
The song of the birds for mirth—
One is nearer God's heart in a garden
Than anywhere else on earth

—Dorothy Gurney

A LITTLE PLANTER HANGS ON THE INSIDE POST of our screened-in porch. It is a small round can painted dark green. Attached to it is a black trivet with white writing and two blue birds on either side, and a shiny yellow sun above the verse. The poem is the one that opens this chapter. The planter was made years ago by my Dad and I keep a bunch of lovely life-like artificial violets in the can, symbolic of my Mother "Violet." Years ago I embroidered this same verse in a sampler and framed it as a gift for my mother-in-law for her back screened-in porch in Pennsylvania that overlooked her small garden. Later it was given to my daughter Laurel who hung it outside by her front door and near her garden in Pennsylvania also. This is a sweet verse that has touched me and many others through the years. It is only recently I learn the author when I buy a notepad with the verse on. Always the verse has been left with no credit to Dorothy Gurney. I do not know of her, or any other of her poetry, but admire this little poem that is so well known. It speaks to me of the love I have for my own gardens, and the feeling becomes so much deeper as I actually kneel and dig and tend my flowers and plants.

*Little planter made by my dad
with violets*

*Who bends a knee
Where violets grow
A hundred secret
Things shall know*
—anonymous

I have not been a gardener all my life but I have always loved and appreciated flowers. Growing up in the outskirts of Philadelphia I watch as my Mother Violet, plants and tends her gardens filled with violets, marigolds, pansies, petunias, zinnias, asters, and so many flowers I do not remember. She has our small fenced in yard that is facing a back alley, lined on either side with brilliant blooms that attract attention from passers-by, and create a glorious sight for the eyes. She does not want my help to plant and tend. This is her joy, and almost a need. But I am allowed to water the gardens with the hose. Her favorite hymn is one she plays on the piano and that we sing in our Methodist Church, "In the Garden." The first verse begins:

*My mother's
backyard gardens*

I come to the garden alone
While the dew is still on the roses
And the voice I hear, calling on my ear—
The Son of God disposes—

And it goes on to say how "He walks with me and He talks with me, And He tells me I am His own," and each line is more moving than the next. Perhaps she sings that in her heart as she gardens, and perhaps too, she meets her Lord in the silence of tending the flowers. I know that I do.

On the front lawn of our city row home is another outstanding garden flanked by brilliant fuscia azaleas. My Dad also cares for these flowers. I last drive by my childhood home in 1994 and those azaleas are in bloom just as they were when my parents tended them. I wonder if they are blooming still in this new century, in the gardens they love so? They bloom in my mind and heart for reflection at a moment's notice, a forever garden.

My mother's azaleas still bloom after all these years.
Our little granddaughter Maxine is standing in front of them.

A poem by an anonymous poet is lovely to me, and seems appropriate to share and leave in spirit in my Mother's gardens just for her.

ORIGIN OF VIOLETS

I know, blue modest violets,
Gleaming with dew at morn—
I know the place you come from
And the way that you are born!

When God cut holes in Heaven,
The holes the stars look through,
He let the scraps fall down to earth,
The little scraps are you.

Jenkintown Gardens

As my children are born and raised I do not do much gardening around our big old home in Jenkintown, Pennsylvania because there are so many other things that fill my life and time. But we plant many new trees to blend in with the older ancient ones, and on occasion I make small gardens along the side of our home near the huge pale blue hydrangea bushes that bloom every year that we live there, and that were blooming long before we moved in.

Our youngest daughter Janna becomes a gardener creating a garden in the back yard for many years, and too, even after she married and lives in our home there with Bill she continues to garden, while we spend more and more time in New Hampshire.

Gardens in the Woods

My garden is a forest ledge
Which older forests bound;
The banks slope down to the blue lake-edge,
Then plunge to depths profound.
—Ralph Waldo Emerson

Finally it is my time to become a gardener here in the woods that I love so. We are here in New Hampshire more than in Pennsylvania, and so I begin some limited gardening in 1994 so that flowers will be blooming at Janna and Bill's wedding by the lake in August. It is then following their wedding, they move into our family home in Jenkintown. Now in the present however, Janna and Bill and children live in Riverside, Rhode Island, and their gardens bloom in fullest beauty in their secluded back yard.

PETUNIA

Inverted leaning petunia bloom
    you look like a pointed elfin cap
        soft and violet
            with fluted brim.
Bring me your nature spirit and softness
    and Holy Beauty—
And your constancy,
    that though I be
        turned upside down—
            I shall remain unwavering—
                to those I love—
                    to my beliefs,
                        and to Him.

JGK

Moving permanently into our cottage in these woods in January 1996, I become a true gardener that spring and ever after. The seven beautiful rock walled garden areas Bob creates, I complete by filling them all with flowers year after year. I am partial to petunias of every hue and they are interspersed among all the other blooms, as well as having one entire small garden to themselves, filled entirely with their glorious gentle blossoms. This is the "Prayer chair garden."

Mine is just a little old-fashioned garden where the flowers come together to praise the Lord and teach all who look upon them to do likewise.
—Celia Thaxter

Each rock walled garden is named; the St. Francis garden (His statue stands in it), The Path Garden (the path leads to the dock), The Beach Garden (it overlooks the beach), the Deer Garden (it has a sweet statue of a reclining fawn in it I named "Dawn"), the Lake Garden (right above and at the water's edge) and the Gnome Garden (due to as the gnome figures in it written about previously, and the tree I refer to as "the gnome tree."

The Deer Garden

Soft white and lavender petunias sway
In the old fashioned garden created this day.
And brightly hued marigolds stand stately and tall—
Guarding the edges 'round the hand made rock wall.

A dear fawn figure lies amidst the flowers—
Enjoying the fragrance and passing the hours.
And brilliant green of the plush velvet lawn—
Enhances white snapdragons encircling the fawn.

Blue and white ageratum are tucked in the rows
Blossoms are refreshed with the spray from the hose.
We stand back and admire the colorful array—
Of our lakeside garden on this breezy June day.

Dedicated to Bob   JGK
who built all the rock walls—
and to the Angels

Each year the gardens are different because although I plant perennials that should be here year after year, they are not always here. The harsh winters destroy some of the plants, but I always replace them. Also bulbs are often dug up by the little squirrels and chipmunks, but this is all part of nature.

Cone Flowers

Cone flowers are also plants of beauty standing tall above all the other flowers and with the blue lake as back drop to their bright purple color. These daisy-like flowers known as *Enchinacea* are also one of the most important medicines to Native Americans. It is written the spirit of the flower draws all the systems together so they act in perfect harmony. They grow wild on the prairies but are also here in New Hampshire.

CONE FLOWER

I am the pink cone flower growing by the lake,
My blooms sway in the prevailing breeze—
        four buds will explode into blossoms
           under the starry sky.
In a garden beneath trees—
        I was planted in the wake
          of a passing—
In memory of a precious creature
        who too once blossomed on earth—
But now graces a place on high;
        who lives—and did not die.

                              JGK

Other Cone Flowers were later added to my gardens in memory of my friend Bertha's two other beloved little cats. All three passed away in 1996 and have Cone Flowers on Higher Ground, and low Phlox.

Memory Plants

My gardens vary each year because I am continually adding new perennials, and lovely annuals interspersed among the new and the old treasures. Many phlox plants bloom in various colors as "memory plants," flowers chosen and lovingly placed in the gardens to be a memorial to loved ones, both humans and animals. Some are beginning to become green as I write . Due to freezing temperatures, come spring, I often replace a large phlox plant or other memorials.

These are memory plants for parents, an uncle, a dear friend, and there are cone flowers and a lower blooming phlox variety planted in memory of other beloved animal friends who passed away in Jenkintown, Pennsylvania and New Jersey, but who are remembered faithfully here. The phlox so loved, also has it own poem.

BUD

I am the phlox bud.
I woke up this morning
     and saw the sun for the first time.
I felt its warmth on my outer petals
     and the breeze brush my stamens.
The sparkle of the blue lake
     caught my eye—
And the glistening wings
     of a visiting butterfly.
I see tall trees and clouds up above,
     and grass, and flowers stretching out before me.
I rejoice at my birth!
     O—this must be earth!

JGK

Lilac

It is the season now to go
About the country high and low,
Among the lilacs hand in hand.
And two by two in fairy-land.

—Robert Louis Stevenson

Begonias, marigolds, tulips, yarrow, impatiens, and many other lovelies grace the rock wall gardens. This year we plan to have lilac and purchase a new plant as before. Others planted in the past did not survive. Lilac is so beautiful to me, and a huge bush of it was at the back of our yard in Jenkintown. Vases and pitchers held it indoors and the scent and those memories remain. Lilac is New Hampshire's state flower so we surely want it blooming in abundance. I learn through reading in a local paper here that back in 1750 New Hampshire's Royal Governor Benning Wentworth imported "laylacks" from England, and ordered gardeners to plant them at his new seacoast mansion in Portsmouth. I wonder if he knew he was making horticultural history? These sturdy English "Laylacks" were the first to be planted in the New World. It is recorded they happily took root and flourished and produced their colorful blossoms for many generations of visitors to the home now known as the Wentworth Coolidge Mansion. Again, this spring, 250 years after they were planted, Wentworth's trees are once again bringing forth the fragrant and long lasting purple blooms we admire as "lilacs." The Wentworth Coolidge Mansion's lilac trees are believed to be the oldest in this country. Surely then I can believe our new lilacs will take hold and bloom for us and take root despite the cold winter! Our new lilac is a "Donald Wyman Lilac" and will be 18 feet tall and 10 feet wide. Tomorrow we will plant it on the edge of a wooded area between the Deer Garden and the Gnome Garden, and here it can be seen well to be enjoyed, and its fragrance will float oe'r Higher Ground.

I learned too, that George Washington planted lilacs at his Mount Vernon home and Thomas Jefferson made them part of the landscape at Mount Vernon. And in early nineteenth century, my friend Thoreau wrote about the "vivacious lilac" that bloomed for generations near the doorways of old family farm houses—or homes—often as "sole survivor" of the family that once lived in the now abandoned homestead.

I had never known that lilacs were said to have originated in the mountains of eastern Europe and to have been carried by travelers to England in 1620. (I have this recorded in an old nature journal because I love lilacs) Today lilacs are in countries all over the world but just not in bloom yet in my gardens. Surely I can depend on them this year!

I learn too in my reading that you NEVER, NEVER prune lilacs until after they have finished blooming. You can leave some of the blooms on the branches to dry too. Birds love the seed and will spread them all around. Lilacs should be planted in full sun, and spring planting is best, so mine are going in the ground tomorrow. Perhaps these lilac notes will help you in your gardening or inspire you to plant this beautiful flower, and too, remember New Hampshire.

Marigolds

Marigolds are abundant in my gardens also, and I particularly plant the very large ones. I have read in various sources in the past that the marigold is a valuable medicinal plant and inspires receptivity and compassion, and often it is woven into wedding garlands for luck. In some places it is known as "Summer's bride." Marigolds are so happy and delightful to see, you have to greet them with a smile. You cannot help yourself. Last summer my lakeside garden held only the very large yellow and orange marigolds and you could see them clearly when out in a boat on the lake. The colors were so bright! They inspired a poem.

MARIGOLD

Yellow marigold
    your immense round blossom
        is like a ball of sunshine.
Bring me your orb of brilliancy—
    that once mine,
        it may gleam forth from my heart
            in sunbeams—

Each like a spiritual dart
    injecting other hearts with streams
        of radiating lovelight.

JGK

Marigolds in rock wall garden by the lake

RHODORA

And as I read I reminisce
This book is bridge across abyss—
For I am once again with him—
As if there's been no interim
And there he sits in radiant aura
Once more reciting—"The Rhodora"

JGK

Rhodora

A number of years ago we planted a Rhodora in loving memory of my dear friend Francis, mentioned in an earlier chapter. Francis loved the poem "The Rhodora" by Ralph Waldo Emerson, and each time I visited him he would recite it for me by memory. It fed his soul . Before he died (he knew he only had a short time) among many other treasures, he gave me his old, narrow, brown poem book titled *One Hundred and One Famous Poems.* In this book was "The Rhodora." I too memorized it after Francis' death to honor him, along with writing my own poems for him. I am ashamed to say I have not retained it all after ten years because it made me sad to recite it, and so through neglect I have lost portions. But as I write now it has given me new resolve to learn it by memory again in time for the tenth anniversary of Francis' entrance into Heaven. July 15, 1990. The poem that begins this segment about "The Rhodora" and Francis is the third verse of a poem I wrote for Francis ten months after his death. The complete poem is in my previous book, *The Enchantment of Writing,* where I share even more about this dear friend.

"The Rhodora" by Emerson is lovely and begins:

In May, when sea-winds pierced our solitudes,
I found the fresh Rhodora in the woods,
Spreading the leafless blooms in a damp nook,

Because of these lines we planted the Rhodora in Francis' memory in our woods to the left of our cottage. There it remains unseen except to us, because we wanted it to be in a secluded place exactly as written about in Emerson's poem. The only difference being Francis' Rhodora is covered by lake breezes instead of winds from the sea. It is comforting to have this memorial in our woods, and I believe it blesses Francis deeply. We both particularly liked the lines buried in the middle of the poem in regard to why the Rhodora is in an unseen nook.

Rhodora! if the sages ask thee why
This charm is waste on the earth and sky,
Tell them dear, that if eyes were made for seeing
Then beauty is its own excuse for being:

The poem is moving and ends by saying the poet never thought to ask why the Rhodora was there in the woods, but in his simple ignorance he concludes and supposes "The self-same Power that brought me there brought you."

Perhaps it is a poem you may want to find and read. I will be re-memorizing it so that it can bless me wherever I am within my heart and mind, as I envision the Rhodora in our woods, and Francis smiling face.

Dahlias

Standing quietly by the fence,
you smile your wondrous smile
—Quach Thoai

The above is a portion of a beautiful brief poem about a Dahlia, written long ago by a friend of Thich Nhat Hanh. The poet goes on to say that the beauty of the Dahlia leaves him speechless, and the beautiful song he hears from the Dahlia fills his senses. And there is more; lovely closing lines that inspire.

Hanh is a combination of mystic, scholar, poet, and activist, and lives in exile from his native Vietnam since 1966. This poem appears in his journals, *Fragrant Palm Leaves*, written from 1962-1966 and in another of his books. In 1962 through 1963 he lived in the United States as a student and teaching assistant at Princeton and Columbia. He also tried to negotiate peace and a better life for the Vietnamese for many years. This poem touches Thich Nhat Hanh as it also moves me from the minute I read it. I copy it in my journal and the comments about it, and plan to share it with my daughter Janna. The poet ends the poem by saying he bows deeply to the Dahlia.

But Thich Naht Hanh's remarks about the poem are as beautiful to me as the poem itself. He writes, "Do you see? The moment appeared. The curtain was drawn back for a second, and the poet could see." He elaborates by saying that though the Dahlia is commonplace and that most people do not truly see it, if you listen for and hear its eternal song and see (with the spirit, I would add) its miraculous smile, than it is no longer an ordinary flower. Thich Naht Hahn feels it is an ambassador from the cosmos.

The words Hahn expresses should be words to guide us all. He tells how his friend passed the fence and saw the flower very deeply and so struck was he by the sight of it he wrote the poem.

I understand this, for I too write poems for many things "from the cosmos" that others might not be inclined to notice. Perhaps it is because I am blessed to live in the woods amongst nature for many years. Hahn states his friend was a simple, ordinary person and not a mystic. He uses this all as an example of how we can practice mindfulness. We are to look deeply and try to be in touch with life as we walk, sit down, drink tea or in doing any of the ordinary things in life. He states that you are really yourself then at these moments and then you are able to encounter life in the present moment.

I am particularly drawn to this poem because my little granddaughter's name is Dahlia June. She is the daughter of Janna and Bill. Her first name is after the lovely flower and her middle name is for our daughter June. Just recently Dahlia does a beautiful presentation of Dahlias through her art work and own words at her nursery school in Rhode Island, and is acclaimed for the beauty of it. She is only four and a half years old but she loves her floral name. She appears in my *Journal of Love* next to a Dahlia plant in a big terra cotta pot on our deck.

In spring I give her a large packet of Dahlia seeds which she plants in her own little garden. They are growing now and visible, and Janna calls to say how Dahlia is looking for the gnomes in her garden. She has a framed picture of the "Gnomes Tea Party" I spoke of earlier and I send her two more photos of the gnomes, this time in snow, and explain in a note they are symbolic of the unseen ones she is hoping to spot. She has a book about gnomes, and this has sparked interest in the subject anew.

Growing Dahlias in my gardens is a must. We buy more bulbs this spring to plant. Aside from my mother, Violet, with her flower name, we have only one other floral name in the immediate family, that of our daughter, Laurel. But we do have two daughters and a granddaughter bearing the names of spring and summer months when flowers bloom, that of June and Jessica's middle name of Mae, and granddaughter Leslie's middle name of June. She has her mother's full name but in reverse. Her sister Julia also bears a flower middle name, that of Rose. I hope Mother Nature is as happy with us as we are with her. Luther Burbank's words are so true. "Flowers always make people better, happier, and more helpful; they are sunshine, food, and medicine to the soul." This man and his work are amazing and are a chapter in my *Journal of Love.*

Wildflowers

Earth laughs in flowers.
—Ralph Waldo Emerson

DANDY FLOWERS

We've chosen here to be exiled
Where lovely flowers grow so wild
Along the path and by the rock.
He says we'll be the laughing stock—
To keep those long stem flowers there
Blowing in the summer air,
Because they're dandelions tall
And should be cut down one and all!

I said he had a "city mind"
Permitting him to be so blind.
In woods all things grow wild and free—
I became a referee!

We parted then—I said a prayer—
Soon he called me out to where—
The flowers stood by rock and tree
He left them all there just for me!
He thinks I'm strange and yet somehow—
I know he sees their beauty now.

Dedicated to   JGK
the dandelions

Besides the gardens that God and I create together, He does an exceptional work without me in scattering large patches of wildflowers everywhere, especially near our cottage and the birch trees in front of Bob's "Birchgrove" office at the base of our big hill. Large dandelions, buttercups, and other varieties unknown as yet to me abound, and blue delicate asters so sweet. When we begin spending more and more time here in the early nineties, Bob spots these flowers and mows them down! He considers them weeds, and to me, some of the prettiest flowers are considered weeds. And so we lovingly disagree consistently. Years pass and he now respects my wishes to let the wild flowers grow any place they please. That they deign to grow about our cottage is delightful, and to slay them not understandable. Flowers shall grow spontaneously in these woods. I continually write poems for them, and all the flowers in our gardens.

> *Nothing's small. . . .*
> *Earth's crammed with heaven,*
> *And every common bush afire with God.*
> —Elizabeth Barrett Browning

NEW ENGLAND ASTERS

Soft velvet flowers shyly peer—
    from hidden places. Dear
Blue Asters fill the spaces—
    in crevices—and lift their faces.
Decorating rocks most ancient—
    waiting, blooming—ever patient—
For the glance of one who'll see,
    their clumps of beauty on a spree.
Wild, tenacious, grace-filled, strong—
    their presence—joyful, whispered song.

JGK

Water Lily

Water lilies evoke a feeling of holiness as they float upon our lake like apparitions. So serene, they give off a sense of innocence and divine peace. Janna wants to use them as center pieces, one per table and each floating in a dish, for her wedding and reception by the lake. But they open wide in morning and close not long after, and so she chooses instead chrysanthemums not yet in bloom, vibrant and green against everything white, green like all of the woods. Later as the guests take them home they shall have the joy of the full blooming plants. The water lilies are still appreciated by the guests as they stand by the lake, and the lilies become a part of her wedding. Better not to take them from the water, and thereby they are present in their natural setting. Claude Monet's paintings of water lilies have always been meaningful to me, and now I have my own water lilies upon the sparkling lake just footsteps from our front door.

Grass

the fragrance of the grass
speaks to me. . . .
and my heart soars.

—Chief Dan George

The grass of "Higher Ground" is simply magnificent; planted, cultivated and tended and mowed by Bob. It is only in the last six years or less that we have had this beautiful enormous lawn running along the front of our cottage and on either side. He plants the seed to help to beautify the space in which Janna and Bill will be married. Thereafter it becomes somewhat of an obsession, to tend this lovely soft grass, that even rises from under the hard winter's ice and snow a brilliant green! It is between our cottage and all the rock gardens that are by the lake, and stretches to the woods that surround us.

GRASS

I am the bending grass cradling the morning dew.
Each droplet sparkles in the rising sun.
Each blade has an Angel whispering—
"grow, grow."*
I hear echoes of elementals
Running through my denseness.
I hear joy at my greenness—
And laughter as they splash.
I am one with the new day.

*from the Talmud   JGK

Bob is relentless in his mow-ing, and there is no place to escape the sound of that mower until it is finished its work. Never once does he turn the mower off. It is like an abomination to the bird song and lap of the lake and soft unknown sounds of the woods. I call him "Gerald McBoingBoing," the title of a child's story book that belongs to our now grown son George, about a little boy who makes a great deal of noise. That does not apply to George but most certainly to his father. It is a joke between us. It happens today for the first time this spring as I write here at my desk and see him walking back and forth behind that mower down below and passing in view of my upper windows here at my desk. But I appreciate his work and the luxury of green grass in the woods.

Bob wearing screen-netting hat in black-fly season in May as he rakes

I believe we are the only inhabitants of these woods to have a lawn. Its glorious color (green is favorite color of us both) enhances the gardens and cottage, and children and adults both love being barefoot in it. Many a picnic has taken place upon it, and little homemade tents set upon it for grandchildren in summer. Teen age grandchildren, Jesse and Leslie and their six friends from Pennsylvania, set their larger tents upon it also last summer and camped here for five days by the lake. Croquet and Bocce Ball are played upon it every summer by family vacationers, and family dogs love rolling in it. Birds hop all over its softness throughout each day.

Richard Jeffries says, "Every blade of grass, each leaf, each separate floret and petal, is an inscription speaking of hope. Consider the grasses and the oaks, the swallows, the sweet blue butterfly—they are one and all a sign and token showing before our eyes earth made into life." Such a beautiful and inspiring thought and we experience this inscription daily, again and again from the grass and all of nature. Close your eyes and walk barefoot in our grass by the lake. Hear the birds singing and know you are in a wooded paradise. An anonymous poet speaks of greenness I see before me in a poem titled "The Voice of the Grass."

> *Here I come creeping, creeping everywhere;*
> *By the dusty roadside,*
> *On the sunny hillside*
> *Close by the noisy brook,*
> *In every shady nook*
> *I come creeping, creeping everywhere.*

The Third Feather

In late summer of 1997 I found three unusual feathers, each on separate occasions and all in a period of a week. I believed them to be messages from the Angels in response to prayer inwardly in my heart. The first two poems appear in other books and the last I will share with you now. This was not the last feather that came as a sign, however. Others have come since in various ways and I have them all in my writing room—all so significant to me and comforting.

THE THIRD FEATHER

I am the third feather that descended
    onto the lawn.
I was suspended
    by the soft winds of morning
        and arrived with the dawn.
Slim and golden I hovered
    on the last wisp of a breeze
        before touching earth.
An Angelic message of expectation,
    I was discovered
        in the brightness
            of the sparkling sun.
I bring light and elation
    to the one
        who believes
            in signs
    and the presence of Angels.

JGK

House Plants

Over the past five years or more I have collected a number of Jade plants and a Christmas Cactus, and each has a name. Emerald is my oldest and largest Jade at the living room window that I call the "guardian plant" of the cottage. Her continuous growth has been amazing, so much so that we have had to transplant her to a larger container twice. Sophia, Jasmine, Sweetness and Eleanor are smaller plants on the opposite side of the cottage. A Christmas cactus named Winter is at a front window. I think of them all as a little family and imagine them communicating amongst themselves. I call them "the girls." I also say little prayers for them holding my hands over them. Like George Washington Carver I place my indoor plants outdoors on the deck in summer "to play in the sun" and they truly enjoy this. Winter particularly thrived and grew larger and burst into early glorious large pink blossoms in mid-October these past two years, instead of in December.

WINTER'S PLAY

I put you out to play today—
      your many arms now swing and sway,
While each and every fuschia flower—
      in dance can feel its inner power.
And as prevailing breezes stream,
      to move you as you sit and dream—
Your pot with *flower fairy* face—
      adds to this scene of joy and grace.

Dedicated to Winter —   JGK
my lovely Christmas Cactus—   November 3, 1999
at play on a warm November day

And too, last month in April shortly before Easter, three blooms burst forth! Never had this happened! I interpreted the blooms as signifying the Holy Trinity—Father, Son and Holy Spirit—just to glorify the Risen Christ at Easter. They fell off shortly after.

I talk to the plants outdoors as well as the indoor plants, who are also outdoors when the warmer weather permits as I have shared. This is especially easy to do to the indoor ones because my planters cause one to be inclined to talk to them. All the pots are identical except for various sizes, with the face of a fairy on each, (as mentioned in the poem) with greens and fruit and flowers as "Hair," though all ceramic. When I talk to the plants they seem even more to have definite personalities because they all have faces.

I have added one plant to the family recently, that of a pretty African Violet that is at the kitchen window where I have created my little shrine on a very wide windowsill. Her name is "Violet," of course. She is the only one in a pot without a face. Her pot is violet in color.

Rochester too has a special plant or two of his own, that of tubs of rye and oat grass. I plant the seed and it grows into lush green fullness in a few days and lasts several weeks. This veggie added to Rochester's diet has given him enjoyment through the years, and is a healthy cleansing snack.

When I shared some of these thoughts about my house plants in my *Journal of Love*, I also included a poem that this snack garden for Rochester evoked. Perhaps you would enjoy it. Even such a seemingly insignificant thing as this can seem lovely enough to deserve a poem.

SNACK GARDEN OF LOVE

On our kitchen table—which is in the hub
Of life here in our cottage—there is a small white tub
Exploding with a shock of bright green rye and oat grass.
Grass—so thick and tall I spontaneously smile each time I pass
Wondering often if anyone else might have a centerpiece like that—
And surely if so—it is someone in love with their cat.

Rain

A journal entry of June 4, 1996 in my nature journal speaks of a lovely summer rain, rain we feel blessed by. I call these "rainforest" days and they continue into the present.

It has been a rain forest sort of day most all the day, at least all morning and into mid-afternoon. It was cool and lovely with gentle rains, and everywhere is the lush grass Bob has nurtured, and the green shrubs and ferns and trees. I am so thankful as I gaze out my window as I write at my desk, and I thank Christ and my Angels that we have been given this paradise by the lake to live in.

Yesterday and today as I write we are experiencing terrible thunder and lightening and heavy rain. A weather forecaster on a channel coming from Maine often tells us the present forecast, but adds that if we wait ten minutes the weather will change. This seems like a little nonsense, but actually it is pretty sound and true. We live within a few minutes walking distance to Maine here in our woods (I may have told you that before) and half of our Lake Balch is in Maine, so the weather from Maine often applies to parts of New Hampshire. And the weather does change abruptly! Storms rise up seemingly out of nowhere as they did yesterday and do today, and suddenly we are engulfed and over powered by major winds, lightening bolts and thunder claps that astound! The lake becomes like an ocean with huge white caps. It is at times like this I worry about the sweet wildlife and wonder where they take cover for protection. As the storm begins harshly today I worry about the two mallards I was feeding who flew into the winds and rain when it arrived while we stood together on the deck. A poem written ten years ago applies to the storm we are experiencing at this very moment!

SUMMER STORM

From upper window as I wrote—
Observing sun and lake and boat—
The atmosphere turned dark and mean,
Obliterating summer scene.
Instead of peace and benediction
Entire view was contradiction!

Gentle breeze that once blew mildly,
Grew to gusts that ranted wildly—
Creating havoc as aggressor—
Became in seconds full transgressor—
Whipping lake to frenzied motion,
White capped waves turned lake to ocean.

Thunder rumbled; then the lightning—
Cracked above in sounds most frightening.
Branches snapped and blew around
Before crashing to the ground.
Suddenly there came conclusion—
From these moments of confusion.

Little birds and chipmunks small
Returned as if to Nature's call.
All the woods green in profusion
Seemed to have a new infusion.
All outdoors was washed and bright
When that summer storm took flight!

JGK
July 21, 1990

As reported in the poem, each storm leaves "Higher Ground" beautiful, with soft sparkling wet green grass and trees vibrant and green. The lake calms to its placid state and all the birds return singing. Minutes from now when this present storm ends I will experience all I am sharing here with you and I will leave my desk for a few minutes to especially welcome the mallards back.

Some of our loveliest days here are "rain forest" days and they are especially appreciated in these past six years when we have a screened-in-porch and can experience these gentle rainy days outdoors. Several special days come to mind now in the present as I write, days spent on the porch with our beloved friend Joe Clancy. Dennis (extended family of ours I mention) has brought his Dad to spend the day more than once, and each time we choose to sit and talk on the porch rather than indoors, because the gentle rain is so beautiful. How I wish for these summer afternoons again, but Joe was ill when Dennis brought him here to be with us and he went to Heaven shortly after. We cherish those days and are thankful for the photos we take that illustrate the memories in our hearts and minds.

There were many years of spending time here with Joe and Terry when he was not ill, and we remember these great times continually. One sweet thing Joe always did for us was to make iced coffee. He had a special touch and method and it was incredibly delicious. He also frequently wanted us to pray together, and we would always join hands as we prayed. Loving memories like this come to mind as we drive to his viewing and wake in Wakefield, Massachusetts in December 1995, and a poem arrives just for Joe.

MEMORIES OF JOE

He made iced coffee with a flourish—
Yet 'twas not with this he'd nourish.
It was his love and charm and fun—
That fed our souls when day was done.

We keep those moments that we shared—
And all the times our hearts were bared
In confidence; hands held to pray,
Those are the memories that will stay.

Dedicated to our friend   JGK
Joe Clancy   December 18, 1995
Written as we drove to
Wakefield, MA to his wake

Other summer afternoons a crowd of grandchildren of all ages
gathers on the porch to talk and play games taking a reprieve from sun
and swimming in the lake. Often I retreat to the porch in the hot days of
summer to write because it is too warm up in my writing room, and Bob
and I love to read on the porch and sometimes have a light breakfast
there. Many wind chimes above, several from Jessica, and on the front
deck make it all magical, as well as numerous plants, several "Gardening
Angels" (a play on words) with gardening tools, and a dream catcher
swaying with the wind chimes, a gift from Terry, Joe's wife. Moments to
remember and treasure.

THE MUSIC OF ANGELS

There is music so disarming—
Utterly, hauntingly, supernaturally charming.
Known to induce an inner calm
Washes o'er one like a balm.
Winds pour forth from off the lake
Delicate instrument may now partake.

What prayer and mystery's in the air
To capture souls quite unaware.
Prevailing breeze—tinkling sublime—
Mystical, magical, melodic wind chime.

JGK

The porch is the favorite place to gather in rain or fair weather in summer, especially with Dennis, Patti, Sarah, Jenny, and baby Michael, and often Terry. Joe is so pleased, I know, to see us all together where once he too shared hours and love. The Clancys and our roots are entwined as well as our lives, for we bought our cottages and land here in the woods one year apart, and that was all gift from God, one we never take for granted, here in this Granite State. So many loving memories are connected to the rain. A poem written following one of Joe's visits in the final year of his life is appropriate to close this meditation on "rain."

RAIN

The rain pours down into the waters of the lake—
All the woodland trees are drenched for their own sake.
I watch—and listen to this wondrous sound—
Of rains that pound the earth on *Higher Ground.*
A gentle mist softens twilight's darkening scene—
And birdsong's heard as everything's washed clean.

JGK
April 21, 1995

Statuary

Tucked into all my gardens are various statuary that add to the enchantment of the glorious blooms. There are mainly small and different angel forms, but also a set of gnomes as written about earlier. St.

Francis too is at the center of a small garden named after him with a large bird at his feet and a dove in his hand, a gift from our daughter June. She is also responsible for the magical blue gazing ball on a wrought iron stand that is in the center of the *Deer Garden* where the fawn reclines close by. In the *Beach Garden* an unusually enchanting bird bath is in the form of a beautiful Cherub Angel sitting with her small feet dangling into a lovely large shell. The shell is continually filled with fresh water for the birds. The sweet Angel holds a dove in her hand. This is a gift from the Clancys, a surprise for our December birthdays two years ago. When I request Sarah to name the Angel, she responds "Gabriella." The little bird in her hand I baptize "Maraglo" from a poem by E. B. White that I have included in my *Journal of Love*. It is sweet and so worthy of repeating now for you.

> "My name is Maraglo"
> said the bird, softly, in a small voice.
> "I come from fields once tall with wheat,
> from pastures deep in fern and thistle;
> I come from vales of meadow sweet,
> and I love to whistle."

And lastly but not least, there is an unusual small Angelic fountain with continual flowing water nestled in the green bushes and trees near the St. Francis Garden. This fountain is a loving gift from our daughter Jessica and her husband Michael. Angels abound on Higher Ground!

And too, Jessica surprised us with a wooden wishing well painted green and brown that sits by the stone path leading down to the dock. It is filled with Petunias.

Not termed "statuary" for the garden but in the realm of decorative beauty and usefulness, is a wooden butterfly house on the side railing of our front deck near the bird feeders, and a wooden bat house attached to our green shed. These are recent gifts from Patti and Dennis and we await visitors in both, though some may already have frequented them and gone unnoticed. I often look up inside the bat house.

Communication

Flowers abound in the gardens, and the angels and other statuary are just small additions that seem to dwell there, symbolic of true heavenly angels. I talk to the flowers as I garden and listen for answers "in spirit," guidance as to where they might like to be planted, or if the ones already securely in the earth might have a message. Angels guide me, I believe, for I ask them to help me. I talk to wildlife, the chipmunks and squirrels, the birds and "Mrs. Mallard." Often I hear mental replies and write them down. Everything living communicates in some way and if we wish to tune in and learn to listen, then we can ask God's help to have a perceptiveness and openness to these little ones.

Once you begin writing things down in a journal, your faith is strengthened and doubt does not destroy what comes to you "in spirit." The written word is powerful. All of creation is speaking if only we learn to listen—and then record what is given to us.

In my *Journal of Love* are amazing accounts about George Washington Carver, the man to whom plants revealed their secrets, and of Luther Burbank. George Washington Carver said: "I like to think of nature as an unlimited radio station, through which God speaks to us every hour, if only we will tune in."

Once you read about George Washington Carver you can never look at a plant or flower again in the same way. He was a marvelous and intelligent and educated man. Why then cannot I, cannot we all, talk to the plants and animals and expect a response as he did and who told us that "Everyone can if only they believe it."

Luther Burbank is another who communed and talked to plants and dramatic results occurred in their growth. Helen Keller said about him, "He has the rarest of gifts, the receptive spirit of a child. When plants talk to him, he listens. Only the wise child can understand the language of flowers and trees." May we too, like these two great men who had child-like spirits, learn to become like a child. When we have that innocence we are receptive. Jesus too requests that we become as a little child so that we may enter the Kingdom of Heaven. In surrender and littleness secrets are revealed to us.

A Childhood Legacy

As a little girl I was in a Brownie Troop. Brownies are for smaller girls, and later one usually becomes a Girl Scout as I did. To this day I remember the joy of having a "Brownie" name, a name each girl in my troop had in addition to her real name. I no longer remember if the name was given to me by my troop leader, or if I picked it out of a Brownie hat, or if I chose it for myself, but I thought my name was magical and most beauteous. To this day I love its charm and sweetness. My Brownie name is "Blossom" and it has remained a part of me. It is particularly meaningful when I garden, but living here in the woods has brought it to mind in a more permanent way, and it truly has significance to me. Perhaps it is a love name of my "inner child" or "my shadow." (I believe it is.) It only passed lovingly through my mind on occasion in the past when reminiscing, and during the years of raising our children it would bring a touch of my own childhood and an inward smile, but now it seems to be wanting recognition. I believe it is because I live in the woods where enchantment reigns, and too, because I have become even more child-like living so totally surrounded by nature. And that is the way George Washington Carver and Luther Burbank were, most child-like (not "childish"), but they were intelligent men making yet unheard of discoveries. But their spirits were like that of children.

Perhaps we are all supposed to experience this throughout life, and feel amazement and awe at the tiniest living things God created. When we view life through the eyes of a child our wonder and delight returns and joy wells up within, and no matter what others say we still believe in magic. And this is life-changing! I would not have life any other way.

Jameson Ronald Kolb

One day last summer when our then second to youngest grandchild Jameson was 9 months old, and with us alone while his parents George and Valerie were on a "whale watch" outing out of Portland, Maine, I was just overcome by his preciousness. He was so sweet and mild, and out of love for him I did not know what to do next, but he was totally content sitting on my lap or playing on the porch or grass. Though I had already

taken pictures of him (my camera always an extension of my arm), I decided on more. All our gardens were in full bloom, and Jameson like a little flower himself, I decided to intermingle them. Going from garden to garden I placed Jameson in amongst the flowers, or on the surrounding rock walls, or occasionally on a little wooden chair in front of a garden. This chair had belonged to his Daddy who had sat on it at Jameson's age and longer. Jameson thrived in the flower beds, smiling as I snapped picture after picture while he patted the blooms. It was other-worldly and I wondered what he and the flowers were saying to each other, he in his innocence and still so fresh from Heaven, listening to and truly looking at the flowers as a new little one to this world. After completing a roll of 24 pictures, the film jammed and became torn and ruined while Bob was

removing it. It was so sad and it made me cry at the loss, for now a summer rain storm came and we had to be on the porch. I prayed that the sun might be bright again before George and Valerie returned, and my prayer was answered. Carrying sweet Jameson (he sounds like a flower!) to the gardens, we began anew, and he seemed even more delighted at being back to visit his floral friends. I did not have to coax smiles, it was as if I had not even taken the previous pictures. He was so enraptured by the gardens! In a very short time I completed another full roll and am thankful we all have those remembrances of a memorable day. Flower gardens fill us with joy and that joy nurtures our "inner child." Jameson thought his "Grandmom" was taking pictures of him, but actually it was a little girl, a little Brownie named Blossom, not very many years older than himself. That's why we had so much fun.

Musings

When we enter into the presence of gardens it is as if time stands still. We find a place of peace and beauty and we seem to be in another point of time. Gardening can be healing. Last summer I experienced a broken heart being ever so slowly but gently mended as I planted and pruned and mingled with my beautiful flowers clear into fall. It was the blooms and blossoms, and the earth and the sun and wind and the toil that nurtured my heart. I could become lost outside in a heavenly and healing realm tending to the gardens, down on my knees as the prevailing breezes washed over me. It was the most spiritual and cleansing and healing experience in those months, and tears well up when I think or write about it here or in journals.

The garden helped me, because, as Thomas Moore states in *The Re-Enchantment of Every Day Life*, "it addresses the soul so directly and gives it the things it needs much more plentifully than does the culture around us."

Through the years the Virgin Mary has frequently been described in writings as "an enclosed garden." She has been at times depicted in such a garden with a unicorn and I have given this very image on an embroidered throw as a gift to a friend. A unicorn is a symbol of Christ. Perhaps that is why my healing began in my gardens last summer. I was in the Holy company of Christ and the Virgin Mary, and too the Angels, in my enclosed gardens. It is said that entering a garden is comparable to passing through a mystical gate. It is so. As in the words of the hymn "In The Garden" my Mother loved so: "He walks with me, And He talks with me, And He tells me I am His own"—and like my Mother I met the Lord in the silence of tending the flowers.

Moose

It is significant to me as I write now about the unicorn that a notice appears in the New Hampshire Sunday News of June 4, 2000 about the return of Moose and that they are on the move, Moose, too symbolic of Christ to me as a form of deer. Many collisions with Moose on the roads are being reported and some moose sadly killed. The yearlings, the ones born last spring and summer—are being pushed away by their mothers and the cows are ready to give birth at this time of year. The yearlings are wild and confused looking, for they do not know what to do or where to go. It is said a collision with a moose, which weighs in at twelve hundred pounds or so—nearly always kills the moose. So very sad to report is the death of a driver also. Warnings are given to drive slowly at night. Where is our Matilda? Will she return to us in October? I await her and I will know her. We have looked deeply into each other's eyes and souls.

Garden of Verses

Just as Robert Louis Stevenson created his book, A Child's Garden of Verses, so the child Blossom has made a "Garden of Verses" for her garden musings. My Shadow likes to write poems too.

NATURE'S LULLABY

As we settle down into our dreams
outside the open window water streams
down into the green forest—
and we are blest

        to drift off to nature's torrential refrain
            as the lyrical sound of pounding rain
              resounds in the night air.
                  Magic is everywhere!

JGK

Written in the early AM hours as the rain pounded down outside our open window, the sound of it evoked this poem.

ASIAN TULIPS

All winter long I would remember
Bulbs I planted last September.
I dug the holes eight inches deep—
And kissed each bulb—then put to sleep
Each tiny roundness in the earth.
Then blessed them to insure safe birth.
And now some leaves are sprouting forth—
Right after all this snow up North!

Bulbs planted upside down, I fear—
Grew south to bloom in China this year!

JGK

Petunias in garden and gazing ball

Still new to gardening, I discovered I planted many of the bulbs upside down. This poem is in memory of those who never grew.

BUTTERFLY WEED

O sunny yellow butterfly weed
      bring me your innocence
           and cheerfulness—
                 your sense of the wild—
That my heart may nourish and spring forth
      with simpler joys
           and a sunny nature
                 and the spirit of a child.

                              JGK

Some of the dearest and prettiest flowers to me are weeds.

PETUNIA GARDEN

We are the purple and pink petunias
      newly planted
           by the tranquil blue lake.
Each has been granted
      for love's sake
           and our old-fashionedness and beauty—
A garden surrounded by rock—
      to delight in the peaceful scene
           of grass, water and dock—
               and towering green trees.
The prevailing breeze
      bestirring each graceful flower
           to dance and sway—
Caresses our delicate blossoms
      this summer day.

Dedicated to my beloved friend   JGK
Francis J. McGeary on the 8th   July 15, 1998
anniversary of his entering Heaven

TO A WILDFLOWER AND HER FRIENDS

Another June—another year—
Again I greet you here, my dear!
Swaying gently 'mongst your fold—
So tall and slender—topped with gold.

A fine ballet troupe has assembled—
O my dear—your group's resembled—
Dancers all in syncopation.
Through the woods you cause sensation!

Beneath our window in a crowd—
You burst in yellow right out loud!
Brightly blooming as we gaze—
With brilliant color all ablaze!

As we experience the riot—
That came in silence and in quiet—
Lining paths of rocks and earth—
We welcome you—wildflowers of worth!

JGK

There are many more poems in my "Garden of Verses" but I will just include these. Hopefully you will plant a poem in my garden too, and then begin to create your own "Garden of Verses" in your journal.

And, I am happy to say that we just planted two more new Lilac bushes as I finished sharing with you about our gardens. They are the same Donald Wyman Lilacs and same lavender color as the one I told you about earlier. One is planted to the left of our beach in a thick green foliaged area, and the other behind and to the right of my prayer chair and platform in the wooded greenery there. I named the three bushes Lilac (the first one, it seemed right), Amethyst and Violet. My indoor African Violet does not mind that a Lilac bush shares her name of Violet. Plants are that way, loving and spiritual and unselfish.

Reflect and Journal

☆ Through imagination sit in a beautiful blossoming garden. Enjoy all its mysteries. Now plant something in it that hopefully will bear fruit for you: a project, a relationship, a dream etc. Imagine how it sprouts and blossoms and bears fruit, and give thanks to God. Record it all in writing if you wish.

☆ Is there a garden from your childhood or teen years that holds meaning for you still in your heart? Sit quietly and envision this with eyes closed. Try to see as many details as possible.

☆ Write about all you saw and all you remember in your journal.

☆ Have you ever planted a flower or shrub in memory of a loved one? Is it something you might like to do? If so, consider buying one while reading this book. Perhaps have a little ceremony by yourself as you plant it.

☆ Write about it in detail in your journal from the first thought, to the purchasing, to the planting.

☆ Perhaps too, you might like to plant your state flower in your garden as I planted my state flower (Lilac) in mine.

☆ If you cannot plant a memory plant or state flower, perhaps with your colored pencils or crayons, draw the flowers or shrub you would plant for a loved one or for your state. Think of this drawing as a symbol of the real thing and respect your drawing, perhaps displaying it. Take a picture of your drawing to glue into your journal near the written entry about the flowers.

☆ Or if you prefer (or do both) draw a picture of your childhood garden to display. If you had a garden you will treasure this picture you took time to draw from memory.

☆ What would your hidden nature name be if you chose one? Would you like to? Write about it in your journal. It could change the way you look at nature. If you are woman it will be a flower-type name, and if a man, a tree or woods-like name. If this retreat you are mak-

ing through the reading of this book is meaningful to you, your chosen name will be significant to you now and as time passes.

☆ Have you had some "rain" in your life? Write in your journal to ease
your heart.

☆ Imagine you are a flower. What kind would you be? What color?
What would you do? Relate it to your life in some way. Journal about
it all.

☆ I hope you have come to realize how spiritual a garden is, and how
we can be healed spending time in a garden. Write a poem about a
garden or specific flowers that you like. Enter it in your journal. Write
many poems like this. If you do not have a garden or live near one,
your drawings and poetry and nature name will enhance your life.
Read your poems in your sacred space often and admire your drawings.

☆ Perhaps buy a house plant for your sacred space and give it a lovely
name during your retreat.

Try writing an acrostic poem pertaining to a flower you love, or
flowers in general. Enter it in your journal. Maybe you would like to try
writing these poems for other subjects too. Here is mine for the

FLOWERS

F   loral beauty
L   avishly abounds
O   verlooking the lake—
W   here birds and butterflies
E   nhance the gardens as
R   egal appreciators
S   ublime.

☆ Perhaps you would enjoy reading my *Journal of Love* or books about
George Washington Carver or Luther Burbank. Also *The Secret Life
of Plants* by Peter Tompkins and Christopher Bird and *Talking With
Nature* by Michael Roads.

☆ Throughout the summer, if you have a garden or are in a vicinity of wild flowers, press lovely little blossoms between the pages of a book. During the cold winter months these can be included in your cards and letters or used for your own pleasure. You could keep a pressed flower in this chapter on "Gardens" in this book as a memento— and, remember to take time to smell the flowers.

This chapter on gardens has been filled with the beauty of things seen. Now be prepared to learn about the unseen, who are remarkable in their own right.

CHAPTER THIRTEEN

Beaver Tales

Let me have wider feelings, more extended sympathies, let me feel with
all living things, rejoice and praise with them. Let me have
deeper knowledge, a nearer insight, a more reverent conception."
—Richard Jeffries, *Nature and Eternity*

JUST AS WE HAVE HAD INTERESTING ENCOUNTERS with the squirrels,
chipmunks, raccoons and birds—so too, have the beavers of
Higher Ground made themselves known to us. The difference is—they
have made known their presence but never have we been permitted to
meet even one beaver personally. For this we are sorry and hope one day
we shall have that privilege, for they have aroused our interest in them
keenly. Because of their mysterious presence amongst us we were inspired to learn some things about them, for in the learning we felt that
might hasten the day of such a meeting. We knew, of course, that beavers
bite down the trees with their teeth, but what actually happens to the
trees after that is what we wanted to learn—and how they reached their
destination chosen by the beavers. First of all it is hard work to cut down
trees with teeth and the beaver works by a stream or lake in order to
transport what he has accomplished. The tree is cut into smaller logs with
a team effort, and beavers then swim with the logs to the place where they
are building a dam. One by one the logs form the walls of the dam as the
beavers push mud around them to keep them firmly in place. Sticks are
added also and the dam becomes as tall as a man. If the dam is made in
a stream, the water is held back by it so that a deep lake is created and the

beavers then can make their home which is called a lodge. In the case here on Higher Ground and in our Lake Balch that already exists - they proceed with the lodge building at once. A pile of logs in the middle of the lake or in a cove has had two tunnels made in it at the bottom of the pile. The other ends of these two tunnels come up inside the lodge. It is inside this room in the lodge where they sleep. They live in colonies of up to 13 members, including the adult pair, kits and yearlings. In spring, yearlings leave the lodge to form their own colonies.

After the tiring work of building a dam, beavers will rest and feed on water lily leaves, abundant on our lake, or chew the bark from sticks. I have discovered through reading that beavers are vegetarian. Along with the water lily they live mainly on leaves, grass, and small herbaceous plants like cattail, bulrush, duckweed, goldenrod and waterweed. If an animal pursues them they can rush to their lodge and slip down a slide built on the side of it and from this they splash into the water and dive into it deeply and go up into their lodge to hide. They are very fast swimmers and when they escape in this way no other animals can get into their lodge.

In the winter when the lake is frozen the beavers rest inside their strong home, and snow covers the roof of the lodge. They do not sleep throughout the winter but wake to feed when they are hungry. Near the lodge they keep a supply of logs and sticks and the beavers can leave by way of the tunnels that do not freeze and are deep under the water, and thereby they can get additional sticks for food. Adult beavers can remain submerged for fifteen minutes by closing their mouths behind their large teeth and using their protective eye membranes and earflaps. They have good senses of hearing and smell but poor eyesight. I have read that their average life span is three to four years, but to reach eight years of age is not uncommon and in some rare instances individuals live to fifteen years.

Soon it will be mating time for the beavers, and in sixteen weeks the babies are born. When the snow and ice have melted and spring has come—it is then the female will have her babies. Growing big now are the young beavers born the previous year and soon the Mother and Father will send these young away in order to make room for the new little ones.

We learned beaver babies are the size of a small cat and have soft, thick fur. After only a week they are taken out of the lodge by their

Mother and swim beautifully. As the baby beavers grow bigger they too help to fix the dam and after summer is over they all put more mud on the lodge in preparation for winter. And so as with the squirrels - another cycle begins. It is all so amazing and there is an intelligence that truly surpasses human understanding. God has indeed instilled within them abilities that are remarkable.

Though the beavers have managed to stay out of sight they have freely let us know they are present. We have been incredulous at their close existence to us even though we have never seen one. Our first evidence of beavers on Higher Ground was the absence of two slender poplar trees on our property after we had been away from our cottage for a week before moving here permanently. We could see the teeth marks on the stumps of the trees and also the tracks in the sand on our beach of the beaver, and tree branches obviously being dragged to the water.

Our next proof of existence came several weeks later when one morning we could not open our door because a tree was lying on our deck outside blocking it. Finally managing to get out we knew again it was the work of the beavers. We never touched the tree but each morning for the next week we would waken to find more of the tree missing—until at last the entire tree had been taken away to use for the beavers' lodge. We found this to be extremely interesting and it was the main reason we decided to read about our little invisible friends and become more informed. I am sure they will call again but it has been about five years since this last visit.

We have hundreds of trees on our wooded property so we certainly do not feel threatened by future loss. Beavers seem to select trees with thinner trunks. The shavings all about the ground and the very obvious teeth marks and finally the gradual disappearance of the tree they took down while we were asleep, were all worthy of photos, which we did take. Along with pictures of the raccoons hanging over the high red barn birdfeeder feasting, and of squirrels, chipmunks and birds on the deck outside our sliding glass doors with Rochester observing all from within and often reacting in wonderful ways, we truly have captured in part some of the magic of living in the woods. The rest is seen in day by day existence here and held in our hearts. How blest we are that God has permitted us to share life in harmony with such wondrous creatures. It is pure gift from the Creator whose same Breath breathed life into us all!

As to the beaver, he truly has played a tremendous role in the human and natural history of North America. When streams are dammed the land becomes more fertile, and new plant growth enables other animals to live. Amazingly beaver dams have created mountain valleys, raised water tables, and distributed water runoff. In addition they have made possible new habitats for waterfowl and fish, and also—stimulated re-growth of vegetation.

Perhaps he is a symbol to us that we must go beneath the surface and into the deep. Unseen, he teaches us that there is so much more than meets the eye, so much more that is waiting to be discovered that we can learn from in God's world of nature, and thereby grow closer to our Creator.

BEAVERS

Beneath the surface
  often there are forces
    unseen but sure.
And in the deep abyss
  where the cool water courses—
    they live obscure.

In the depths—
  what thrives
    in our lives
      and shall endure?

              JGK

Reflect and Journal

☆ Are you willing to go beneath the surface and into the deep? Take time now for a period of meditation asking God to show you some-thing from the depths of your being.

☆ Stay with whatever is shown you for a period of time.

☆ When released from your meditation write in your journal about what you were shown.

☆ In a future meditation, like the beavers, build yourself a small lodge. Yours will not be built in actuality but by means of imagination. This can be a place to return to often in future meditations, a spiritual haven in which to rest, dream, heal.

☆ Place items in your lodge that will bless you and comfort you each time you visit it, yet keeping it sparse and uncluttered.

☆ Describe your lodge in detail in your journal and the accessories you have placed within it. Write about how this all affects your peace and being whenever you visit it in spirit and meditation.

☆ Perhaps the beaver experiences some of your same feelings. After all he is capable of building this complex lodge. Comparing his thoughts and lodge to yours can be future journal entries.

☆ Your retreat is not a time to be "busy as a beaver." It is a time to be quiet and reflect, write, read, and meditate.

Just as you may experience a metamorphosis on your retreat, so do creatures much tinier than you are, and this change is moving to witness.

CORONATION

Caterpillars all around—
On the cottage—on the ground
Little bits of fur and face—
At their pace search for a place.
Soft and fuzzy—dear and small—
Golden brown upon the wall.
Who would guess the transformation
In metamorphic coronation?

Butterflies now here abound,
Surround, confound, deeply profound.
Mystery, beauty from soft fur—
Does occur—now flitting blur!

Dozens of them fill the air—
They're everywhere—sent to declare—
The One Who Changes Not—can be—
The One who changes us, you see.

Dedicated to all caterpillars   JGK
and butterflies

And now listen to words of the lovely butterfly.

BUTTERFLY

I am the butterfly lingering on the pink cone flower.
My yellow and black wings flutter in delight.
The flower and I commune in the August sun
    of an early hour—
While the wind causes her blossoms to sway.
We whisper secrets of the eternal
    before I take flight—
And have spun
    a mystical friendship—
On this summer day.

For the butterfly I watched   JGK
 on the Cone Flower
August 19th, 1997

This event I will share also. I realize these things occur in nature, but
I could not allow this to happen right before my eyes.

RESCUE

While writing at my desk upstairs
I saw a being filled with hairs—
Outside my window dangling there.
Invisible thread I knew was snare—
    And acting as a silken stair

Leading to a spider's lair!

The baby caterpillar hung in view,
Through the screen I forcibly blew—
To try to free that tiny one—
The thread began to come unspun—
And lower captive—to expel—
Then drew it up again quite well.

I ran downstairs—a spoon I found
Then rushed outside to stand my ground.
I tossed the spoon and hit the strand—
Making then my firm demand.
The little creature fell to earth
And crawled away in new rebirth.

I watched him as he made his way
His rescue surely made my day!
But here I'd also like to note
I saved a spider who could not float!
And so I then think that all is fair—
That she's denied little guy with hair!

Dedicated to   JGK
the baby caterpillar

Now we will think and learn more about trees, aside from their purpose for the beavers. Perhaps you can sit beneath a tree as you read the next chapter if weather permits and you have a tree. If not, sit beneath one on Higher Ground through means of imagination. Welcome!

CHAPTER FOURTEEN

Trees

I think that I shall never see
A poem lovely as a tree
> —Sergeant Joyce Kilmer, "Trees"

S A CHILD IN GRADE SCHOOL I both memorized this poem as
required, and also sang it with all the other children and the
teachers in school assemblies. It was a favorite of mine and has even more
meaning to me today. Each verse is lovely. "A tree that looks at God all
day, and lifts her leafy arms to pray." How beautiful! And verse four I
have witnessed again and again here by the lake,

A tree that may in Summer wear
A nest of robins in her hair.

Trees, so majestic, mysterious and magical! They have powers we
will never know and draw birds, animals and humans to them for
hundreds of different reasons.

Tonight on television we see a young woman twenty-five years old
who has just spent two and a quarter years up in a tree and written a book
about her experiences. She is mocked on the show and ridiculed, and
rather than centering in on all they could learn from this woman, they
seek to embarrass and destroy her. They ask her humiliating questions
and never hear any of the wisdom she is attempting to share while she
graciously avoids conflict with her taunters. We are anxious to hear all

259

she has to say but it is impossible. Instead I return to the article that was written about her approximately a year ago that I have saved. In this fine article she is referred to as the tree's "Guardian Angel," and at that writing is still in the tree in spring of 1999. It relates how she decides to live in a thousand-year-old redwood rather than let it be cut down by Pacific Lumber, after visiting in 1997 this ancient Northern California redwood forest. She finds this to be a "transcendent experience." The tree is nicknamed Luna by environmentalist activists, and is on land owned by the timber company in Humboldt County, California.

In December 1997 Julia Butterfly Hill begins her "tree-sit," occupying two tarp-covered platforms about 180 feet above the ground. Food, water, and other supplies are brought to her about once a week by a support crew. She uses candles for light, and a propane stove for cooking. She hauls her supplies up by rope, it is reported.

"Constant prayer and belief in the power of love and healing" help her endure life in the tree. The article tells that she is the daughter of a traveling evangelist. All her water freezes due to extreme cold while winter winds encircling her are up to seventy miles per hour. Other terrible travails assail her; a timber company trying to dislodge her using helicopters, starvation, and gangs of men.

Her high calling and goal is to save not only Luna but all the ancient redwoods in Northern California. To fill her solitude she writes poetry and via a solar powered cell phone she conducts media interviews. Her reports by phone are reported on a web site. Despite harsh conditions and vicious harassment, she is strong and shows unconditional love. "I tell them this is about respecting the gifts that nature has given us," she reports as her reason for doing all of this.

In response to questioning how long she will live high in this tree, she vows that she will do everything in her power to make the world aware of the destruction or her feet will not touch earth.

She lives day by day, prayer by prayer and does not accept agreements proposed as yet proper, believing the timber company to be dishonest. She states "If Luna could talk, I know she'd say thanks."

Because we can learn little from her television appearance due to the men that were present, or what she has accomplished, we plan to read her book. Perhaps you too are interested in what one woman is trying to do by giving of self to save trees. I can not write about trees without sharing Julia's story.

There is another woman, Joanne, close friend of ours, who too has an unusual experience with a tree. Though of much shorter duration the encounter is mystical, and she follows an impression on her heart to discover a huge oak that is in need of spiritual help. Upon finding it in a location she is not at all familiar with, she ministers to this tree. It is a moving account that can be read in entirety in my *Journal of Love*. We can never doubt our spiritual connections to all of life in this world, when happenings like these occur. Joanne, in turn, experiences the healing the tree is ministering to her. It is a true story you will not forget, should you read it. Each of us can have an encounter with a living tree if we live in the sacrament of the moment and are fully alive and aware. We can have many such brushes with the mystical.

Today as I write the wind is whistling through our trees, and broken boughs are all about outside on the lawn and in the rock planters and by the lake. There are white caps on the water and unknown things are hanging here and there. A nuthatch hangs onto one of our feeders desperately with his tiny feet as the long cylindrical silver feeder swings in the high wind. The wind continues now for the third day! These blasts are not the lovely prevailing breezes from across the lake, but great gusts that surely make many little creatures take cover. A poem from the not too long ago comes to mind—written in a zephyr momentum such as now.

WIND

I am the rustle of the wind sweeping through the trees.
I loosen pine cones from their branches—
And carry them in their downward flight.
I fly with birds—
And rush through grasses when fairies play.
I cause the flowers to sway—
And small white caps to rise upon the peaceful lake.
I accompany Angels creating celestial notes
    upon the wind chimes—

I swish the fuzzy tail of an upside down squirrel
        on the birdfeeder.
I am spirit.

JGK

We walk through the forests of physical things that are also spiritual things that look on us with affectionate looks.

—Baudelaire

This quotation describes how I feel when I walk about our property. Every tree, shrub, and rock is so personal to me, and they hold great meaning because this is the home and land I love so. But I believe also they all feel this love from Bob and myself, and in turn are radiating it out to us and all our surroundings. People sense this here.

When you approach our property after driving a mile through the woods, you pass along and behind a great wooded area before reaching our road. It is filled with many kinds of trees and this huge area is a hill that rises behind our small cottage. Turning left at the end of this area is our personal road leading down to our home and the lake. I have mentioned earlier that to the right of the hill at the top is the Clancy's cottage, extended family whom I write about often, and who do not live here year round. Driving down our dirt hill one sees rows of Fraser Firs, Colorado Blue Spruce, and many pines. These were planted by Bob years ago in the seventies when we bought this property. In his hand he held them all as tiny seedlings, a hundred or more. Now they enhance the entrance to "Higher Ground." At times Bob thins them out by transplanting some in other areas around our home. In December he digs one up at Christmas time to be used for our Christmas tree indoors. Then after enjoying it for several weeks it is taken outside to wait until the ground is not frozen so he can transplant it to a new place. Each of these trees brought inside for Christmas is named by our granddaughter Sarah at my request. The most recent two have unusual names given at once by Sarah as if she had been prepared for my request, which she was not. So spontaneous was her answer each time that it left no doubt that the name is truly the one meant for each specific tree. One is *Rafiki Modare* meaning "Friend of nice people" and the last, *Ipendi*, Swahili for "love."

IN GRATITUDE TO IPENDI

Thank you, dear little tree
For the joy you've given to me—
With your tiny colored lights
You have filled my quiet nights—
With pure delight and peace and calm.
Your presence like a lingering psalm
Of praise and gratitude for being—
Has touched my spirit and is quite freeing—
From all conventionality and rule,
You've stayed a month and been a jewel.

Brightening home—and yes my soul
I sensed your beauty like a stole—
That wrapped me warm, kept me aglow!
But ah, sweet tree, its time to go.
I shall undecorate each bough
But I simply do not know how—
        To say good-bye.
          I will try.
            I will sigh.

                    JGK

Trees abound all over here, along the lake front, and surrounding our cottage in the back (the wooded hill) and on the sides. A green lawn stretches out front and beyond that in two areas are sandy beaches by the lake. All other area along the lake is filled with trees, giant pines and firs, shorter oaks and some still unknown. They are backdrop to our large green dock that Bob built, and also to my prayer chair on the green platform.

BENEATH THE PINES

I sit beneath the trees of pine—
Their height and strength symbolic sign—

Of our Creator—infinite source,
The One to whom we have recourse.

The Crucifix upon the trunk—
Of tallest pine is an adjunct—
To chair of prayer—and upward glance -
From my own stance of vigilance.

And though I daily make my way—
To this sweet place at which I pray,
The wonder of it does not cease—
And by the lake I find my peace.

JGK

Prayer chair on platform under Trilogy of Trees—
with lake view and rocks and gardens

Trilogy of Trees

Three main trees embrace my prayer chair and platform (the platform built by Bob many years ago) and they are very significant to me. Several years ago in prayer I asked the larger pine tree its name, a tree so tall it is amazing, and so thick I cannot embrace it. Instantly in reply in my mind came the name "Pensive." Since it did happen instantly and because that word was not even remotely in my thinking, I truly believe it is the tree's name given to me either by Angels or the spirit of the tree itself. It is such a beautiful name to me and a most appropriate name for the tree, and also for the condition I am usually in when sitting in the prayer chair.

As I have written in my *Journal of Love,* I have been blessed by being able to see the Angel that guards the tree or the spirit of the tree in two separate photographs I took one year apart. One picture is in *Journal of Love.* The Angel image of light is in front of the tree about four and a half feet from the ground and the same height from the earth as my platform that I climb to by way of the steps. But there is no platform where the Angel is. The Angel aglow has its back against the tree and is in the air beside my platform. I obtained these images when I was standing on the platform at night taking pictures of the full moon. One of these photos is in a frame in our living room and most people upon seeing it will ask, "Is that an Angel?" Angels are beings of light, and each time I was talking to God and my Angels and praying in the dark when I took the pictures. Why should I doubt?

The other two trees were named by Jenny, Sarah's sister, names given to me as instantly as Sarah gave me the names for our Christmas trees. All were truly inspired and given by God. I never doubt. Jenny's names for the other two trees are "Alisha" and "Mikey" (short for Michael), and their meanings found in a baby name book are most significant. Alisha, meaning "truthful," and Michael or Mikaleia, (Mikey) means "Who is like God?" Of course Michael is the name of the archangel who defeats the dragon. I truly sit surrounded by noble and spiritual trees who chose to reveal their names

I enjoy putting my back against Pensive when praying and I feel his energy and comfort. Often I put my arms around his big trunk in a hug, though my hands cannot meet. To sit in my prayer chair with my head back gazing into the tall overhanging branches, that create a sanctuary above me, is most inspiring. All of these little love rituals are part of my spirituality.

The Spruce

An extremely large Colorado Blue Spruce is guardian to the entrance of our cottage to the right of the door. It was a tiny little thing when planted and now it is about 20 feet tall. Her name is "Rhapsody," and she truly is a rhapsody in white in winter, with dozens of tiny sparkling colored lights shinning through the snow. (I have mentioned her briefly to you in my chapter on snow.) We leave the lights on all year and light the tree for especially happy moments that occur, or when expecting company, or for any reason at all. She looks beautiful in the dark of a summer's evening in her festive colors. By day the tiny bulbs can barely be seen. Here in New Hampshire many folk leave their outside Christmas lights up all year on their homes and restaurants, even their wreaths and other decorations. It is unusual but very special. As we drive through our woods many of the cottages tucked in the trees are lit up year round, not extravagantly, but sparingly and sweet. Many are with these newer lacy strings of light that hang from the roof in a scalloped pattern. We too have them on the side of our screened in porch.

The Gnome Tree

One very giant pine tree not far from our cottage (perhaps 30 to 35 feet) I call "the Gnome Tree." Its bark near the base of the tree is unusual, and various underlying layers are revealed. An interesting opening at the base seems other worldly and I imagine it to be the home of gnomes or other elementals. In spring and summer there is a garden all around the base of it surrounded by a rock wall, and two of the gnome figures mentioned in a previous chapter, stand guard at the base of the tree in amongst the flowers. It is a sweet sight to see. This tree too has inspired a poem.

THE DEVA*

On the edge of our woods just by the ascending dirt road—
There is a tall giant pine tree and it is the abode
Of Gnomes! Yes, Gnomes! Not obvious to a casual passerby,
Unless one is attuned and with an observant eye—
The ancient and unusually layered bark formation
And the enigmatic openings—draw me to station
Myself at its base—upon the hand assembled stone wall—
To be a sensitive, silent listener. And on my ears befall
Stirrings from within the trunk - mysterious and unexplainable!
Sh-h-h!! it is the wee inhabitants—ever cautious—
and as yet unattainable.

*Angel-like beings—Nature Spirits—   JGK
Sanskrit word meaning "Shining One"

Birches

The Paper (white) Birch is New Hampshire's State tree, and our property has many of these exceptional beauties. Some bend gracefully over of their own accord and stand out in loveliness amongst all the evergreens and taller pines and firs. Some have been extremely bent over by the Ice Storm of 1998 and may not lift themselves for years to come. The white birches on our land have deep meaning to me, especially the three in front of our cottage that I view all day as I write here at my desk. They suffered the loss of some major branches in that ice storm, but now seem recovered. Two of these are joined at the base like Siamese twins. They are said to shed some of their bark in July and I have found this to be true.

My dear friend Francis, an obstetrician who also loved to study about nature, and knowing about my love of the birches here, told me about the loosening of the bark on or about July 15th of each year. Though I had observed this because it was evident, I did not give it full attention thinking there was no particular date or pattern. The following year on July 15th my beloved friend entered Heaven, and to help myself accept his absence I wrote a series of poems for him then, just as I had in the period before his death. He was a poet who had inspired me to again write poetry after a long period of silence on my part in its regard. I have written about Francis in each of my previous books and have written hundreds of poems on endless subjects since meeting him and having his love and encouragement. The poem that follows is about Francis and the Birch Tree and the knowledge Francis shared with me.

EMBARKED

As in nature we see change
Mysterious, subtle—often strange—
So we humans undergo
Metamorphosis as we grow.
The scientific research states
July fifteenth amongst all dates—
There need not be extensive search
To note the change in tall white birch.

The white bark loosens on the tree—
And on that date—with touch is free—
From solid trunk, can move with ease
Shift and flutter in the breeze.
Like yearly rhythm of ocean tides
There's rhythm too, the birch confides!

And so same date we also marked
A gentle loving soul embarked—
Freed from confining link to earth
With breeze from Spirit had rebirth.

In luxury of remembrance of   JGK
Francis J. McGeary
Written on the date of his
Mass of Christian Burial.

We also have a clump of beautiful birches in front of Bob's small office across the dirt drive from our home, thus the name he gives this building, "The Birchgrove." It is the name of an old hymn. In an antique poem book for children I read that beautiful fairy maidens, the Dryads, are supposed to live in trees, and one poem tells the story of one who is imprisoned in a birch tree and is titled "The Spirit of the Birch." It begins:

> I am the dancer of the wood—
> I shimmer in the solitude;
> Men call me Birch Tree, yet I know
> In other days it was not so.

It goes on in poetic form to say she is the Dryad of this tree, and because she danced too long one summer night, she was found and imprisoned by the Dawn and made captive. She (the Dryad) relates how she sways and bends and dances forevermore. The poem is by Arthur Ketchum. Our home and woods is lovelier because of the birches interspersed with all the other many trees.

Spring

At this time as I write the woods is coming alive with returning wildlife, and some small green perennial plants. Soon there will be a greening of all the trees that are not evergreens; the birches, poplars, maples and others still not identified.

Awakening

The trees in wood
In silence stood,
All winter long
Awaiting song—
Of little birds
To sing the words—
Locked in tree trunks,
As words in monks.

Intercessors in the branches—
And their presence now enhances—

Woodland scene
Becoming green.

The birds now chirp
Sweetly usurp
The swish of leaves—
Translate with ease
And sing the words
Of trees and birds.

Harmony in soft elation—
Announcing Spring in God's Creation.

JGK

In direct contrast to this glorious evidence of new life, are words in a poem expressing the death of the leaves of a Poplar tree by the side of our cottage, but with death, the promise of resurrection. This poem is in the chapter on "Snow," (Chapter 6).

The Blessings of Trees

Our trees bless me as I sit at my desk and window writing. Trees create beauty and shade, and these same trees witnessed out daughter's wedding here and many other family gatherings. Trees create a spiritual atmosphere, and Thomas Moore states in *The Re-Enchantment of Every-day Life* that "trees are not mere material objects but have a body, soul, and spirit." And I say yes to that! I believe there is divinity in a tree, and remembering that Jesus was crucified on wood from a tree emphasizes that divinity to me. That I love and treasure both trees and books is understandable since books are made from trees.

Michael J. Roads, in his book *Talking with Nature*, converses with trees as I often do, and receives answers. He states, "Talking to a tree is easy. The very grandeur invites conversation. I would no more walk beneath the branches on my way to the river without a word of greeting than you would pass your family pet without a word of recognition."

Living amongst trees invites such a relationship, it is true. Trees here are my friends and I treat them with respect in acknowledging them.

I consider Pensive my guardian tree and have for years. I thought it was original in my thinking, yet only recently, in Denise Linn's fine book *Sacred Space,* did I read more about Guardian Trees. She writes that they are a source most important of healing. She feels the honor and love that you give your tree will make it become an even more powerful center to bring in light and energy, and a Guardian Tree can also be a powerful transmitter of healing and energy to an entire household. One suggestion she makes in a lovely tree-of-light meditation is to leave a gift for your tree after meditation with it or near it. This little loving act I have been doing for many years so it moves me to read it in her meditation. Many of my tokens are special rocks I find for this purpose but I leave other personal things also.

Search for a Heartbeat

TREES

T enderly shading
R oads and gardens
E legantly standing watch—
E nergizing earth and life
S acredly.

Trees are magnificent and living creatures. In his unusual book, *Sharing Nature with Children,* author and naturalist Joseph Cornell relates how we can hear the heartbeat of a tree. Since a tree breathes, eats, and rests, the heartbeat of a tree is a wonderful crackling gurgling flow of life, he states, and the best time to hear this heartbeat of the forest is in early Spring. The first surges of sap are sent then upward to their branches. This prepares them for another season of growth.

Author Cornell suggests choosing a tree that is at least six inches in diameter with thin bark. He states that certain trees of a species may have a louder heartbeat than others, and that deciduous trees are generally better for listening than the conifers. If you press a stethoscope firmly against a tree and keep it still so as not to make noises that will interfere, you will be able to listen. Occasionally you may have to try different places on the tree trunk to find a spot that makes for good listening. Amazing! This book is enlightening in so many ways and is wonderful for adults learning as well as for children. I am happy to discover it.

Pinecones and Acorns

Pinecones of several varieties abound here and little grandchildren have gathered them often to make Christmas decorations. When our daughter Janna was preparing to be married here I gathered several hundred pine cones. Gradually I hand-printed Janna and Bill's names on equal amounts of small pieces of paper (in green ink of course) and added their wedding date. These were attached to the pine cones. We heaped the pine cones into several large pretty baskets and some of our little grandchildren gave each guest as they left, a pine cone to take home. The guests loved the idea and many asked for extras to take back to Pennsylvania to friends and family not present who knew Janna and Bill. We have a number of these wedding pine cones in a corner of a bookcase in our living room as mementos.

Natural objects given off by the trees are so appealing to me. On my desk within a circle of stones and rocks I have numerous acorns. Acorns have attracted me since I was a tiny child. I have shared in the chapter "Diane and Friends" about the squirrel who safely stored an acorn in Dennis' water pump pipe and created havoc. That is so tender when you think upon it for it was done in innocence and need. Little creatures are so inventive as they learn to live in all the elements and seasons. We humans have to be sensitive and learn from them and appreciate some of the amazing things they do even if we are initially not particularly appreciative of an act because it does not benefit us. Would we be as instinctively intelligent if placed in similar situation?

Not long ago I wrote about an acorn. I write about every thing within sight and unseen as well, it seems, because I am in love with this place of enchantment. Even without a written poem, life here is a poem.

Acorn

Acorn,
　　　Squirrel's favorite nut
　　　　　he finds on the ground—
　　　　　　　that he stores and hides
　　　　　　　　　and on which he has fed—
　　you look like a round
　　　　brown little head
　　　　　　with a pointed cap.
Bring me the fairy that in you resides—
　　　　or so I have read
　　　　　　and I shall tap
　　　　　　　　into a magic realm.

Since childhood I have been delighted with the belief that a fairy lives within each acorn, and to bring them indoors welcomes the nature spirits into your life.

And so, from the very simple to the sublime, I shall close these thoughts on all the magnificent trees surrounding us with a poetic meditation upon the shadows created by the tree filled woods.

Shadows

I am the shadows weaving themselves in
　　the depths of the forest.
I conceal rocks and stones
And protect creeping, crawling things.
I become a haven of rest
For the hunted—
A sanctuary from the hunters.
I protect my own.
My coolness refreshes—
The shade restores—
From the heat of the sun.
My darkness holds silence and secrets

Too wondrous to imagine.
I am profound mystery.

JGK

Reflect and Journal

☆ Think of a tree (or trees) that has meaning to you. Close your eyes and envision it. If it is near by take time to visit it today and then write about it in your journal. Did you see it in a new way? Did it speak to you? Include these thoughts in your journal entry.

☆ If you have never named a favorite tree, pray about this as you envision the tree, and then ask for a name for your tree. Giving it a name will make it even more special and personal to you.

☆ If you use a camera, take a picture of your tree so you can keep an image of your tree in your sacred spot, or make a sketch or crayon drawing of it, or do all three.

☆ Visit your tree often, either in spirit through prayer and the picture you now have of it, or in actuality. Learn to talk to it. Say a prayer each time you visit it and bless your tree in some way, through a verbal or meditative phrase, or the sign of the cross over it.

☆ Record all that you do in regard to your tree in your journal.

☆ Perhaps your favorite tree will become your Guardian tree.

☆ Have you ever felt you were "up a tree"? Write about this experience in your journal.

☆ Pray for trees all over the world so they are not ravaged by unjust cuttings, and that rainforests and other sanctuaries are not destroyed that are necessary for the wildlife.

☆ If there is one fairly close to you, visit a forest, and just enjoy sitting against a tree in stillness. Later record that experience in writing. Perhaps also take your camera along.

☆ The book written by Julia Butterfly Hill is *The Legacy of Luna: The Story of a Tree, a Woman, and the Struggle to Save the Redwoods*.

The article I have shared from in this chapter appeared in *The Journal for Holistic Living—New Age* and was written by Pete Brady.

A portion of a white birch tree here became a significant sign to all of us. Our son-in-law Michael made the cross for Katie's grave (beloved dog of Michael and Jessica).

KATHERINE ELIZABETH

A rugged cross
Made of white birch
Marks our deep loss,
Creates a church—

In woods by lake
With mound of rock,
And hearts still ache
Recalling shock.

Carved in the bough
Her name is there
And we somehow
Can say our prayer—
Remembering still
Her girlish way,
The daffodil
And heart-break day.

Dedicated to   JGK
Katherine Elizabeth (Kolb) Drakely
on the 3rd anniversary of her death
March 28, 1992

☆ ☆ ☆ ☆ ☆

We go now from the majestic to the minute. Everyone loves trees, I can assume, but what about little mice? Will you give me an opportunity to share with you our experiences with these tiny creatures? They were not in my realm of existence before living here, and now - it is time for you to meet them on your retreat. Please do not judge before you read. Remember, this retreat should be filled with epiphanies for you. Perhaps this is one!

Oh yes, I almost forgot to tell you, yesterday we bought three large hydrangea bushes, which really will grow to look like trees. These are filled with nostalgia as we remember the hydrangea that grew beside our home in Jenkintown even before we moved in, and all during our many years there. Also in childhood and teen years on vacations in Ocean City, New Jersey, the hydrangea was a special highlight in that town on the Atlantic Ocean. We will plant our new bushes in the woods at the end of our property. A smaller vine-like hydrangea plant grows up the sides of our white trellis.

CHAPTER FIFTEEN

Our Sleekit Timorous Beasties

It is probable that man is perceived by God to achieve his greatest stature when he humbles himself to help an animal.

—Robert A. Kolb Jr.

ONE CANNOT LIVE IN THE WOODS and not expect to have mice. They are seasonal, however, so they are not always present. Even when they are there is little evidence of them, and if it were not for Rochester, I am sure we would rarely meet one. He does manage to frighten them out of hiding at times with his sense of remarkable hearing, and then acting instantly to respond to the sound. Even out of a deep sleep in bed or on my lap he can immediately be called to duty and patrol by a noise we often do not hear at all. Many a time there has been a chase through this small house.

EARLY MORNING MOUSE CHASE IN A SMALL COTTAGE

My little cat curled deep in sleep—
Awakens suddenly—makes a leap—
From off our bed—runs out the door,
His speed is such he skids on floor.
Noises here—noises there!

277

I sense out there—there is a pair!
It seems to me a mouse he's chasing
Lots of action—now some pacing—
    Near the closet of the broom—
    But mouse escapes into our room.

Around and 'round the big brown chair
    Cat and mouse are circling there.
The chair sits by my husband's face—
He lies in bed—sleeps through the race.
Because I have some apprehension,
    I ask him please to pay attention.
"Let me sleep—you're always worried."
(By his nose they both just scurried)
He makes it seem that I am crazy—
When we both know he's being lazy!

    Lots of clatter under bed!
    Quiet now—my cat instead
Jumps on me—puts paw in hand—
Stares in my eyes—I understand.
As he lies down—we're face to face.
    I commend him on the race,
I thank him for his swift detection—
    And his marvelous protection.
He's never killed a mouse, you see.
Each one's a gift he's brought to me.
Rochester only wants to please—
We set the mice free in the trees.

    I'm overjoyed they called a draw.
    I gently squeeze that dear small paw.

                                        JGK

Other times Rochester's incredible immobility and patience for extended periods before a door or area he knows a mouse is hiding, pays its reward through the mouse's capture. Once this occurs this is not a scene you would observe in another home, I feel certain. He proudly brings the little creature to us in his mouth and we in turn congratulate him and make quite a loving fuss over his success. Then we direct Chester to the door and allow him out on the screened-in-porch. Winter or summer this is the plan. Never changes. Once outside he parades around a bit still quite proud. Meanwhile Bob (or myself) has gotten a cereal bowl and we begin to urge Chester to drop the mouse. He knows it all by heart and conforms. Once the mouse is dropped the little thing is in a stunned condition from his flight around the cottage and his eventual capture, and Rochester's prolonged moment of strutting and glory. He does not run, and Bob places the bowl over him while I take Rochester off the screened-in-porch. We allow a short space of time for the mouse to recover, then Bob slips a piece of cardboard both under the bowl and the little creature within.

The final step is to take bowl, cardboard and mouse outdoors, carefully closing screen door. Then Bob lifts the bowl and the little mouse runs off the porch as if his tiny pants were on fire, if he wore any. And thus ends the saga of how we capture mice.

I forgot to mention one very important point. We never kill any living thing! And so this is the only humane way we have discovered to capture and release a mouse that Rochester catches first. Fortunately he too is a humane and pro-life little cat, so he acts in complete cooperation with us. Naturally, we are not so naive as to believe that the little creatures humanely captured and released do not immediately return to enter our home, perhaps even before we are inside and have closed the door.

There are many little hidden entrances for a tiny mouse to enter. We have laughed and joked often over the fact we could very well be capturing the same mouse repeatedly! But that is the way it will continue to be. As friends of God's creatures and vegetarians, we do not eat anything with a face nor do we kill any living thing.

If a man . . . can make a better mouse-trap than his neighbour, though he build his house in the woods, the world will make a beaten path to his door.

—Ralph Waldo Emerson

We have not noticed any such worldly activity at our small door, but then Bob's marvelous inventions are not well known.

The procedure of capture I have just explained is used when there are no humane traps set in the house. It is rare we have to use the method devised by Bob and Rochester when the traps are set about unseen. Only occasionally. The traps I speak of have evolved over the years as Bob has continually refined them and become more and more creative. It is impossible to list all of his creations.

Mouse House

In our home there is a House.
It's decorated for a mouse.
Invented by a man of God—
Whose hope it is no one will trod,
Or torture, poison little mice.
That's why this Mouse House is so nice.

It is a Pro-Life trap, you see.
He catches mice and sets them free!
Peanut butter and jelly beans—
Entice each mouse and are the means,
To tempt his entrance through the door.
Then it closes—that's the core—
And it's the basis—to enwrap
Each tiny mouse in Mouse House trap.

Then man takes the House outside,
Raises door up very wide.
A wiggling little nose peeks through.
Little eyes then search for clue—
To see if there is anyone—
To block his path when he will run.
If you could see this little face—
Never again could you erase—
Or take a life in apathy.

Thou shalt not kill is God's decree!

Dedicated to Bob, to mice—   JGK
and to all non-violence

Bob's houses have been so inventive and the mice so cute, that I
have actually written a series of children's stories about a little mouse that
roams in our rafters and continually gets caught in Bob's humane trap
where he briefly enjoys capture. Once released each day he goes out and
has adventures of the humane sort that help and rescue others, only to
return each time to our basement and the trap to be deliberately caught.
There he is fed jelly beans and peanut butter (the lure for him to enter the
trap) and sleeps until released for another adventure. He needs no lure.
He cannot wait to return to the amazing trap to eat and rest!

In periods when the traps have broken down or Bob is too busy to
create new ones, or he has a lull in his ingenuity, we use the "Rochester
and bowl" method. It all has afforded us much fun over the years and a
sense of satisfaction and joy that we never hurt or kill these little tiny
mice.

*Are we to pity only creatures whose appearances please us? It is not
because they are small or ugly that mice and rats don't suffer when they are
torn apart.*
—Bruce Marshall, *Thoughts of My Cats*

Others are astounded we would go to such effort for a mouse's safety,
but I promise if you ever looked carefully at one of these little creatures,
looked him in the eye, I do not think you could kill him either. Their lives
are important and created by God. They are frightened too, and desire to
live just as we do.

My sweet friend Rose-Beth in Pennsylvania who loves her dear cat
Willy, is also kind to the wildlife around her. Before sleep each night she
puts little pellets on the kitchen counter top so that her "house mouse"
will not go hungry that evening. She is interested in and loving to all
creatures she meets. She occasionally has referred to her mice as "wee
sleekit timorous beasties."

When we hear a noise and know it is a mouse, it never alarms us. We know what they are like and they will be treated with kindness and set free if captured.

I believe a man speaks loudest of his spirituality when he silently holds and comforts an animal. We attempt this comfort toward mice through allowing the mouse to rest and recover under the bowl after having been caught by Rochester. I often talk to him quietly or say good-bye as Bob gently transports him in his bowl to the outdoors. The mouse is also permitted to rest and eat in any of Bob's mousetraps until his eventual release.

Several years ago I wrote an account in my journal of Bob's current adventure at that time only in mousetrap building. It was a rather extraordinary period and worthy of recording for posterity. I think you might be astounded by it all too and so I will share it.

Entry from Jan's Nature Journal—April 9, 1996

On March 14th—Bob built a better mousetrap and perfected it on March 15th. It was made from a Shop 'N Save All Fruit jar (empty) which is rather narrow and about five inches long. It was attached to a wooden base with a wooden platform inside so the mouse did not have to sit in its own waste. It had a wire mesh door that snapped shut—the mesh allowing the mouse to breathe when the mouse entered and tripped a device. On the night of Friday, March 15th, the day he perfected it—Bob set his trap downstairs in the bathroom with peanut butter inside. On Saturday morning he was in shock to find he had caught not one mouse, but two—in the same trap. This was incredible because it meant that both mice had to enter the trap at the same instant and tripped the spring together!!!! After admiring them and talking to them and giving them a blessing, Bob took them outside and released them. The interesting thing about these little mice was that they were brown and white (white tummies). We have never seen or caught this type before. Our mice have been little gray mice and/ or little brown voles. But never a mouse of brown and white. And here were two! Sunday he caught one mouse, and Monday March 18th again—he caught two mice in the same trap. They were adorable. Jessica and Renee were here and little Renee loved them and waved gently good-bye to them after I gave them a blessing. Bob took them outside and released them by the lake.

Starting Tuesday morning Bob set two traps and again caught another mouse. From then on for twenty-one days exactly (total) he caught at least one mouse every day. Sometimes two or three. There were two exceptions to this because there were two days the trigger mechanism did not work because the trap was not set properly, but we still had "visitors" to the traps that day because the food was gone. Each capture and release was accounted for and at the end of twenty-one days it totaled thirty-four. We believe that some of these mice might be repeats because they are always released unharmed and may have found their way back into the cottage. At the end of this period the traps continued to be set for several weeks without one indication that they were visited. We assume that we have completely depleted the mouse population— at least temporarily. During this entire period we never saw a mouse in our cottage or evidence that mice were around—despite the fact that Rochester patrolled regularly during this period. This is thirty-four captures in twenty-one days!

A man is truly ethical only when he obeys the compulsion to help all life which he is able to assist, and shrinks from injuring any thing that lives.
—Albert Schweitzer, *The Philosophy of Civilization*

Never since have we had anything occur that was similar. There are only certain seasons, usually late winter to early spring, that there is evidence of mice, by Rochester's reactions and what we experience.

There is a Buddhist vow to "save all sentient beings" and God has stated "Thou shalt not kill" in the Ten Commandments. Whoever added a codicil to either? With that in mind we three shall continue our rescue missions for mice here on Higher Ground.

We believe our mice are truly contented after experiencing this extraordinary day in the presence of one written about in this poem.

HOME AGAIN

A humane mouse trap in the basement rafter—
Has achieved success—and caught what it was after.
Through its wire mesh windows we felt the stare
Of the little creature we carried out in the air.

And the trap sits amidst three chrysanthemums
Blazing with color—and that about sums
Up all that has occurred.
And with not a squeak or a word—
The little mouse sits within enjoying his new home.
Breezes blow in from the lake—the trap rests in the loam
With its door wide open. The mouse aware of the reprieve
To his life through this humane trap refuses to leave.

For hours he has sat beneath the tall firs
And to our invitation to come forth—he demurs.
With supply of peanut butter and an orange jelly bean
He washes his paws and face and relaxes—ignoring the scene
Of two humans who periodically visit his trap—
With coaxings and camera—that they might snap
His picture as he comes through the door.
He's been through this before!
Dear humans—they don't know he's the same mouse
Trapped in the humane house
That was caught last Sunday
And stayed over 'til Monday!

The open door holds no allurement!
How he loves this securement!

JGK

Reflect and Journal

☆ Are you timorous like the mice? Perhaps only on occasion? What causes you to hurry about trying to remain unseen?

☆ Write about this in your journal and keep writing until answers surface. Write without stopping until you are guided to stop.

☆ Do you often feel the size of a mouse, diminished in some way in the land of giants? If so, explore this also in your journal.

☆ What makes you feel trapped? Is it something you should pray and write about at intervals on this retreat?

☆ Imagine the joy of the little mouse when set free! You too can be set free from anything imprisoning you. God can set you free.

☆ Pray about this—and then write about anything that comes to you in your journal as a result of prayer, even if it does not seem relevant.

☆ Has this chapter in some way made you look at mice differently if previous to reading it you had only negativity concerning them?

☆ Practice looking at *all* beings with the eyes of compassion no matter where you are or where you go. Continue to enter and explore these matters in your journal.

☆ Would you like to draw a picture of one of our mice using your crayons? Perhaps in doing this and creating a sweet image, it will help you to look at mice differently along with all I have shared with you. How about giving the mouse a cute name? Yes?

Come with me now after pausing to bring some refreshment to you—and we will touch on some matters of the heart. Take a little walk first if you would like to stretch—then join me. I will wait for you. Take notice of all the bees in the flowers. If you stand silently and observe they will never hurt you.

BEE

Buzzing bee
　　　in airy fold of the lavender
Bring me your sweetness and steadfastness—
　　　that I may cast seeds of love
　　　　　and grow to be a flower child
　　　　　　　imparting fragrance and laughter—
　　　　　　　　　hereafter.

JGK

A butterfly speaks now telling of her encounter with that bee. All of nature interchanges it seems and we are beneficiary to all of its sweetness and beauty.

BUTTERFLY AND BEE

I am the black and white butterfly
    languishing on the lavender.
A bee takes sudden flight
    from the center of the slender blooms
        and I tarry alone now—
           my wings shimmering in moonlight.
As the returning bee zooms
    downward into the lavender's depths—
I fly into the night.

Written for the butterfly and bee   JGK
I witnessed August 10, 1997

I have almost forgotten to tell you that we have had four more new blooms on the Christmas Cactus. It is a bewilderment as to why it has bloomed twice this year but such a blessing.

And, too, I have some sad news to share. This morning we found a dear bird dead on our deck under the feeders lying on its back. We do not know its name. Never in the history of our living here have we encountered a bird's death. It was extremely sad to me and we do not know the cause. Bob buried him in our cemetery with words of prayer for his eternal rest. It is very disturbing to find a sweet creature in this way, but we are thankful he can be buried in dignity. Now—to the matters of the heart I referred to. . . .

CHAPTER SIXTEEN

Remembrance

*And now here is my secret, a very simple secret: It is only with the heart
that one can see rightly: what is essential is invisible to the eye.*
—Antoine De Saint-Exupery, *The Little Prince*

TODAY IS MY DAD'S BIRTHDAY and had he lived and not died in 1977
shortly after he turned seventy-three, he would be ninety-five
years old. Because I miss him so much I continue to honor him in many
ways. But today I want to do something totally different. Inspired by a
movie I saw this past year titled *Fearless,* in which the two persons who
star in it buy gifts for their dead in order to aid in their own healing (the
woman for her baby who was killed, the man for his father who died), I
decide to do this also. This man and woman are survivors of an horrendous plane crash in which the woman's child has been a victim. Having
escaped death, now they are trying to help each other survive life in the
aftermath trauma they are experiencing. Together they shop, and today
I too shop.

After Mass we drive to a Rite Aid store on Route 16. When I had
prayed about a gift to give my Dad while in church, instantly came the
name of Larry McMurtry. This author is not one I have ever read or is he
in my realm of thinking, so I believe the direction has been given to me
by the Holy Spirit. My Dad liked to read and he occasionally enjoyed
westerns. In my mind previous to prayer, I had briefly had the thought to
buy him two books. I knew now after prayer I was to get a book by this
author whom I have never read but whom others enjoy immensely. As we

near the store another title comes to mind, *Travels with Charlie* by John Steinbeck. Years before my Dad had read this book and loving it so much he gave it to Bob to read. I read it when Bob finished and that copy long ago was put on our shelf.

In RiteAid I walk directly to the paper back book section, and though there are two racks filled with books, a copy of Larry McMurtry's *Dead Man's Walk* catches my attention. That title (there is only one copy) is the only title by this author, and I find that exciting. Because there is no selection, I believe in my heart this is the very book I am being directed to buy my Dad. It was waiting for me! Once it is in my hand I feel I am accomplishing a spiritual mission, and I too remember the exact shelf at home where that copy of *Travels with Charlie* sits waiting.

In my mind while driving to RiteAid I feel impressed to also buy Dad a sketch pad or a special tool. But suddenly on a shelf before Bob and me as I begin to look for a sketch pad, is a display of Hummingbird Feeders. Instantly in complete agreement Bob and I feel this feeder is the other gift to get Dad because he enjoyed watching the birds and caring for a small garden. With some inner overpowering emotion I purchase the book and birdfeeder.

Back at our cottage I immediately take *Travels with Charlie* from the shelf, an old paperback, and inscribe both the old book and the new with words of love to my Dad. I light five candles and display the books and the birdfeeder on the long wooden table, and also our gifts to Rochester whose birthday is being celebrated still, though it is three days previous. I take pictures of this display so I will always have them to keep, and then some too, with Rochester sitting next to the books. He is fond of books and is an author himself. And my Dad would have loved Rochester in life. He knows him only from heaven. Rochester is my angel.

Bob hangs the Hummingbird feeder out on the high wooden bar on the front deck where other feeders hang. It is up only ten minutes when Bob calls to me to hurry and see. A hummingbird already is visiting the new feeder and drinking the red sugar nectar Bob had prepared for it. It all happens so fast I miss the bird. Incredible! We did not see any hummingbirds last year, but the year before had many. We had smaller feeders for them then, none like this fine large globe one just placed there. And now a visitor appears minutes after the new feeder is placed outdoors!

I tell Bob it is the spirit of my Dad, coming in the form of a Hummingbird to greet us, and to thank us on his birthday. Minutes later the tiny wisp of a bird returns and I see this remarkable miniature creature in all his beauty. He flutters to each opening in the feeder and stays in our company. The feeder and its spiritual visitor are so precious and meaningful to me, and cause me to feel my Dad's presence.

The two books I carry upstairs to my lovely writing room and place them in view on a white chest. They are his and I say prayers over them. If anyone should want to read them while they stay here in this room on Higher Ground, that would complete the intention of these gifts. My Dad likes to share his books. And as I leave and descend the final stairs into the living room, Bob awaits and tells me he will borrow my Dad's *Dead Man's Walk* for he has never read this author. Synchronicity again—for I am planning to do the same. I sense Dad's smile upon us for his new two volume library.

The next day I have a desire to make a sketch of the feeder, the gift for my Dad and the birds. There are several colorful pictures of it on the carton and I sketch one. I am not very good at sketching spheres, but after much erasure I believe I have drawn it as good as it will ever be. My colored pencil has filled in the brilliant red of the fluid within the globe but cannot match the radiant globe of nectar that sparkles out on the deck in the sunlight. A little hummingbird puts his long beak into the yellow sculptured flowers around the base of the real feeder. We watch him. It suggests on the carton in the information given to put a trumpet bloom of some sort into the yellow plastic flowers and it will be even more an attraction to the hummingbirds. I have done that and replace them when they fall.

After drawing the globe for my own enjoyment and gluing it into my large nature journal I begin reading anew the information on the carton to add to our knowledge of hummingbirds. I already know it is the smallest bird in North America, but Bob and I do not know that this tiny bird can fly backwards and upside down. Many times we have seen them fly sideways, and Sunday we watched them hover as well.

The smallest hummingbird, the 2 1/4 inch Cuban Bee, weighs only two grams! The largest hummingbird, the 8 12 inch long Patagonia, weighs less than an ounce. I am inspired to read about them and learn even more in the tiny print on the carton. The hummingbird's wings beat over seventy-five times a second! Hummingbirds have an incredibly high metabolic rate and consume 1 1/2 times their weight in food each day. Imagine! And the male is the only hummingbird with streaked throat feathers. There is a type with more green coloring and also the ruby throated. They are such a gift to have here.

Upon reading this information I write in my journal and remember then I wrote a poem about hummingbirds several years go after Bob made a number of feeders for them out of small plastic bottles. I find it amongst my poems and begin to read. It seems new to me and I barely remember it. Now it seems appropriate to share.

THE WHIRLY BIRDS

Needle beaks so thin and slender
Miniature bodies—iridescent splendor.
Feathered helicopters soar and glide
Our questioning spirits they've defied.

Of sweet crimson nectar each is lover—
At feeders tiny beings hover.
Beating air—dear wings are blurred
Vibrations hum is softly heard.

Attracted by the color red—
And three and a half inches long—'tis said.
A title earned—duly conferred—
In all the world no smaller bird.

And yet they've won a big man's heart
Loving them right from the start—
Creating feeders in the basement
To hang on wire at window casement.

He is seen with beaming face—
When humming birds his feeders grace.

Inside the window like a lector—
He urges them to drink his nectar.

Dedicated to   JGK
the humming birds and Bob

I find it interesting the poem written years earlier, was in the same period as in the present when we purchased the feeder. The poem is written two days previous to my dad's birthday and one day after Rochester's.

What a thrill today to again see a little hummingbird come to the new feeder. I do not know if it was the same hummingbird that came twice today or a different one each time. Bob claims they were different ones yesterday because he saw green on one that he did not see on the other. Today the second one feeds long, then flies to our big front windows as we watch. He flutters there up close to the glass as if to greet us. I moves me deeply and I again murmur to Bob that I feel it is the spirit of my dad indicating "thank you" for the gifts we bought him yesterday.

But I share these happenings not to just speak about hummingbirds, but to speak also about those we love and who are in another realm. Buying gifts for my dad is heartwarming and the gifts bring his presence closer. I have not shopped for my dad in years and in doing this it truly helps me. I feel like the child again who surprises him, or the teenager, or the grown daughter who with my family celebrates his birthday with full heart. One of our daughters, Laurel, shares his birth date and these combined celebrations were ones of joy. To suddenly have the sweetness of his real presence missing is overwhelming. Now, through a unique celebration for those who died, depicted in a very tender movie that touched out hearts, dad once more is permitted to receive gifts of love from us on his birthday. And I shall do this again, and again.

Life's journey is circular it appears. The years don't carry us away from our fathers—they return us to them.

—Michael Marriott

FAREWELL

The last time I saw him
So ill and so pale—
He lay in a bed
Confined by a rail.

I kissed him then gently
Then walked to the door,
I glanced back to see him—
Another time more.

Our eyes met then briefly
On the rail lay his hand—
One finger raised weakly,
Knowing I'd understand.

That this sent his love—
It was all he could do,
I did not know then—
What my father knew.

With that one sweet finger
He bid me good-bye.
And each time I remember
I sit down and cry.

Dedicated to my father,   JGK
Ellis George Gray
Died August 21, 1977

The day after I finish this chapter about my dad, a synchronism occurs. In the Sunday paper is an article about an author who has written a book about the middle aged who lose parents. She claims that midlife "orphans" feel their parent's loss strongly particularly if the second parent dies close to the first. In my case my parents died one year apart, first my dad, followed by my Mother with a broken heart. Eighteen years later I still miss them, grieve unexpectedly at times with tears coming out of the nowhere and into the here, and I have the need to write about them often. Dozens of poems have been written for them along with much prose. I still had young children when they left, my youngest of six only eight years, the same age I was when I too lost the only grandparent I ever knew, my mother's mother. This author tells how people stand at her booksignings to tell their stories of loss to her, and how after losing both parents these middle-aged children truly feel "orphaned." As an only child I too experience this ever since their deaths. One person states that though she is without her parents a decade there is still an emptiness that she cannot describe. Author Jane Brooks too was overwhelmed by her mother's death, so overwhelmed by grief she worried something was wrong with her. Her father had died two years previous. The book is a result of that grief after six years and contains an exploration of her own experience as well as those of fifty-two fellow "orphans" she interviewed along with assorted grief counsellors and therapists. The name of her book is *Midlife Orphan* and one can learn more from her website also (www.midlifeorphan.com). In time I intend to investigate both.

Reflect and Journal

☆ Meditate for ten minutes or so in your place of retreat about this true story of mine.

☆ Is there someone you have cared for or loved deeply that has passed on, for whom you might like to buy a gift?

☆ Write about it in your journal for ten minutes without stopping.

☆ If you have been given directive, act upon what you have been shown through your writing as soon as possible.

☆ If you buy a gift for your loved one, record about the shopping and selecting of the gift and take a picture of it to put in your journal with your writing. You will have this event then thoroughly recorded to inspire you in future readings about this tender experience.

☆ Rent the movie *Fearless* if you think it would appeal to you as part of your retreat experience.

☆ Has another creature in any form ever caused you to believe it was a visitation from a loved one you miss and long to see? Even for a fleeting moment and a surreal sense? Perhaps reading this has caused you to remember. Write in your journal about it if it is so, so you do not lose the experience.

☆ ☆ ☆ ☆ ☆

My Dad would have loved to visit the place I am about to ask you to visit. I do not think you would expect to find such a place in the woods. It has been here near you all during your retreat. Come.

Before such a place existed however, this poem tells my dream for this cottage. It has come true since it was written some years ago.

WALL TO WALL

Books for walls
That is my dream,
In rooms and halls—
On every theme.

Great minds so deep
And so astounding—
Who could sleep
With books surrounding?

The written word—
Has silent power.
And my heart's stirred
Hour upon hour.

JGK
March 13, 1992

Be careful as you go to visit this special place. I hear a familiar noise approaching.

TRACTOR MAN

He's just below my window now.
He's on his tractor—and somehow—
I know his heart is singing well,
No words are said but I can tell
Because his face reflects his heart—
He's working at his special art—
Of moving earth, and shifting loam,
Creating beauty 'round our home.

In red plaid jacket and a cap
He circles now for one more lap.
His yellow tractor whirs and sputters—
Adding joy while he still putters.
The birds all sing—the ducks cry out—
And all the while he drives about—
Just like a kid upon a toy—
Because within he's still a boy.

Dedicated to Bob   JGK

Oh yes, and before you do make the visit, I must tell you that "Mrs. Mallard" had eleven baby ducklings, so tiny and precious, that she brought to visit us immediately. They could barely walk and toddled across our grass after her. The other lady mallard had five babies. We are thrilled with this new life. Perhaps some of the second mallard's babies were harmed by predators, but I pray not. We saw her in the lake several days later with the ducklings all in a line behind her. The male mallards are not with either female mallard. I hope they return to give support as they had been doing—and now to that visit. . . .

CHAPTER SEVENTEEN

The Bookshop

*The magic of a bookstore stems in part from the depth of literature
it contains, its surprises and mysteries—A magical store
has its own character and spirit and the browser gets the impression
that the store will never reveal all its mysteries.*
—Thomas Moore, *The Re-Enchantment of Everyday Life*

B   eneficence awaits
O   ccasions of reading
O   ffering opportunities
K   inship to the
S   acrosanct.

JGK

OOKS WERE A PART OF MY LIFE from my earliest childhood and my love for them grew deeper as I grew. Reading and writing were enchantments in my world and are increasingly so in the present. As a younger mother caring for and raising my six children, I extended myself through the giving of books and the writing of letters in order to reach out to others. This was discussed in great detail in my previous book, and both were a joy to do then as they are now. While my children were still at home I had two dreams that were not fulfilled, that of owning a bookstore and or operating a food kitchen in my home to feed the poor.

The first would have fed the heart and soul, the other the body and soul. As to where the bookstore would have been I knew exactly. A small corner building that was for rent not far from our own home, in my vision was a delightful bookshop in the middle of our town. It remained unused for years and seemed to be crying out for me to set up shelves of books within it.

And the food kitchen residence? That was to be in my own home! We had just had a new kitchen put in our home in the early 1980s, very large and open and lovely, after living with a very large family and small kitchen for years. I have told you about this enlargement briefly in Chapter Two. It seemed too wonderful not to share with those who had no kitchens or food, and I envisioned people coming down the path to our back door and into our cheerful pale blue and white kitchen. The pale blue to me was called "Blessed Mother Blue," though not a term that originated with me, and I felt she and the Lord would be there to help me prepare all the nourishing meals.

I had taken and completed a course for many weeks on Saturday mornings in the art of Macrobiotic Cooking. I learned this way of cooking and eating so that I might help a friend who had cancer, and also so that my own family might benefit. Many cancer patients have been healed through this manner of eating. It totally interested me and I personally cooked for a precious Peruvian woman who lived miles from me across the city of Philadelphia. My friendship with her is written about in detail in my book *Higher Ground* and also about this period in our lives. She and I could only communicate heart to heart for she could only speak Spanish and I only English and a stumbling Spanish. But so much love was shared between us as I cooked her macrobiotic meals for a period of many months. Eventually I taught her daughter Martha how to cook macro-biotically too, and she took her Mother back to Peru and in turn taught another woman in Peru how to cook in this way. This woman then cared daily for her Mother feeding her with this nourishing healing food. My Peruvian friend Magdalena had previously been dismissed from a Penn-sylvania hospital before I began preparing her meals, with the belief and certain knowledge given her from her doctor that she could only live a couple of weeks. There was nothing else they could do. Through this special cooking and diet she lived two and a half years and did not die of the cancer. It was a period of my life that was most moving and rewarding. Our deep faith that Magdalena and I shared in Jesus also created a bond between us when we were alone together that made the spoken word not really necessary.

Cooking in this way for my family was also a great experience. It was a time in my life when I enjoyed cooking more than any other period, even though it took twice as long to prepare the meals. Though our family did not remain strictly macrobiotic, Bob and I never ate beef from that time on and eventually became total vegetarians in '1989 for the sake of the animals, not our health. The Macrobiotic Diet was hard to implement with children and teenagers, and though they ate it, it was not always with joy, but Bob and I thoroughly enjoyed it. At times my teenage son George would bring several friends in the kitchen to watch me as I prepared these unusual dinners, and their respectful silence while George made hilarious remarks about the ingredients added to the fun of trying to feed my family in a very nourishing way even though they were not fond of the food. To this day I get teased about the aduki beans, a favorite of mine, but one of the courses that was disliked by George and my other children. Though they teased, I believe they understood how very nourishing and healing it all was and that I was trying to keep them healthy. It is ironic that it is George who most enjoys our vegetarian food now in recent years when he is here, and often buys some products for his family, even though they are not vegetarians.

A book that influenced me and others greatly in that period was *Recalled By Life* by Dr. Anthony Satillaro, a physician at Methodist Hospital in Philadelphia at the time. Later two of my daughters and I heard him speak at a local church. He had been at death's door because of cancer, but through eating this diet was healed. Because of this he went all over the world sharing his healing and his before and after x-rays, substantiating the Macrobiotic Diet. His healing also brought him back to his Christian Catholic Faith as well and he returned to attending daily Mass in thanksgiving for his health. The book is worth while to read, a man's spiritual and physical journey. This book was an inspiration and one of the reasons I wanted a "soup (Macrobiotic) kitchen" in my own new kitchen to help the poor.

Tape Ministry

Before these endeavors of which I dreamed, a bookstore or soup kitchen, I had a Christian tape ministry in my home for eight years. I have written about this in detail in my book *The Enchantment of Writing*. What began as a small act of love in taping the weekly sermons in our Methodist Church, turned into an enormous ministry. When once we taped the sermons and I would take them to local sick people who could not attend church to hear them, later I would be mailing out hundreds to those in spiritual need all over the United States! What began as a small two cassette player operation turned into multiple units plus a high speed duplicator, dozens of mailings daily, and continuous work. But a faith ministry filled with love that I operated in a front hall former coat closet under our living room staircase while still attending to my family's needs. This also required the writing of personal letters with each tape mailed, a large part of this ministry. It was an extraordinary eight year period. As I have shared in my previous book, my youngest daughter Janna, just a very little girl then, and her best friend and our neighbor Eileen (the same age) used to play in our yard outside my tape closet. They often rapped on the window and asked when I could come out and play. It was very tender and I remember it to this day with much love. They did not apparently think it strange that a mommy seemed to be forever in this small closet. It was also a place of meditation for me, for I could turn down the volume and be in silence while the messages were being recorded, or raise the volume to hear inspirational music and words. It was a prayer closet as well as a tape closet where I was surrounded by one small window and dozens of shoe boxes filled with cassette tapes. A small wooden kitchen chair that had belonged to my parents and that I had sat on as a child, was the only other item in there except for the matching kitchen table that held all the tape players that recorded the sermons. It was a wealthy time in Spirit to me. I thrived on doing this ministry. Eventually after many replacements and repairs by Bob on the equipment used, we decided it was coming to its natural end, this very marvelous eight year tape ministry that had helped so many in soul and spirit. Both the tapes and the letters, letters that were even more necessary than tapes, touched hearts, and I am so thankful for that period in my life. But because it ended, it was then that the dreams of either a food kitchen or book shop began to loom larger. Bob felt at that time they could not happen and discouraged them to my disappointment, perhaps remembering my eight years of disappearing into the front hall closet. (You can understand now why in Chapter 1 I suggested using a closet with a window as your sacred space.)

Dreams Fulfilled

It was only a matter of time that my biggest dream of writing became a reality and I began to write books. This had been my dream since childhood, long deferred due to marriage and the rearing of my six children. And that is my ultimate dream come true, that God would use me to write books that hopefully would touch hearts and souls and help others, a dream I will substantiate forever.

But—more recently God has given me answers to my prayers of long ago, delayed to be sure and in a different form than I had imagined, but an answer. Most definitely! What a surprise that it should come so many years later! I, along with Bob am now the owner of a bookshop! Not the one I imagined in the attractive small building in the center of my hometown of Jenkintown, Pennsylvania, but a bookshop in the woods! Not the type bookshop where people come in to browse and walk out with a bag of books, like the type I visit. No! Our bookshop is "on-line," on the world wide web, and operates out of the green painted trailer I have told you about earlier where Bob has his office and computer, and that he named "The Birchgrove" because of the lovely surrounding white birches. And the name of our bookshop? You will like the name. It is "The Enchanted Forest Bookshop." I welcome you to it anytime you wish.

When we decided to be shop owners we each made lists of possible names for our shop and I feel blessed one of the names I created was the chosen one. Since I feel like I live in "The Land of Enchantment," the name seems most appropriate. Our little shop only opened May 17th online, and now as I write on July 5th exactly seven weeks later we have sold 101 books. We just mailed out eight mailing bags of books this afternoon. It is a wonderful thing to do and I am thankful to at last have a bookshop, one totally different than I could ever have imagined.

Bob receives the orders and confirms them online, then we locate the books. Not unlike my tape ministry, I enclose little notes, though not extensive letters as before unless I am answering a question or giving additional information. I try to personalize the books in this way as well as wrapping each book in colorful tissue paper. Even though the majority of our books are not brand new, each is treated with care and respect. The paperbacks are color coded and displayed on a beautiful book shelf that wraps around our screened in porch on three sides and was created and built by Bob. I may have mentioned that book shelf earlier in another chapter. It holds hundreds of paperbacks of all subjects, non-fiction and fiction. The hard back books are kept in his "Birchgrove" trailer on shelves until ordered. I cannot begin to tell you the joy I have at now being the co-owner of a bookshop and being able to dispense books all over the country just as I used to do with cassette tapes. Each day we carry packages of books to the Post Office as I used to do with tape orders, and it is a great satisfaction of heart to be able to please people. If for some

Birchgrove—Bob's office and now our on-line bookshop,
The Enchanted Forest Bookshop

Paperbacks are color-coded and displayed on a book shelf that wraps around our screened-in porch on three sides

reason we cannot send a book in the exact condition they wish (though all are in good and mostly excellent condition) we always include an extra book as a little surprise. Since the bookshop is basically on our lovely porch and Rochester adores being out there in the warmer seasons, he is our little bookshop angel and guards those books just as he inspires and helps me to write my own books.

Our small cottage is filled with books on shelves in every room, shelves created by Bob, and books I will never part with and that I add to the volume of with new ones every two weeks when we go to Maine.

Thomas Moore has written in *The Re-Enchantment of Everyday Life:* "A book is a book, and in these times in particular, when information is becoming available in many different formats, especially on computers, it may be important to remember that a book is more than its text. It has a presence, and in that presence lies its magic."

To this I say Amen and Amen.

That we should now actually have a bookshop of our own is like the icing on the cake, for it is wonderful to dispense books to others.

THOUGHTS FOR FOOD

Books are other minds on earth—
I must search the shelves to find—
The ones that have the greater worth,
The books that best will feed my mind.

When I'm within a room of books
I seem to hear the silent voices.
They fill the crannies and the nooks—
Deep in my soul—and it rejoices.

I wait to feel that gentle prod—
Before selecting ones to read.
That soft impression comes from God—
For He knows best the books I need.

JGK

For years I inhabited book stores that fed me spiritually—three very unique ones that I lost one by one and each in a different state. During an extremely difficult decade in my life (the 80s) and into the 90s as well, I frequented the Encore Bookstore in Jenkintown, Pa. It was an outstanding store and part of a large chain. As I have written previously in another book, each Saturday night during those years I would go to my church for confession and remain for prayer. Following this I would visit the Encore Book Store which was like a church to me also, or at least an annex, not far from my home and church. Surrounded by books and alone in the aisles brought such joy and peace. Oh the books I purchased too in those years! I have every one! Often I would slip into the store during the week too, because I could not pass it on an other errand and not go in for at least a few minutes to have that aura come over me.

While this store existed I often visited an incredibly stocked and huge bookstore, "the Booksmith," in the large mall in Newington, New Hampshire. We would drive all night from Pennsylvania, (Nine hours and often more) and make only two stops, one for breakfast and one at this bookstore. Bob would give me one hour in the store sometimes joining me part of the time and other times napping in the van with Rochester. Oh the things I accomplished in that one hour in that store! Yes, I bought books always, but also made notes of things to purchase in the future. I would actually run through the huge parking lot and the mall when at last loose from the van so as not to take up valuable time of my "gift of the hour" in merely walking to the store. It was a little bit of heaven (well, actually a lot) when I entered the wide open front of that store. Up and down the aisles I would go to all my favorite subjects, and all the while feeling like I was carrying a bag of spiritual wealth when I walked back to the van. It was and still is spiritual wealth! While stopping there each time on our trip up to New Hampshire every several weeks (we commuted back and forth a great deal after Bob retired early) I became so dependent on this store for "soul food" as I did the Encore Store. But they were totally different in size and atmosphere. Soon I learned Encore was closing. It was a deep sadness to me. It had been there for me through difficult years and I paid my last respects to it with tears. It really was overwhelming to me.

Not long after the Booksmith also closed and I was again devastated. I went back repeatedly (50 miles south from our cottage) in its last weeks because all books were on sale, and I truly built up my own personal library with many purchases. The closing of this store as with Encore was extremely painful to me and the end of an era.

Eventually on our excursions to Sanford, Maine (I believe I told you that we, our lake and woods, are on the border of New Hampshire and Maine) I discovered a fantastic bookstore called Bookland. What happiness! For seven or eight years in the 90s I visited this store every two weeks when we went to Sanford to do other necessary errands, and also have the treat of going out to dinner in a little country restaurant. After dinner was my time in Bookland before we headed home. It was magical, and my purchases are all on shelves here in our cottage along with all the other books bought before. I made wonderful friends there, Rob, the manager and Cheryl a sweet saleswoman, and also they invited me to give two booksignings there of my *Compassion for all Creatures* when after several years of shopping in Bookland I told them I was a writer. Such sweet and lingering memories are attached to walking through those doors and spending a precious hour there browsing, and clutching the filled bag when I left. (Yes, always a filled bag.)

But as before, notice was given that Bookland was closing in early 2000. It truly was heartbreaking to me. As before to the Booksmith, I went to all its closing sales to purchase books of worth, until at last the door closed forever. Every two weeks when I go to Maine I still stand with my face pressed against the glass and peer in at the empty store that once held such wonders, and also delightful friendships, and the tears come. It was a holy place. Cheryl and I still see each other occasionally in Maine, and we write, and we e-mail. We will always be friends no matter where she goes. But our bookstore is gone! So tragic!

I found one other little bookstore after Bookland closed in Springvale, Maine, a small town before driving into Sanford, and after shopping in it only four weeks it too closed! I was in disbelief to find the sign on the door when I returned. What is happening to our much needed book stores! One needs the store, the aisles, books in our hands, and too in the bags when we leave. Bookstores are for the soul and mind. Nothing can replace them!

So you see, I need a bookshop desperately and I long to "feed" others, so we have created our own. I believe, however, that soon another bookstore (not online) will appear, for I am praying. In fact each time I press my face against the glass at the empty Bookland and lay my palms on the cold panes, it is my prayer that it will soon be once again filled with books. Bookaholics need books, you see. But it is an addiction so worthy and healing to the soul.

Where would we be without books? Nothing can ever replace the joy of books; holding them in your hands, reading, absorbing, and imagining, and learning. And rereading them, something I do constantly!

Years ago in the early 90s I broke free of reading only spiritually, something that fed my soul for years. While raising my family my reading time was limited and I felt this was the most important type reading for me then. A close friend Dottie soon gave me a lovely novel and I did not think I would be able to read it, but I forced myself. It was a tender story that totally captivated me and from then on I began to broaden my reading interests. This poem expresses these discoveries found in books that opened up new reading adventures in my life. Nonfiction is still my favorite however, especially the spiritual, animals, and nature, books concerning writing and the writing life, but oh, so many more.

FORGIVE ME!

I never knew that I who read
      the spiritual classics—and who feed
On hallowed soul food such as these,
      (and biographies, journals—yes, they please)
Could enjoy a mystery now and then;
      in fact I find I have a yen
For marvelous historical novels too
      and now have changed my point of view
That God cannot be found in fiction.
      (said aloud—that would cause friction!)
For I find God in all I read
      and very humbly now concede—
That I can hear Him speak so softly
in other books—not just the lofty.

Dedicated to my friend   JGK
Dottie Borkowski

    Who would suspect that here amongst the trees and gardens, the birds, bees, butterflies and lapping lake, that there is an enchanted bookshop in a little green trailer encircled by birches? A few feet away across the grass, is the screened-in porch containing all our additional wonderful inventory that we can enjoy seeing in display when we sit and eat breakfast on the porch or come out before sunset to eat a late dinner. Just being in the presence of books is an enchantment. And Rochester's presence adds charm to it all. So many old bookshops have a cat as a companion or mascot but Rochester is part owner, of course, to this one. You will even find him on the cover of two very fine books sold here, written by his companion and the feminine co-owner of this shop. Actually, he is somewhat of a celebrity.

    Though you and I many never meet in person, we do meet in spirit through books, this one and the others I have written, and that too is another precious thing about books. Readers and authors meet through the expressing of heart thoughts and the written words on the pages, and the intermingling of their spirits.

This poem written for Bob explains his fine creations.

A Wealth of Shelf

My husband's a builder of shelves
On which are housed "other selves"
We allow to live in each room.
And while some might assume
The shelves are for storage and convenience,
They actually symbolize my husband's lenience
For my obsession with books.
He creates shelves in all crannies and nooks—
For the presence of great souls and minds—
That I term "blessings" and "finds."
These then we consume with a need—
For it's for learning and pleasure we read.

I know my husband will continue creating—
For in his heart he's just basically waiting—
For the next books I bring through the door—
Then you will hear his hammer once more.

Dedicated to Bob with love—   JGK
builder of shelves   August 29, 1996

I know you would enjoy visiting our Enchanted Forest Bookshop and you can, for I will close this chapter by giving you our address. But even if you do not actually visit it online, you can close your eyes as you have done before and see yourself in spirit here in the woods. And in doing that you can browse through and read any of my books here in the cottage or on the porch through imagination. They are here to be shared with you on your retreat. Please enjoy them.

Reflect and Journal

☆ Are books important in your life and if not, why not? In your journal write about a books from your childhood that left a lasting impression.

☆ Now write about another book that you read as a teenager or adult that has remained a fond memory. Perhaps you will want to find a copy and reread it if you do not own it, to see if it has the same effect upon you now. Write in your journal about this if you should reread it. Often books fondly remembered become dearer to us upon rereading, and sometimes they no longer interest us.

☆ Write in your journal about any dreams that you had that did not materialize, such as my "food kitchen" or neighborhood "bookstore" did not for me. Do you still carry the disappointment? Perhaps you have never written about them and put them to rest.

☆ Now write about a dream you have now that hopefully will come to pass. What can you do to facilitate the dream into becoming a reality aside from prayer?

☆ Did you ever have a secret place like my closet where I made tapes and prayed? Write in you journal about it. Perhaps you had forgotten it until reading about mine. Did it enhance your life or was it detrimental to your well-being? In writing it all out healing will come if there was negativity involved.

☆ Like my three beloved bookstores, what in your life "closed down" on you that had fed you spiritually or emotionally and gave you joy? Was it hurtful? Did you ever journal about it non-stop for fifteen to twenty minutes to let it all pour out on paper and give you peace? Just writing about my bookstore closings here helps me anew, even though I had written about each in my journals.

☆ Close your eyes in meditation and visit our bookshop here on our porch in the woods, or one that has meaning to you elsewhere. Be specific in seeing titles. Perhaps the ones that surface in your mind are ones that you are being led to read or reread. Spend at least fifteen minutes in meditation amongst books. You will be blessed.

☆ You may visit our online store, The Enchanted Forest Bookshop, by accessing www.half.com and putting in the name of this book. Or you can send us E-mail: enchantedforestbooks@yahoo.com Welcome!

☆ This verse describes our Bookshop. Perhaps you too can write a poem about a book you love, or the entire concept of books in your life.

> The Bookshop has a thousand books,
> All colors, hues and tinges,
> And every cover is a door
> That turns on magic hinges.
>
> —Unknown

UH-oh, I hear that cricket again! I was hoping he would not bother you while we were discussing books. Did you notice him?

HELP!

> There's a cricket with us here—
> And he loves to sing I fear.
> He's been chirping all night long—
> We have memorized his song.
>
> He's unceasing through this day—
> Can it be he's planned to stay?
> There's no discussing it with him—
> We are captive to his whim!
>
> I've never known such deft persistence—
> We've gone limp from worn resistance!
> Help!

JGK

I think he likes to be near books too! Rochester often enjoys a cricket chase but he never harms one. He is intrigued by them.

When you are free after reading this chapter and doing your Reflecting and Journaling, perhaps you would like to sit outdoors on the grass, or on the dock, or in my prayer chair at night under the moon and stars. Meditating at night in this way is incredibly moving. You will feel like you are actually here. I have done this in spirit many times while still living in Pennsylvania. You may want to write about it later in journal as I do. I have even taken pictures of the moon.

Come into my thoughts now about the moon and stars that bless this precious "land of enchantment" I love so.

Just turn the page.

CHAPTER EIGHTEEN

Stars, Moon and Sunsets

O give thanks to the Lord of Lords,
for his steadfast love endures forever;
Who by understanding made the heavens,
who made the great lights;
the sun to rule over the day,
and the moon and stars to rule over the night,
for his steadfast love endures forever.

—Psalm 136 : 3-9

CELESTIAL PAGEANT

I am the brightness of the moon lighting up the darkness—
    My aura shines out upon the heavens
And the stars twinkle.
We together give a celestial pageant as gift—
Showering love and moon beams and stardust
Upon all creatures and mankind below.
We illuminate oceans and seas and earth
And radiate the flowers with our presence.
In sunshine they will blossom and flourish

Giving beauty and light—
As we give to the night.

JGK

Stars

In our former home in Pennsylvania our lifestyle was different. We were indoors more in the evenings, yet we were outside enough there at night over the many years to know that in comparison, the heavens here in New Hampshire are a phenomenon. Whether it be the difference in atmosphere making visibility truly clearer, or the huge expanse of openness that we are afforded here in the natural world as opposed to the suburbs of a city, I cannot say. But there is a difference, so remarkably so, that it has overwhelmed us continuously since this cottage in the woods became ours. The beauty of it all struck us from the first evening spent in this state.

We have loved the stars too fondly to be fearful of the night.
—inscription in crypt of Allegheny Observatory,
University of Pittsburgh

It is written that there are billions and billions of stars, but that we can only see about 2000 of them because most of the stars are so far away. And it is recorded that even great astronomers through their mighty telescopes cannot see all the stars, yet still they know they are out there with a certainty. But it seems to us that we are witnessing these billions (trillions?) of stars while standing right outside our cottage, heads back in awe, in every season.

STARS

S   prinkled across the heavens of night
T   rillions of infinitesimal dots of light
A   stonish seekers
R   everently
S   ubdued.

JGK

The stars have blessed us so much here these past twenty four years that we never get over their awesomeness, never take them for granted, and I continually write poems about experiencing their grandeur and their affect upon us. So many significant things too, are associated with the stars, and glorious night skies here with brilliant moon. The poems arrive to help me express myself, and my journals are filled with writings about the utter joy of living here and being privileged to attest to the wonder of it all night after night. So many personal memories, both beautiful and sad. Never will I forget the night we arrived here after my dad's sudden death and his funeral service and burial in Pennsylvania. I climbed into my prayer chair under the stars and trees by the lake and sat numbed. And then the flood of tears came that I had somehow stored within in my shock and grief up until that moment of ascension into my prayer chair. I wept and wept and felt closer to God here beneath His stars in my deep sorrow.

> *Listen a while, the lake by night is a lonely woman, a lovely woman, circled with birches and pines mixing their green and white among stars shattered in spray clear nights.*
>
> —Carl Sandburg

Night after night Bob and I have been appreciators of this exquisite beauty and are continually drawn outside to view the stars even in very cold weather. But on summer evenings we often roam down to the dock to view them all by the lake.

Surveying them from my prayer chair is other-worldly, for wrapped around by trees and high plants and green growth of all varieties below, and covered by a night sky blanket studded with a million (or so it seems) sparkling stars, I seem to be in another dimension. Through the years I have sat there for hours in the evenings in the silence of God, the night and woods, only the insects, bird song, and unknown sound keeping me company. Deep meditation and contemplation occur. It is written; "God determines the number of stars; And gives to all of them their names" (Psalm 147:4).

Too, we have sat out under the stars when our large family has gathered while on vacations and told stories around a campfire. Memorable events. Last year two of our older grandchildren Leslie and Jesse came up when school was out with six of their friends and pitched three tents to the left of our cottage by the lake. They too were awed by the stars and sat up half the night each night under the display. Our son George, before his marriage, used to gather with friends from Jenkintown, and Fordham (where he was working at the time) for a long weekend here each July. We were not living in New Hampshire permanently then, so we always went back to Pennsylvania while they were here so they could use the entire cottage as well as pitch tents. They too were mesmerized by the night skies above and spent hours out on the dock each evening so as not to miss the wonder. George and his wife Valerie later gave us a marvelous telescope so we might begin to view the stars in a new way and learn more about them, a gift deeply appreciated.

SUMMER STARS

Bend low again, night of summer stars,
So near you are, sky of summer stars,
So near, a long armed man can pick off stars.

—Carl Sandburg

In my previous book I shared a poem that expressed how we are affected by the gloriousness of the stars, and it is a writing I would like to share again with you also. I am attempting to express the inexpressible. Though it was written several years ago I have not come any closer to trying to exclaim the awe and gratitude we feel under these heavens at night.

STAR OWNERS

Returning from Sanford, Maine
On dark country road devoid of cars—
Our headlights guiding us on the lane
And the heaven above packed tight with stars—
We felt alone there on this planet—
And driving into our State of Granite
And through our woods so black and still—
Saw the lake at last—just down our hill.

And there—under majesty of velvet dome
We stood silently outside our home—
Heads back—gazing into God's vast spaces—
While millions of stars shone on our faces.

It seemed we owned the world and night—
We two together in starlight.

JGK
from *The Enchantment of Writing*

Previous to writing this poem another was penned several years earlier, one of many, again trying to share the awesomeness we perceive. This latter one was written telling of returning home on a snowy evening in January. As before, though I may not seem at a loss for words, I truly am. This poem is only an attempt to capture the beauty and the emotions we were experiencing.

COMING HOME ON A WINTER'S NIGHT

As we walk through snow so deep—
Descending crunchy hill quite steep—
We savor stillness all around us,
O—the night it does astound us!

Here in woods alone together
In most frigid winter weather—
We are grateful for the essence
Of Our Lord's most Holy Presence.

We approach our home and lake
Thanking God for each snow flake.
Falling delicately on our faces—
Leaving magical wet traces.

O—the glorious black above—
Is His Velvet Heaven of Love,

As human soul reflects through eyes—
So God's Stars are His Disguise

Sister Moon is in her place—
We commune with outer space—
View His wondrous heavenly display
Vow anew to Our Lord's Way.

JGK

As we live with this gift of the night heavens we are truly blessed. That after all these years we still speak of it, write of it, and silently gaze in wonder, should perhaps convey the splendor of it all.

Those who are wise shall shine like the brightness of the sky, and those who lead many to righteousness, like the stars forever and ever.
—Daniel 12:3

This next poem tries to again say that what we see above is incomparable, that no earthly imitations or attempts of lighting the night can ever compare with the heavenly, and the work of God.

NIGHT SKIES IN NEW HAMPSHIRE

Thousands of lights bursting in the night sky—
Lights—crackling, popping, exploding—that defy
The imagination in color and intensity—
Each with the possible propensity
For multiplying into infinitesimal sparkling dots—
With flaming comets of brilliance racing across in knots
Before them—and lengthening into streams of fire—
Descending at great speed only to expire
Into the air causing cheers of delight—
From those of us below on this fourth of July night.
And then we returned to our woods and lake—and in the deep dark
Stood gazing up at the splendorous arc
Of luminosity, millions of stars—radiant, resplendent

Filling the heavens—each singular pendant
More intense and glorious than any man-made meteoric spray—
And we are transfixed in awe at God's dazzling display.

J.G.K.

And yet after all is exclaimed, there is still yet one earthly star who
lights up my life and delights, and is an expression of God as well as His
personal blessed gift to me. I am sure He is pleased I am overjoyed with
His gift.

MY STAR

I gaze up at the heavens
    and see the brilliant, shimmering stars
        in the night sky—
And in wonder feel that I
    am one
        with all creation.
And yet this inward elation
    cannot compare
        to what I feel
When I gaze upon the radiant star
    who shares my nights and days—
        shining his love in tender ways
            everywhere we are!
He is my Angel of Light
    my one true star—
        more beauteous
            than all the stars of night.

For Rochester   JGK
with inexpressible love on his birthday
May 30, 1998

Rochester asleep on a quilt in the writing room

As I have written in my previous book, it is not unusual that I should see Rochester as a STAR in my life for he has brightened my heart and soul all these past years, and travelled a healing path with me. He has brightened my existence with the light and height and depth of his love and reveals God to me.

When I read the following lines of a poem by William B. Yeats that I have always been moved by and copied into my journals, I think of the "two men" I share life with under the stars.

Had I the heavens' embroidered cloths,
Enwrought with golden and silver light,
The blue and the dim and the dark cloths
Of night and light and the half-light,
I would spread the cloths under your feet;

But the poet goes on to say he is poor, and has only his dreams to spread under the feet of the one he writes to and asks they tread softly on his dreams. We three share dreams under the stars and moon, and tread softly.

Star Envoys

Reach high, for stars lie hidden in your soul, Dream deep, for every dream precedes the goal.

—Pamela Vaull Starr

Stars have played a roll of importance in my life in another way, though not like the actual stars on high. For the past seven years I have experienced the enchantment of being surrounded by stars, star cut from yellow poster board to symbolize the glowing and sparkling stars of reality. With the twinkling stars above so present it gives me joy to create stars for others. Mine are carefully and personally cut out and seem to be in a dancing pose. I have written about this star ministry in great detail in my previous book, *The Enchantment of Writing,* and even illustrated the dancing star for readers to copy. The dancing yellow cardboard stars bring messages of love and healing as do the real stars on high. Each year the number stars I must cut out has increased and now is approximately 400 in number. Since each star must be cut by hand it is quite time consuming but is a work of love. Each star is prayed over by myself and a loving and uplifting word is written on its surface. Each star is accompanied by a "star letter" that explains the ministry and the affects it will hopefully have on recipients. Since this ministry is explained in my previous book and invites each reader to consider the possibility of perhaps creating a star ministry also, I will not write all the details here. I can only say it is a ministry that blesses others and myself and my family. I have also included the "Star Letter" in my previous book that you are free to copy if you wish if you should desire to have such a ministry. You do not have to do it all on a large scale. My ministry just grew over the years. My friend Ginny who is a pastor in a church in New Jersey first started the ministry there for her congregation and I felt it worthy to do also. Perhaps you will enjoy reading about the creating of it all in my other book. It is a blessing to self to do it, not to mention the recipients of the stars. All my "stars" (star words) are right here on my desk from all the years I have been receiving them, and each has had special significance in my life. Ginny used to send me a star each year until I began my own "star giving." It is an outreach ministry like my former tape ministry, though far less expensive to do. In the "star ministry" one only needs yellow poster board and postage (well, envelopes too). But if you keep the ministry confined to local family and friends, you will not need any postage. Please read about it if you can. It is very meaningful I promise you, or I would not have written about it briefly here in this book after having written at length about it in *Enchantment*. Stars bless in all their various forms and are expressions of the Divine.

> *When it gets dark enough, you can see the stars—*
> —Lee Salk

We know that through the years the tiny points of light we see in the dark sky above us have been used to plan navigational journeys, and that they are a dependable and trusted means of guidance. Perhaps the stars are trusted much more than all the instruments of sophistication. Just as each one of us is a gift and has meaning as no other human on earth, so each star has meaning. It can be twinkling and shining all alone up there in the heavens or be part of a well known constellation, but the star has a reason for being.

The stars can teach us this as we gaze upward, that we too are like the stars. In fact we are each gifts, each a star of God. And we should never feel alone for we share the gloriousness of the heavens and the glittering stars with all around us and we are His. We each, like each star, have a purpose. These thoughts have been inspired by my own experiences and the healing affects of the stars upon me, and by a brief meditation in Night Light by Amy Dean that confirms my own reflections. Keep your eyes upon the stars, please.

FULL MOON

M ajestically suspended in blackness
O pulently beauteous
O racularly mysterious
N onplussed we gaze skyward.

JGK

In my lifetime much attention had been paid to space. In a personal sense our youngest daughter Janna was born two months before man landed on the moon in July 1969 and our son George was born on the very day John Glenn orbited the earth, February 20, 1962. Many boy babies in Temple University Hospital in Philadelphia, Pennsylvania, were given this famous astronaut's name that day, or portions of it. I could not watch with all the world because I was giving birth, but I did see many accounts of it later as this enormous achievement in history was reviewed and discussed. That this famous man should again go up into space last year was a wonder after thirty-eight years following his first space encounter. Many other brave men and women have also made such journeys since then, some very sadly losing their lives in doing so. Neil Armstrong's "That's one small step for man, one giant leap for mankind" on the moon gave us all a new perspective when viewing the moon, one of extreme awe. Not that it was not there before as we looked up at this amazing light, but to now realize men have actually travelled there and walked upon it just boggles the mind, or it surely does mine.

> *The moon rains out her beams, and heaven is overflowed.*
> —Percy Bysshe Shelley

BY THE LAKE

O beautiful moon
Shining on me
Streaming your light
From eternity

Creating a pathway
Straight from the sky
Out onto the water
Beckoning me nigh

Did you wish me to tread
Ever lightly your beam
Or am I imagining
As if in a dream?

Oh, now I see clearly
Why you gloriously glow
God's in His heaven
And you're telling me so.

JGK

When we view the moon here in its various forms, each so magnificent, above the trees and lake, it is never done casually or in a detached way. It just never ceases to amaze us. We pause and spend time in looking upwards when outdoors or deliberately go outside to see it. Like the stars it is a phenomenon here.

Even though I do not have a special camera for taking pictures of the moon I still do it occasionally when the weather is clear and the moon is especially awesome. I just must. I just did it again last evening! The pictures mean something to me personally and always turn out. As I write I am looking at a picture I took several years ago while standing on my prayer chair platform on a summer's evening. It is a meaningful picture to me with a full moon shining and the branches of the trees in the foreground but not obliterating the moon in any way. But there is an image in front of the tree to my left, one of the three trees that surrounds my platform. It is a white image of an angel, with the edge of the form in the lower portion slightly aglow. I have written about this in the chapter on "Trees" in this book. Thomas Moore, in *The Re-Enchantment of Everyday Life,* has written:

> *Trees are the teachers, revealers, containers, companions, and protectors of the sacred - and Divinity resides somehow in the marrow of a tree and in the sanctuary made of the overarching branches.*

Is this Angel seen because of the full moon, and why did I not experience her with the naked eye? Was I too busy taking pictures? I think yes. Or was I only meant to know the image later through the picture as a means of letting me know of the Angel's existence, and to believe while not experiencing it in actuality, but only through the lens. Bob tries to explain it away offering numerous unethereal possibilities, but I would be disappointed if he did not because we are so different in nature. Meanwhile this picture blesses me daily and I sense the presence of the Angel as I sit in my prayer chair. How could I doubt?

A number of years ago my friend Jeanne sent me a magical greeting card with a painting on it titled "The Moon Fairy" by H. Kaulbach—circa 1918. It is so lovely. It is a picture like "The Moon Fairy" (and the photos I took) that makes my heart dance. This picture card too is in a frame.

Through poetry I will describe her to you, the only way at the time I could fully capture all I felt in my heart about this mystical picture when I received her in the mail. Perhaps some readers may be familiar with this painting.

MOON FAIRY*

The sky is black—but you are there—
Subtle image fair, and long, dark hair
Descending upon your pale pink iridescent gown—
A single sparkling star tiara as a crown.

Sitting barefoot in the slender arc of the quarter moon
with delicate grace
And charm and tenderness upon your child-like face—
You look gently toward earth with love.
Your left hand scatters glistening stardust from above.

Luminous clouds in dark heavens create a soft light—
Suggesting your mystical presence on this magical night.

Dedicated to Jeanne Quinn   JGK

Crescent Moon

When the moon is a crescent as in this poem, the unlit part of the moon is often visible. This is called earthshine and is due to light reflecting off Earth's atmosphere. It is also called "the old moon in the new moon's arms."

Viewing tips: Earthshine is visible just before and after new moon.

I have learned these facts from the June newsletter of the Protestant Community Church in Medford Lakes, New Jersey sent to me (monthly) by my friend Ginny who is Pastor there. Ginny of the STARS!

It is written that the new moon is a time of dreams, vision and magic. This seems to be so in the vision of my Angel. A fine book based on the moon created with empty pages to use as journal but filled with inspiring thoughts and information to motivate writing and prayers and actions is *Prayers to the Moon: Exercises in Self-Reflection* by Kay Leigh Hagan. It has insightful quotations and knowledge too about the moon at the bottom of pages. You may be interested in this book.

> *On the road through the clouds*
> *Is there a short cut*
> *To the summer moon?*
>
> —Den Sute-Jo

I share with you now another poem, and though written several years ago I remember that night as if it were last night for the beauty of it. The moon was the magic for it all, lighting up each detail I saw in an otherworldly fashion.

Please share this scene with me now on your retreat through rereading the poem, then closing your eyes and letting your imagination create for you that artistry of a moonlit summer's night.

MOONLIGHT ARTISTRY

In the night cool winds blow.
Outside the window wooded hill is aglow
With moonlight, and I upon my bed in the dark
See the ferns sway and the birches' white bark—
Captured like an art print in the window frame.
I search in the cobwebs of my tired brain to give it a name.
On the sill—my cat sits silhouetted against the glimmering green—
Having left his sleep upon my legs to be immersed in this scene.
Breezes drift in washing over my mind

Cleansing it from the heat of the day, and I find
Mystical moments in the hush and the quiet.
God gave these as gifts. I cannot deny it.

JGK

It was through this same window at sunrise that I was privileged to
see the massive majestic male moose with full rack of antlers pass across
that hill and before my eyes as if he too was an art print framed in my
window.

And from another perspective I have been encompassed by refreshing night beauty through the open sliding glass doors in the front of our
cottage and the glowing moon above it all.

WOODLAND NIGHT REFRESHMENT

From our little cottage looking out through the trees
On this glorious night I am cooled by the breeze—
Washing through softly sliding doors open wide—
Causing wind chimes to dance and sway and collide.
Mystical music hauntingly drifts—
Out onto the lake—and rises and lifts—
The tinkling tune to the summer moon—
Seen through the branches; while wail of the loon
Eerily calls out, my heart hears it resound—
As I gratefully drink in woodland night so profound.

Dedicated to Higher Ground   JGK

Reach for the moon. Even if you miss you will be amongst the stars
                                                    —Unknown

The moon has been a great blessing and source of inspiration to us
since being a part of these woods. We have experienced the moon here
in ways as never before elsewhere, and we are grateful. It is a gift from God
for us.

The stars pass
The moon passes
Blue clouds pass above the
  mountains to the north
The years go by.

—Empress Jito

Sunsets

Give me the splendid silent sun with all his beams full-dazzling.
—Walt Whitman

OBSERVATIONS

At sunset pale pink clouds float in the sky.
Three quarter moon hung in pale blue is up on high.
Coral streaks run through the heavens overhead—
As we wait for sun to sink and go to bed.
Soon bright stars will be accompaniment to moon—
I will sit beneath the splendor—while the Loon—
Calls to all the creatures—the night
Is descending in the gloaming at twilight.

JGK
August 24, 1993

The sunsets here on the lake are incredible and I have been photographing them for years. An exceptional one has appeared in a magazine of a corporation, submitted by a family member related by marriage. When published she sent us copies and one is framed in our living room.

One entire album is filled with nothing but sunsets, and yet each different. The orange and red sunsets of deep intense color are overwhelming. In some of the photos the lake is as brilliant in depth of color as the heavens, and if one reverses these photos and views them upside down it is as if the lake is the sky. There is no telling them apart.

Bob at sunset on Lake Balch

Mark Twain has written, "One must stand on his head to get the best affect in a fine sunset, to bring out all its beauty."

On numerous occasions there have appeared shapes of angels in the heavens that are duplicated in the reflections upon the lake. One cannot doubt these forms are angels. Several years ago I took a picture that amazed us, so defined was an angel in the heavens, with smaller ones about the larger. We had duplicates made to use as our Christmas card that year and I wrote a descriptive poem to accompany it. The photograph had an impact on many friends, and family too, and some even wrote telling us of other angels they saw in other areas of the picture. We had an 8 x 10 enlargement of it made that blesses us to this day. I feel it is a Holy Picture, images given to us from God. Is it any wonder I am forever accompanied by my camera around these grounds?

I will share with you the poem that we sent with the cards telling of the night I took the picture.

ASSEMBLAGE OF ANGELS

Standing on our deck and looking out onto the lake
We saw the fiery red upon the waters that only comes from the wake
Of a setting November sun. We gazed in awe of the sight
That was transforming this day to translucent twilight—
When suddenly a new brilliance spread over the sky
Filling the heavens with intense color to signify
And announce an assemblage of Angels engaged in healing prayer
For the bestowal of blessings upon humanity—
and God's creatures everywhere.

When at dawn or sunset a glory of variegated clouds convenes—
It is Angels holding converse—and color is their means.

Dedicated to the Angels   J.G.K.

Angels abound on Higher Ground. I believe that to be true. I record
each moment experienced in their regard in my Angel Journals. Naturally some entries are about Rochester, for he too is an Angel. Although
I mention Bob frequently in these journals, HE IS DEFINITELY NOT
AN ANGEL. Much has been written about these angel signs here in my
two previous books. It is a comfort to be a believer in their existence and
the signs that are given. I would not want to be a non-believer in Angels.

And sunsets too are gifts of majesty unlike anything in this world.
They are given as individual gifts of unique beauty, each in colors that
cannot be duplicated, - from intense reds and oranges to paler shades of
pink, gold, peach and purple, and other tones not known by earthly
names. They turn the lake with surrounding trees into a Holy, mystical,
magical expanse, another realm unidentifiable by name but recognizable
by one's own soul and spirit.

Reflect and Journal

☆ Has the night ever been menacing or sorrowful to you, a period when
   sadness makes its appearance? If possible sit out under the stars and

moon alone in a quiet place. Ask God to heal your heart and mind and believe it is happening. Put your head back and feel the grandeur of the night sky upon you.

☆ If you are living where you cannot do this, seated in meditation in your sacred place imagine our lake and the heavens I have described. See yourself by the lake or in a prayer chair. Actually feel the stars and moon shining upon you. Imagine your face aglow and God sending you healing rays of light. Accept this healing—and thank Him.

☆ Write down your experience in your journal, whether it occurred in actuality outdoors or in imagination in your sacred place. Record every detail so that you never doubt the healing given you and so you will often repeat your time spent under the night sky in whatever form you experienced it.

☆ If you have never paid much attention to the heavens at night because of where you live perhaps, why not try to change? Possibly if you think of it all as a gift you will want to unwrap it in spirit each night and accept it as a present and allow it to become more a part of your life. Begin to learn the meaning of wonder in a deeper way. Look forward to seeing the majesty of the stars and moon nightly.

☆ Is there an earthly star in your life? Write about that person or animal companion in your journal or in a poem relating him/her to the stars. Had you ever thought of him/her in that way before?

☆ Does having a "star ministry" intrigue you in any way? Pray for guidance in its regard.

☆ Do you presently "moon" over someone or something in your life? Write about it in stream of consciousness writing. It will help you.

☆ This very night if it is clear, try to view the moon with a new perspective, in actuality. If you cannot be outdoors then again, do this in spirit by the lake. Ask for a message and listen in silence.

☆ Write in your journal what you were given. Begin to build upon it in the future if it was a directive or words of guidance. Do this often under the moon prayerfully. God is there speaking in the inner stillness of your heart.

☆ Be more attentive to sunsets and keep a camera with you if possible. Draw from memory a recent sunset you experienced using crayons, paints or colored pencils. Draw a scene of the moon and stars also that you saw if you wish. Drawing this will make you feel closer to your prayers expressed while you stood beneath them, in reality or in spirit. You may wish to display them.

Perhaps now go out under the stars and moon in reality, or sit in your sacred space and imagine yourself under the night sky on the shore of Lake Balch. Envision yourself in the prayer chair. Feel the breezes. I will share little vignettes with you about the lake.

CHAPTER NINETEEN

The Lake

I will arise and go now, for always night and day I hear lake water
lapping with low sounds by the shore; While I stand on the roadway,
or on the pavements grey, I hear it in the deep heart's core."
—Wm. Butler Yeats, "The Lake Isle of Innisfree"

THIS POEM BY YEATS, the third verse especially, has had great mean
ing for me through the years as I stood on the pavements in
Pennsylvania while in my mind, the low sounds of lapping lake water in
New Hampshire were deep in my heart's core.

The Lake

Years ago in the late mid-eighties Bob and I sat by the lake in
Autumn on one of our extended trips up here following his early
retirement. I had not written poems in several years and the scene we
were seeing before our eyes was so lovely on this crisp day. Both Bob and
my friend "Friar Francis" encouraged me to write poetry and this following poem resulted after the sweet suggestion that Bob made that the
floating Autumn leaves were like little boats. The poem always brings
back happy memories of that day and when we were beginning our new
life in travelling back and forth to New Hampshire. It was also when I
began to write my first book, *Higher Ground*, and we two prepared
another book we had done together in the 1970s titled *Whispered Notes*.

The story of this latter book and its long delay is written about in detail in my *Journal of Love.* Perhaps in reading the next poem you can see us by the waters edge and envision this glorious day in October in the woods.

LITTLE BOATS, LITTLE BOATS

Rippling waters
Glistening in sun
Where are you taking them
One by one?

Crispy and light
What is their fate?
Hundreds of little boats
Who is their mate?

Winds blowing lightly
Lake flowing brightly
It's never complete
This marvelous fleet!

The season is Autumn
The leaves change their hues
Falling to water
Become boats without crews.

Bobbing in current
Floating on by
Little boats, Little boats
God's fleet from on high.

JGK

The lake holds such meaning for me particularly the nights spent in my prayer chair overlooking the water with shining moon and glistening stars above me. But the family times around it too are memorable when we were a younger age with all our six children and three dogs still with us, or through the years as our children now continually return with their own families and animals. We are quite a crowd now, seventeen grandchildren in all with twins expected (I believe I told you this earlier) in October by Valerie and George. All these grandchildren since we first bought Higher Ground, and our six children's mates whom we love as our own. It all happened so quickly! I am still a kid! I do not know how this can be! In my heart I feel the ages of some of my grandchildren (and act it)!

When our daughter Janna and son-in-law Bill married here by the lake in 1994 (and I believe too I told you earlier they now have three little ones), George volunteered to give our dock a new coat of paint before the wedding. He and Bob dumped all the shades of lovely soft green paint together we had accumulated through the years and a quiet shade of muted green resulted. It was just far enough away from the cottage with a rock garden and lawn between, that it did not seem different than the green paint used on the cottage, also a soft nature green. It took him some time and dedicated effort to complete the job before the wedding, and while he was working I wrote a poem to commemorate the event.

COLOR ME GEORGE

He has been working all afternoon painting the dock
Never watching the clock—
Arm free of a watch that controls city minds
And all else that seemingly binds
One to things in the other world.
He allows thinking to be unfurled—
And there over the lake in the breeze
By the green wooded shoreline of tall overhanging trees—
His work becomes a form of meditation—
Painting each board to background voices of appreciation
And the motors of passing boats
And bird calls and fluttering leaves. He notes
From time to time—standing up—stretching from a strange position—
That his accomplishment is much—and the ambition
That brought him to pick up the brush and paint—
And stride out onto this tri-level dock so near the quaint

Cottage of his youth—was a good force—
And it was a good feeling to be the source
From which sprang this resulting freshly coated wood.
And from the very beginning it was understood
Before the job was even done
That the newly created paint shade would be named for our son—
"George"—"George Green."
His work has enhanced this scene.

Dedicated with much love   J.G.K.
and appreciation to George   July 3, 1994

*Our green dock, built by Bob and re-painted green by George
for Janna's wedding*

The Lake's Secret

As I was writing out that poem I decided I would like to share with you a very moving story regarding the lake (and much more) and received Janna's consent by phone to write this. I could not have done so without her approval. You will soon understand why. I will tell you the story now.

Vast and beautiful Lake Balch is surely the holder of many secrets that shall forever be unknown, but one treasure lost to its depths I suspect, must be the most poignant of all beneath its surface. As I have spoken of earlier, Janna and Bill were married here by the lake, and under a white trellis with a dark green cross upon it, all constructed by Bill on a long weekend trip up here by Bill and Janna a couple of weeks before their wedding. Then, on a bright sunny August 20th morning in 1994 they became Mr. and Mr. William VanDorick. Following this moving outdoor religious service officiated by the Reverend Donald Richards of our Jenkintown Methodist Church in Pennsylvania was the reception in a large white tent on our grounds to the left of our cottage. Lively dancing, delicious food and happy sociability were all present. Janna's dog Frisco, a Siberian Husky, and Rochester watched from inside the cottage at the screened in windows.

Janna and Bill
Wedding day by Lake Balch

Valerie and George,
sister-in-law and brother of Janna

Maxine (flower girl) and
Jessica (niece and sister
of Janna)

Barbara, June, and Laurel, sisters of Janna,
who sang a hymn at the wedding written
by their dad (Bob)

Family picture. Since this photo was taken, 8 more grandchildren
have been born. Bride and groom in center of back row,
Bob and Jan next to them on right, back row.

As the reception drew to a close some family members and friends changed from their best clothes so that they might swim or use the small boats before going up to the Inn in Center Ossipee in the evening. Jessica and Michael had just purchased The Hitching Post Village Inn about twenty-five minutes north of us and moved there from Pennsylvania. They had been living in my parents home that they owned in Philadelphia, and now they were following their dream of becoming Inn Keepers and operating a Bed and Breakfast. Their first guests were to be family and close friends here for the wedding from great distances. They brought their boat to our lake, a much larger boat than ours, so that wedding guests who chose to do so might water ski after the reception.

The groom was one of the first to use the skis with Michael driving his boat, and off they went. A crushing event occurred while Bill was skimming the water's surface, but we did not learn about it until we arrived later at the Inn for further wedding celebration. Tearfully Janna took Bob and me aside and told us that Bill's new wedding ring so very recently slipped onto his finger by Janna and blessed by God, had slipped off his finger and sunk to the bottom of the lake while he was water skiing.

I cannot fully explain the heartbreak here. She was crushed as was Bill and they felt so helpless, as did we, despite words we attempted to comfort. They left on their honeymoon with this painful loss in their hearts.

Janna does not give up easily on things confronting her in life, so once back from their Disneyland honeymoon in Florida, Janna drove to New Hampshire with only their dog Frisco, while Bill returned to work in Pennsylvania. Once here she hired the services of a professional diver from a firm in Wolfeboro (NH), who specialized in the finding of lost articles. He arrived with an array of detection equipment and put on all his gear while learning he was hired to find a gold wedding band in the depths of the lake. A rather startling assignment, and he was very understanding and sweet about it. He truly wanted to find it for her.

Janna took him out in our small boat to the general area on the lake where Bill believed he lost it, some distance across from our shore. We will never forget that scene. There sat little Janna (she is only five feet even) alone in the boat, her back to us, while the young diver searched the bottom of the lake in wide grid patterns around her. Every once and again he would surface, and we could tell they were talking, then he would go under again. Several hours passed and eventually they returned to us without the ring. The diver was so kind and understanding, for he knew Janna's hope had been dashed. She so much wanted the original gold ring again slipped on Bill's finger, but we were all so appreciative for the diver's persistent efforts.

Janna and the professional diver in a boat
headed out to search for the ring in the deeper part of Lake Balch

The ring was soon replaced and then blessed, as was the first one, and Janna slipped it on Bill's finger soon after in Pennsylvania.

They can speak of it now lightheartedly, and I would not have shared it with you without permission, but it was an incident that required healing. Now that they live in Rhode Island these past years they are here with us often, and they always enjoy time here with their three very small children just as Janna did since she was a tiny girl (well, she is still tiny). We always take family pictures of them under the trellis built by Bill. A picture I took of the view in front of our cottage looking out at the lake with the trellis evident, now appears on the new cover on my book *Higher Ground,* designed by Lito Castro and issued anew by Blue Dolphin Publishing, Inc. Janna and Bill have not seen it as yet as I write, but it will be very significant to them. I could not write of Lake Balch without telling you that unusual story.

The poem that follow tells of the spirit of my Dad that I believed to be present at Janna's wedding for he loved her so much in the eight years they had together. His seventeenth anniversary of death was August 21st, the day after her wedding. I believe he shared in the anguish of the lost ring too. Perhaps his attempts to help the diver from heaven were somehow lost in the depths with the ring.

An Unseen Guest

There was a wedding that took place
But in the crowd 'twas not his face
That I could find.
And though I saw it in my mind -
I wanted him—
It was no whim!
For he had held her as a baby
And was there—'twas never maybe—
As she grew.
And she knew
This fine man's ways
For all her younger days
'Til she was eight.
And then the very heavy weight
Of his death was suddenly there;
A young child's deep despair.

I know he stood 'neath woodland trees—
And that the soft and gentle breeze
Was his spirit there unseen—
At her wedding—in the green.

Dedicated to Ellis George Gray
August 21, 1994—
the 17th anniversary of his entering
Heaven—and the day after his
youngest granddaughter's wedding

J.G.K.
New Hampshire

Lakeside Insect

In 1993 I was particularly insect observant and still am, not out of dislike but because I am interested. This particular year must have been the year of the spider for I found the webs so intriguing and still do. Always there seems to be a web in a particular place on the railings next to the steps leading to the dock and a poem would result. I remember too seeing the sweet movie on video *Charlotte's Web* from the book by E.B. White that I and my children had enjoyed in earlier years. First now is a poem with a spiritual theme inspired by the spider

WEBS OF LIFE

Like a spider may we be,
She weaves her web so patiently—
And if it breaks—her sweet repair—
Of broken strands—is like a prayer.

Again and again we too must return—
To reconnect threads—for then we learn—
We need a Center—Holy, Divine—
To pattern *our* webs in His Design.

JGK

The next poem is just joyous observations made while inspecting a web. Everything on "Higher Ground" seems to inspire poetry.

ARCHITECTURAL LYRIC

Sitting on the dock at twilight
I discover a pleasing sight—
A web—spun post to post.
O such intricacy she could boast!

God's tiny insect architect—
Spinner of threads—and each connect

In incredulous perfection!
Making close inspection—
I find lady spider has left her lair
Gone off quite unaware—
That I have found her creation lyrical—
A gentle wisp of an utter miracle!

J.G.K.
July 7, 1993

The Lake's Solace

The lake has been my solace in times of sadness and heartbreak, and has allowed me to share in her solitude and peace when I am in need of aloneness and prayer. She is all things for whatever my need. When I rush to her side and ascend the steps to my prayer chair it is like "coming home," a home within a home, for it is a part of the entire magical landscape and wooded area that contains our real home, the green cottage. But it is in the prayer chair I have poured myself out and found answers and peace in the quietness that can only be found by a lake, a quietness filled with the precious natural sounds of lapping water, bird calls, peepers, and even the buzz off an occasional bug. All of this with stars and moon overhead.

TWILIGHT

It's twilight time upon the lake—
Certainly it's no mistake
I find myself in chair of prayer—
Enjoying now the evening air.

Across the lake a little light,
Goes on in dense trees in the night—
Birdsong fills the silence here.
I'm witnessing day disappear.

The lovely pink of sunset glow
Gleams on the water—breezes blow—
A sliver of the moon in sky;
Are all revealing God is nigh.

JGK

Two poems follow as before that depict my emotions in regard to again being in my prayer chair by the lake. I was always so grateful to be there, for during this period we were still commuting back and forth every few weeks between Pennsylvania and New Hampshire.

The first poem attempts to express my need for being here and for solitude, and the gladness of returning, and getting back to my writing amidst nature.

THE QUIET ZONE

When all is said and done, I know
Within me is a "hermit's glow"—
I can't explain this term unless
You question me and perhaps press.

All the while I'm in a crowd
An inner piece of me is vowed—
To solitude and silence; peace!
An inward calling does not cease.

An oratory is in my soul
To social life you can't cajole
A hermitess lives there deep within
She'll pull me back and you won't win!

And when I've left the outer places
Put aside my social graces
Books and pen and writing pad
Light up my heart and make it glad.

I rush to lake and tall pine trees
Am bathed beneath prevailing breeze
I savor this sweet place I know
And radiate my "hermit's glow."

The birdsong fills me with delight
The wailing Loons in dark of night
Strong friends are here—the rocks and stone
Praise God! I'm in the quiet zone!

Written in my   JGK
prayer chair by the lake

The next poem concentrates more on prayer, and in this case the use of the Rosary. I have many forms of prayer.

If you want to tell anything to heaven, tell it to the wind.
—West African saying

THE PRAYER-FILLED BREEZE

If I could do just as I please—
I'd pray my Rosary in the breeze.
Submit to nature's soft control
To lift and heal my sagging soul.

The beads would through my fingers slip—
While wind would o'er me gently strip—
Those burdens that once held a grip
Send them sailing like a ship!

A precious peace would fill the space
Where once deep wounds held upper place.
And as the wooden beads I'd pray—
Again I'd trod His Blessed Way.

Mother Mary takes me there
The breeze accompanies me in prayer.

The wind and Rosary I acclaim
Hail Mary! Call upon her name!

Written in the prayer chair   JGK
in the breeze

Naturally there is wonderful swimming in the lake, and also boating with our tiny fleet of extremely old row boat (perhaps 30 years old) with outboard and a green canoe, Dennis' small boat, and an older boat (new to us) shared with Dennis, Patti and family. Its name is "Green Bob" after Bob. I did tell you he is known by that name here for many years, yes? Dennis and Patti dubbed him that because of his love of green, but then he too has a wife whose favorite color is green also. It is nature's color and oh how we love living in nature.

Now that you have been here "in spirit and imagination" on your retreat, I pray you too will always hear the lake water lapping on the shore. I pray you hear it deep in your heart's core and return again and again. The lake and its surroundings welcome you.

Reflect and Journal

☆ If you have been in "hot water" recently over a matter or had some "bugs" in your life or been caught in an invisible "web" that has you tied in knots in some way, then in spirit and imagination with closed eyes, gently immerse yourself in the lake under the stars and moon. In your spirit feel the calmness come and the coolness of the water and lake breezes engulf you. Leave your problems in the lake with an imaginary sign above them that reads "No fishing allowed." Now enjoy your time in the lake knowing you will emerge free from these former hindrances. They are deep in the lake. Put your arms up out of the water and thank God—believing! In the future rid yourself of other hurtful matters in this same way.

☆ Do you remember a lake in your childhood or somewhere in your past that held meaning for you? If so write about it without stopping for at least five minutes. You may wish to continue longer as memories surface.

☆ Is there an actual lake near you in reality you could sit by on occasion? Perhaps you never felt inclined to do so before but now after reading this chapter and book you might want to be alone there. If not in reality then visit Lake Balch often in spirit and meditation. Please return daily!

☆ Write about a visit in spirit to Lake Balch. By now you must feel some connection to it spiritually after reading this book.

☆ Draw a picture with any of your art supplies of Lake Balch as a keepsake from your retreat, and to remind you to revisit this book and lake, and to continue your retreat at any times you so choose. Keep it visible so that you feel its presence both through vision and in spirit.

☆ If it adds further meaning, write a poem also about it.

☆ I invite you back again an again. You need only open the pages of this book or meditate in silence, or both, - and you will return. It is such a serene and peaceful place beneath the stars and trees. Will you return often? Please?

As your retreat draws to an end, join me now by the lake so that we may be together. I would just like to share a few thoughts with you. This need not be an ending, but a new beginning.

Afterword

Come forth into the light of things. Let Nature be your teacher.

—Wm. Wordsworth

I go to Nature to be soothed, and healed,
and to have my senses
put in tune once more.

—John Burroughs

SEVERAL HOURS AGO signs of a storm appeared that had been pre dicted on last night's Channel 9 11 PM news. It seemed unsure, this storm, as to whether or not it would make itself known. It vacillated, just enough to let us beware. As it took this course of action a poem came almost instantly to me in content to express the on edge moments occurring, and forming the rhyme on its own as I jotted it down for myself and for you. It needs a title, but I will let you give it an appropriate one.

The sky is moody, listless, dark—
In threatening, overhanging arc.
Now the sun comes out once more—
As we await the storm du jour—
Discussed, predicted, and with warnings—
Too, thunder, lightening, as adornings.
Help creatures, Lord, birds on the wing—
And each and every living thing.

347

You are protector and their source—
Keep them safe from nature's force.
Thank you.

Suddenly the storm did come. I did not fool around anymore but announced its intentions with enormous thunder and streaking lightening that continued for several hours. The lake looked like an angry sea with rolling dark waves. All boats cleared from the lake from its first signs and then torrential rains flooded everything, and large hail stones pounded on roof and deck, even bouncing off them onto the soaked ground as I watched. It was all rather frightening and I prayed for every living being, human and creature, experiencing it including ourselves.

THE GIANTS

Thunder stomps through the woods—
Lightning crackles out its path—
Wildlife hides in the shadows—
'Til the passing of their wrath.

JGK

We each continued our work, Bob over in the Birchgrove and I at my writing with Rochester beside me. At last it gradually let up and then suddenly stopped. The sun broke forth and singing birds were back at our feeders, squirrels and chipmunks running about, and boats skimming across the lake once more. The woods had had a torrential washing and cleansing and everything shone and glistened and seemed greener and more beautiful.

RAIN

R ushing rapidly downward—
A ffectionately administering to earth,
I ndespensable ingredient for life—
N ourishing, necessary cleansing of worth.

JGK

And an added bonus was that we did not lose our electricity, which shuts down almost everything in our home including water; with one exception, as you will remember from the ice storm, our gas range. It happens very frequently here as I have written earlier, and to not happen in this outrageously horrible storm was a miracle. We are thankful!

It all seemed a metaphor in regard to what I hope and pray for you, that when severe *storms* come in all forms, some unimaginable at the moment, that you will be prepared because you made this retreat in the woods. When the *thunder* and *lightning* of life hit as they sometimes do, and the *large waves* of despair drag you down into *deep water*, you will have the life saving reinforcements within you to counter them with works and actions of faith and strength. And like the woods, you will *glisten* and *shine* because you have had *showers* of blessings upon you as you read, and then did your writing in your journal, and drawings and meditations and all things in the "Reflect and Journal" portions to help you counter act any *downpours* in life. You have been fortified by nature and all the beauty of outdoors, even if done only in imagination. What you experience in your heart and soul in that way is like medicine for your entire being. I know that for I have been personally sustained by my past retreats repeatedly through imagination and prayer. We cannot always live in the sunshine but we can carry it within through all the storms of life. And I have been strengthened by nature and all the amazing gifts God has given us in His natural world and that is what I hoped for you through my sharing all the details and blessings of Higher Ground.

> *You drink the scent of the woods*
> *like water from the spring.*
>
> —Chang Chen

Now that you have completed reading this book does not mean you have to end this retreat. If you have not done the "Reflect and Journal" portions at the end of each chapter, now then is the time to do them, to go back and ponder and engage in the suggestions made. If necessary reread the book or portions of it so that you are taken into each "Reflect and Journal" section with thoughts from each chapter to spur you on in your writing, drawing, reflecting, meditation, and other suggestions made. This book can stand alone without the "Reflect and Journal" sections, but in participating in them you will actually feel like you are here in the woods, and anything you are working on spiritually in your heart will have a better chance to be dealt with in the silence of a woodland retreat atmosphere. I know this to be true. When I returned in spirit to my week of retreat in the woods of 1986 I helped myself tremendously each time. In sitting quietly in my adirondack chair in my prayer room in Jenkintown, Pa., I was transported back to my prayer chair under the stars and trees in the woods of New Hampshire. It was very alive to me, very healing. Perhaps one day you will read my book *Higher Ground* (Blue Dolphin Publishing) and you will make that retreat also— along with me. It is very real to this day.

Many places can be made into retreat-like atmosphere even when we must be on the go, until we can return home to our sacred space. Some years ago my green Ford van was a prayerful sanctuary, and when not driving my children about and totally alone, I began to hear soft tinkling music in the rear seating areas behind me. I refused to believe it at first, but then soon began to await it. It could only be described as "Angel music," lovely and ethereal. It made me cry. It accompanied me everywhere I drove when by myself, and I felt blessed. There is no earthly explanation. I accepted it as pure gift from God and the Angels. It was beautiful and lasted several years until the van could no longer be used. I did not ever hear it in my next van. I realized later why the "Angel music" came to me during that period. It is recorded in my journals.

In preparation for reading the "Reflect and Journal" sections for the first time, or rereading them anew, perhaps you could add a mirror to your special table in your sacred space or elsewhere in our home, laid flat to symbolize the lake. Even a small thin branch of green leaves by it to represent the tall pines around the prayer chair, or the entire woods of all sorts of trees, would be most signifying of your retreat. An old bird's nest or a picture of a songbird would be so appropriate too. These are just suggestions. Arranged attractively with your other treasures they can create the aura of the woods and your retreat.

And too, take a few moments today (and each day) to listen to your thoughts and go inward. Sit and be still and close your eyes and look inward. Write down your innermost thoughts when you are ready, even your dreams and desires yet to be fulfilled. Remember to honor God, and who you are and why you are here. There is only one you. You are special!

There will never again be anyone like you in this entire universe. Always write. Capture yourself through writing.

This has been my twenty-fourth summer here and I cannot ever imagine leaving this place. I never shall. My life is connected to all that surrounds me here, a greater whole. Every little thing has great meaning, from the tiniest pebble to the largest tree, and every living thing that shares this magic place with us. We live in a solitude and yet we are continually being touched by streaming life in all forms. When one opens their heart to this sort of living and becomes attentive to the language of nature, it is a miracle and it becomes home forever. To experience life in the silence of snow-boundedness, to observe glowing sunsets at night over the lake, the moon shining down in all its spectacularness, the songs of the birds and peepers, that is the joy of living and is my home, the home we three share, Bob, Rochester and myself. I pray through trying to share it with you, you too have been blessed. Please return often anytime you wish to again make a retreat. You are always welcome for "beneath the stars and trees—there is a place." It awaits you through your imagination and the pages of this book. And do not forget to journal, for it is written: "When the heart speaks, take good notes."

And each time you return to read or to again journal more thoroughly through the use of the Reflect and Journal portions, you will learn more about yourself and go deeper and deeper. Rereading will prompt additional journaling. It will be a gift to yourself. You may never have imagined that a moose, flower, bird or squirrel could be used to touch your life and draw forth more from your inner being, but it is so. It happens to me continually. And I write and write, and pray too—and thank God.

May this retreat bless you now, and again and again, and forevermore. It is your Woodland Retreat. The Angels are with you.

Thank you and God Bless You. Any correspondence to the author of this book may be addressed to

Box 5   or   E-mail
East Wakefield, NH 03830   jan@janicegraykolb.com

SEEKING THE SECRET

In deepest joy I live life on Higher Ground—
Seeking the elusive secret—if found—would astound.

O—if I could just make time stand still
and if only I could will
it to remain—here and now—
to keep it all—somehow
from turning into past—
Then I would cling and hold it fast
and gather loved ones close—to be
in that mystical realm with me.

When I look into a beloved's face—
I yearn for that sweet magic place.

I know if ever it is to be found—
It will be here on Higher Ground

Dedicated to   JGK
Bob and Rochester

Here in This Place

Robert A. Kolb, Jr.

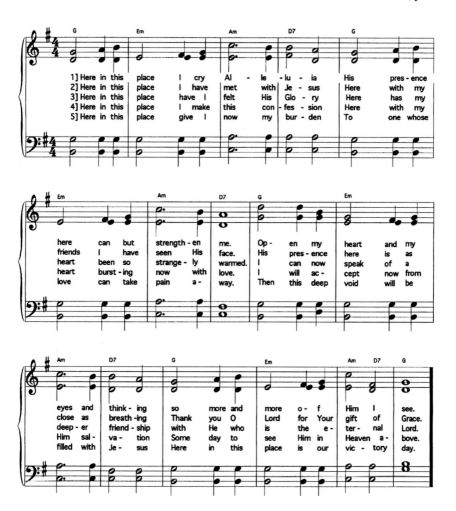

Since the completion of this book,
and just before printing,
the star of this and other books by Jan Kolb
reluctantly departed.
Rochester, who was beloved feline companion,
confidant, counsellor, and angel,
finished his work here—and passed on.
He was a motivator and enabler to Jan
and was much loved and shall forever be with her in spirit
to help and inspire 'til they are together once more.

Rochester entered Heaven
March 8, 2002
5:07 PM

Janice Kolb along with her husband Bob are the parents of six grown children and have nineteen grandchildren. Their life has revolved around raising a loving family with religious values. In addition to raising their family, Janice developed a letter writing and audio tape ministry that gives encouragement and spiritual support to those who need it all over the United States.

Other inspirational works published by Janice Kolb include: *Journal of Love, Compassion for All Creatures, Higher Ground, The Enchantment of Writing, The Pine Cone Journal,* and *Silent Violence.* In a cooperative effort, Janice wrote the book, *Whispered Notes,* with her husband Bob.

Any correspondence to the author of this book may be addressed to
  Box #5
  East Wakefield, NH 03830
  jan@janicegraykolb.com

890055